The Find of a Lifetime

Also by Sylvia L. Horwitz

Toulouse-Lautrec: His World
Francisco Goya: Painter of Kings and Demons

The Find of a Lifetime

Sir Arthur Evans and the Discovery of Knossos

Sylvia L. Horwitz

Weidenfeld and Nicolson   London

First published in Great Britain in 1981 by
George Weidenfeld and Nicolson Limited
91 Clapham High Street
London S W4 7TA

I S B N 0 297 78008 5

Printed in Great Britain by
Redwood Burn Ltd
Trowbridge and Esher

Grateful acknowledgement is made to the following for
permission to reprint previously published material:

T. M. Schuller, Executor of the Estate of Joan Evans: A selection
from *Time and Chance* by Joan Evans. Copyright 1943 by Joan
Evans.

Williams & James, Trustees of the Estate of Sir Arthur Evans: A
selection from *Palace of Minos* by Arthur Evans. Published by
Macmillan (London) Limited.

For Lou, who would
have been pleased

Author's Note

Anyone seeking information about the eventful life of Arthur Evans must turn first to his late sister Joan Evans, whose admirable biography *Time and Chance* welds the man and his forebears, the man and his work, into a single unified story of adventure and achievement. It was my good fortune to spend a delightful day with Dame Joan shortly before her death. Listening to her reminiscences, I felt almost as though I were speaking through her to her brother, so strong was the family resemblance, the family voice and manner. I am most grateful for the many insights she gave me and for her permission to draw on her biography for the facts and quotes which illuminate his life.

I am also indebted to the late Professor Spyridon Marinatos, dean of Greek archaeologists, who told me that Arthur Evans' flair for exploration into the past bordered on "divination"; to Professor Doro Levi, of the Italian School of Archaeology in Athens, for his personal recollections of Evans during the years when their work in Crete coincided; to Dr. Richard Barnett, former Keeper of Western Asiatic Antiquities at the British Museum, for the paths to information he opened up for me; to Dr. Sinclair Hood, former director of the British School of Archaeology at Athens and to Dr. Stylianos Alexiou, former director of the Herakleion Museum, for their cooperation in furthering my research; to Mrs. Mercy Money-Coutts Seiradakis, who offered penetrating observations into both the man and the archaeologist; to Mr. Leon Pomerance, of the Archaeological Institute of America, for his comments and suggestions; and to Professor J. N. L. Myres, who answered my request for help with a most charming and revealing letter about the man he remembered from childhood, when he was invited—along with his father, one of Evans' closest friends—to spend weekends and holidays at Youlbury.

Dr. Donald B. Harden, former Keeper of the Department of Antiquities at the Ashmolean Museum, not only found the time to talk with me about the man Evans whom he knew but volunteered in addition to read the first draft of my manuscript. Professor Trude Dothan of the Institute of Archaeology at the Hebrew University in Jerusalem painstakingly went over the final draft. To both of them I offer my sincere thanks for their advice, corrections, interpretations, and explanations of the archaeological data. If in spite of their efforts there are still errors, I alone must take responsibility.

For facts about his work, there is no better source than Arthur Evans himself. His monumental six-volume *The Palace of Minos at Knossos* remains one of the most extraordinary accounts of an archaeological discovery ever written, and I have drawn heavily on it to describe some of the more dramatic moments in his own prose.

My journey into Sir Arthur's past afforded me many hours of pleasure in the company of people who still vividly remember him. Among them are Mrs. Betty Coxon, who lived on Boars Hill as a child; Mr. P. Denison Haskins, one of the young "regulars" at Youlbury; and above all, Mr. James S. Candy, who shared with me his unforgettable memories of the many years he spent under Sir Arthur's roof. My gratitude to him is boundless.

There are many others to whom I am indebted: the late George Androulidakis, who imbued me with his love for his native Crete; Mr. Victor Waddington, who did so much to facilitate my research; Mrs. Ann Brown of the Ashmolean Museum; the Syndication Department of *The Times* (London); and all those librarians and scholars, too numerous to mention, who so patiently answered my questions and gave of their time.

Contents

Illustrations follow page 182.

Chapter I
Newcomers to History

Thanks to Arthur Evans, the twentieth century greeted spring with the most exciting archaeological discovery since Heinrich Schliemann found Homer's Troy. No Londoner leafing through *The Times* during those early months in 1900 would ever forget the story as it unfolded. A long-lost people had lain buried on the island of Crete, as though for eternity, until Evans reclaimed them from the earth. The news was remarkable from any point of view: that such a civilization had existed, on the very doorstep of Europe; that it should turn out to be so dazzling; and that Evans found it almost on the first day he started digging at the site of Knossos in Crete. He began excavating on March 23, 1900. Less than a week later he had rescued from oblivion one of the oldest of all ancient cultures.

Everything about the discovery contributed to its drama, and not the least the man himself. Nothing in his outward appearance betrayed the mettle, the panache within. He was insignificant in stature, barely five feet two inches tall. He was myopic, middle-aged, and unabashedly Victorian from his polished boots to his homburg. Yet, as his contemporaries would soon learn, Arthur Evans had a way of investing events with resonant excitement and color. The Minoans, as he called his newly rescued ancients after their legendary King Minos, could hardly have chosen a more eloquent advocate to restore them to the annals of history.

No one had ever heard of the Minoans. Not even Evans, as confidently as he approached his task, had expected to find a civilization of such refinement and sophistication. What he was looking for was spectacular enough, in the face of the then-known facts: evidence that a people with a written language had lived at Knossos. What he found in addition to inscribed tablets was a people unlike any other in antiquity, possessed of amenities which even some of *The Times'* readers in 1900 did not yet enjoy.

The Minoans had reached their golden years by approximately 1700 B.C., during the Bronze Age. They had lived in houses two and three stories tall, with windows of four and even six panes; with "flush" toilets and fountains, with flower pots and terraced gardens; with folding doors they could adjust to shut out the hot Cretan sun at midday or let in the cool evening breezes. Their court ladies had spent hours in the meticulous fitting, tailoring, embroidery, and stitching of costumes, each elaborate enough for a presentation at Buckingham Palace. Their slim-waisted men carried themselves like dancers. They had a feeling for beauty unrivaled in their time and rarely surpassed since; even their cooking utensils were painted and adorned. The captivating Minoans, in short, were people after Evans' own heart.

He would have had difficulty in identifying with their contemporaries, the ancient Egyptians, who suffered existence on this earth as a long arduous preparation for life in some obscure afterworld. Instead, these islanders of prehistoric Crete had met each day with exuberance and grace, and with the vital persistence it took to build and rebuild the magnificent palace and villas which Evans' workmen were now retrieving from the earth. How magnificent they were would emerge only gradually, layer by layer, as shovel and pickaxe penetrated Knossos. Evans was still finding surprises thirty years after he began digging. During those three decades what had started out as a passion turned into an obsession. He began with a determination to lay bare the civilization of Bronze Age Crete. He ended up with a consuming need to preserve and reconstruct the Palace of Knossos in such a manner

that "what would have been largely an unintelligible mass
of crumbling ruins" would tell its own story to posterity.

Year by year, as the work continued, he added specialists
to the growing ranks of diggers: carpenters, masons, miners,
concrete-pourers, architects, artists, and restorers. He incurred
"serious expenditures" for bricks, iron, and timber. He shored
up, restored, and reinforced columns, walls, and roofing, and
"recompacted" the Grand Staircase. Fortunately for the Minoans, Evans was able to bring to their resurrection not only
his fervor and immense learning but the advantages of inherited wealth. When the costs of the Knossian enterprise
continued to rise the deeper he dug, he could appeal to
his father for financial help. John Evans was accustomed
to such requests and he responded liberally, as always, to
a letter from a son who was forty-nine years old when he
wrote it.

> It is just as well that I should be in a more or less in-
> dependent position. . . . The Palace of Knossos was my idea
> and my work, and it turns out to be such a find as one
> could not hope for in a lifetime or in many lifetimes. . . .
> If you like to give me the money personally that also would
> be quite acceptable. But we may as well keep some of Knossos
> in the family! I am quite resolved not to have the thing
> entirely "pooled" for many reasons, but largely because I
> must have sole control of what I am personally undertaking.
> With other people it may be different, but I know it is so
> with me; my way may not be the best, but it is the only
> way I can work.

At an age when ordinary men are nearing the end of
their careers, he was just beginning his climb to the top,
but ordinary standards had little application to Arthur Evans.
He came to his rendezvous with the Minoans with no insecurity
or false modesty, fully aware of his own talents and his
need for undisputed authority. When it came to assessing
the Minoans' role in antiquity he was unhampered by self-
doubts. His reconstruction of their great Palace was not dic-
tated by budget; unlike most men, Evans could afford his
obsession. For the Fates, besides favoring the excavator of

Knossos with rare gifts, had also seen to it that he was born at the right time and place.

The year 1851 was a splendid year for anyone to take his rank as the first-born son in an English family of the rising middle class. Arthur Evans, as the heir not only to a fortune but to a unique background, was doubly blessed. He grew up in that best of all possible worlds the Victorian, when nothing seemed unattainable to an Englishman of means and education. The British Empire, having set its course during the first half of the nineteenth century, was about to embark on the second half in a spirit of unbounded confidence. By 1900, when Evans began working in Crete, some 39 million inhabitants of a small island would rule over 300 million subjects—almost ten colonials to every Englishman—never doubting their ability to do so by virtue of superior endowments and enterprise. Arthur Evans, more than amply equipped with both, was born into a Victorian present as promising as the Minoan past.

On May 1, 1851, the center of London was jammed with horse-drawn carriages and thronged with visitors, ranging from robed African chiefs to silk-hatted baronets. The streets seethed with humanity, all making their way to the Crystal Palace in Hyde Park where, in the presence of Her Majesty Queen Victoria and the Prince Consort Albert, the world's first Great International Exhibition was officially proclaimed open to the public. The Crystal Palace was ablaze with gas-lighted chandeliers and its two soaring towers seemed to emblazon the word PROSPERITY on the sky. Admittedly, Arthur Evans had little to do with the event, since his entry into the world on July 8 took place two months after the opening festivities. Nevertheless, neither the Great Exhibition nor his birth could have occurred at a more auspicious time.

By 1851 Queen Victoria had been on the throne for fourteen years—and would still be regally ensconced almost fifty years later—generating a surge of optimism and a sense of continuity that no other people on earth enjoyed. She put her indelible stamp on an age of invention and industrial expansion that produced, along with severe social problems for the lower classes, intoxicating opportunities for the middle and upper

classes in a highly caste-conscious society. The technological
wonders affecting daily life ranged from high-pressure steam
engines to wireless telegraphy. Railroads were beginning to
crisscross England and the Continent. There was talk of building an underground railway system in London. Change was
in the very air; indeed, the most constant factor in Victorian
England was Queen Victoria herself, whose sixty-four years
on the throne historians would call not a reign but an era;
an era of such intense nationalism and comparative peace
and plenty that it left its mark on remote corners of the
globe. By the time Arthur Evans was old enough to travel,
there was hardly an outpost of the British Empire without
its Victoria Hall or Hotel and its afternoon break for high
tea.

The queen was an enduring symbol of empire to the world
and a personification of her times to her subjects. Her Majesty
so emphatically set the tone in morals and decorum that
later generations would still describe any attitude smacking
of prudery as Victorian. Under the queen's watchful eye man-
nered elegance in dress and deportment was encouraged,
wastefulness was not. Yet despite the narrow conventions,
the burgeoning economy at home accompanied by imperial
expansion abroad offered nourishing support for enterprise
and creativity.

The age mirrored by the great Victorian novelists—Thackeray, Trollope, Dickens, the Brontës, George Eliot—spawned
avid readers and prolific writers, and sparked fecund intellectual stirrings in fields ranging from economics to the natural
sciences. It produced men of great and diversified learning,
as able to quote long passages in Homeric Greek as they
were to discuss a mathematical problem or the shortcomings
of the incumbent prime minister. Even such men, however,
and Arthur Evans was among them, followed the accepted
rules of conduct, no matter how daringly they breached the
barriers of rigid intellectual concepts.

Arthur Evans retained the habits of his class and his times
until he died. On the hottest days of a Cretan summer he
never came to the dig in shirtsleeves. Though the son of
a paper manufacturer, he showed his Victorian upbringing
by not squandering a second sheet of notepaper until he

had filled in the margins of the first. His subordinates remained subordinates; servants, servants. Yet underneath this conventional exterior flourished a luxuriant imagination, a love for adventure, and a sardonic wit inherited from his Welsh grandfather; the analytical mind and gift for synthesis of his father; and a flair for the dramatic, a taste for grand living, and a talent for avoiding the banal that were all his own. These attributes were all part of the equipment he brought with him when he began exploring his find of a lifetime, and they helped to distinguish him from a father who was not only a rich man but a famous one.

John Evans was a giant among the polymaths of his day. Long before Arthur was making headlines in *The Times*, John was renowned among scholars for his pioneering contributions to geology, anthropology, and prehistory. Indeed, in a very real sense, some of the spadework in Crete was begun by John Evans before Arthur knew that Knossos existed; and without Knossos Arthur might have remained, as he was once called, "Little Evans, son of John Evans the Great."

The discoverer of the Minoans owed a great deal of his training, much of his knowledge, and most of his drive—perhaps for the very reason that their areas of endeavor were so competitive—to his father. For if the son, with his opening up of the Cretan exploration, was able to fill a gap in human knowledge of several thousand years, the father before him belonged to a rare group of men who had dared to confront the very origins of man himself. The new paths he helped to chart into the human past gave his son Arthur a head start on his journey to Crete.

There were no road signs on John Evans' voyage backward into time. The paths were rough and unmarked, befogged by ignorance and disbelief, smoothed only by occasional stepping-stones along the way to give the explorer firm footing. John Evans found one such stepping-stone, amazingly enough, in the Somme River valley in France, buried deep in a gravel pit where it had been waiting for millennia to chalk up a turning point in his career.

Chapter II
On the Side
of the Angels

His son Arthur was eight years old when John Evans made his first decisive impact on palaeontology, a science still so new that very few people had ever heard of it. On a memorable day in April 1859, in pursuit of stone axes and old bones, Evans set off for France to keep an appointment with his English colleague Joseph Prestwich and a Frenchman neither of them knew. Fortunately, Evans was a good sailor. The ship carrying him across the English Channel from Folkestone to Boulogne afforded "as rough a passage as the strongest stomach could desire," he wrote to his wife. From Boulogne he took the train to Abbeville, where Prestwich was waiting for him at the station, and the two Englishmen proceeded to the house of Monsieur Jacques Boucher de Perthes.

The business which had brought the three men together had nothing to do with the way each earned his living. John Evans, whose prodigious energy his son Arthur inherited, ran a paper mill. Joseph Prestwich belonged to a firm of wine dealers. Jacques Boucher de Perthes was a customs official at Abbeville. What they shared in common, along with a remarkable handful of their contemporaries, was a passion to uncover human history in the almost inconceivable past. Slowly but surely, through their own observation and whatever evidence they could extract from the earth, they were establishing proof of man's existence as far back as the Stone Age.

The English visitors would have liked to spend more time examining the ancient flint axes and implements in the Frenchman's house (it was "a complete museum from top to bottom"), but every hour counted for men whose chief obligations lay in the present. Their destination was Amiens, which, like Abbeville, was located in the Somme River valley, where Boucher de Perthes had found the artifacts now in his museum. In Amiens, he had written them, they would find a stone axe still in its original position, deep in a gravel pit. Evans and Prestwich had recovered similar objects from gravel pits in England. But this binational quest promised to yield even more sensational finds.

"We proceeded to the pit," Evans' letter continued, "where sure enough the edge of an axe was visible in an entirely undisturbed bed of gravel and eleven feet from the surface." That would have been extraordinary enough; but the axe was not all they found. Boucher de Perthes had been maintaining for some years that side by side with arrowheads and flint axes he had unearthed the bones of animals long extinct. What Evans and Prestwich saw with their own eyes in the deep pit in Amiens bore out the Frenchman's claims.

Wisely, they had taken a photographer with them to corroborate their own testimony. Although most scholars had by then accepted these ancient stone relics as man-made tools, fashioned long ago, few among them yet dared to ask the crucial question: *How* long ago? From now on the hoary gravel pits of the Somme River valley would make it impossible to ignore the key question.

"I can hardly believe it," John Evans confided to his diary when he returned home. "It will make my ancient Britons quite modern if man is carried back in England to the days when Elephants, Rhinoceroses, Hippopotamuses and Tigers were also inhabitants of the country." And yet, if the stone axes made by men lay among beds of gravel formed millennia ago, when prehistoric animals had roamed the earth, then surely the toolmakers themselves must have existed at the same time. At *what* time? What kind of men were they? From where had they come? How?

These were revolutionary thoughts in 1859. Not many men would have relegated them to their spare time, as John Evans did out of necessity. Even among the small, erudite group of his friends he was a rare phenomenon. He helped to lay the foundations of modern geology, palaeontology, anthropology, and archaeology despite the fact that he could dedicate only Sundays and holidays to the dim past. His long working days were preempted by the industrial present, to whose opportunities for advancement he was keenly attuned.

In addition to his innate gift for scholarship, which he transmitted to his son Arthur, John Evans possessed a robust talent for business which Arthur did not. John had started his career at sixteen as an apprentice in his uncle John Dickinson's paper mill. Ten years later he became a junior partner by falling in love with and marrying his cousin Harriet Dickinson, the owner's daughter. That was no handicap to success, assuredly. However, the marriage alone could not have substituted for Evans' exceptional abilities and formidable capacity for work. "Flint Evans," as his scholarly colleagues called him with respect, had an equally enviable reputation in the world of commerce.

Evans had a canny way of keeping up with and being ahead of his times. He introduced the manufacture of envelopes just when increasing literacy and the new "penny post" encouraged Victorians, who were prolific letter writers by bent, to correspond throughout the British Isles at a cheap and uniform rate. To facilitate this national proclivity he experimented with his own glazing process to improve writing paper. From the first beginnings of advertising he was quick to grasp the profitable future of this new mass medium. While Arthur Evans, who had a talent for publicity, recognized the power of the written word, John Evans perceived the need for paper on which to print it. Under his management production expanded with the British economy and as it prospered, so did he.

His son Arthur, by his own admission, never acquired "the facility of doing very different things at once." John Evans, on the other hand, seemed to defy the impossible by doing everything simultaneously. Far from neglecting the paper business, he steadily increased the number of mills under his direction. At the same time he became more and more absorbed in his explorations into the past. The evidence literally dredged up from the earth by him and his colleagues was helping to change long-held conceptions about the origin and development of the human race. If his son Arthur grew up with far broader historical perspectives than prevailed only a generation before, it was due largely to the ground-breaking work of men like his father.

For "Flint Evans" the trip to Abbeville helped to confirm what he had surmised for some time. One month after his return home he was ready to formulate his conclusions at a meeting of the Society of Antiquaries: "This much appears to be established beyond doubt, that in a period of antiquity remote beyond any of which we have hitherto found traces, this portion of the globe was peopled by men." Of the many learned papers read before that august body since 1707 (the Society of Antiquaries was the oldest association of its kind in the world), few had provoked more conflicting opinions. Evans' unequivocal statement elicited reactions, even among scholars, that ranged from rapt interest to alarm. It had repercussions in his own home. Some of the conversations Arthur overheard around the dining-room table were as animated, if not as heated, as those taking place in drawing rooms and meeting halls all over England.

For a great many people in the mid-nineteenth century man's historical clock was still set by the Church, which had seen no necessity to adjust the hands since 1642. That was the year when Dr. John Lightfoot published his book with the long and self-congratulatory title: *A Few and New Observations on the Book of Genesis, the most of them certain, the rest probable, all harmless, strange and rarely heard of before.* With admirable precision Dr. Lightfoot had determined that "heaven and earth, center and circumference, were created all together in the same instant and clouds full of water ... this took place and man was created by the Trinity on October 23, 4004 B.C. at nine o'clock in the morning."

However, for anyone who set his watch by the Old Testament, worse shocks than Abbeville were yet to come. In that same seminal year of 1859, five months after John Evans addressed the Society of Antiquaries, Charles Darwin published his pivotal work on evolution. *On the Origin of Species* set out to prove that through natural selection every change in a species was one that had contributed to its survival. That was hard enough for fundamentalists, who believed that God had created every living thing, to swallow. But Evans and Prestwich, by confirming the validity of Boucher de Perthes's discoveries, had pushed back the boundaries of man's habitation on earth and made Darwin's theories directly applicable to Homo sapiens, a recognizable ancestor. And *that* bordered on sacrilege.

There were shocked outcries from the Church. There were savage attacks from the universities. There was even a reaction from a future prime minister of England. "What is the question," asked Benjamin Disraeli, "now placed before society with a glib assurance the most astounding? The question is this—Is man an ape or an angel? My Lord, I am on the side of the angels."

It was a pity that the future excavator of Knossos was still too young to join the fray. Arthur was old enough, however, to be aware of his father's irritation at the letters appearing in *The Times,* some of them so violently antisimian that the usually even-tempered John Evans was provoked into composing an answer. Nevertheless, the furor did not stop him and his friends from doggedly continuing their pursuit of man's distant forebears.

To Evans' Danish friend J. J. A. Worsaae, writing from Copenhagen, it seemed certain that the antiquities from the gravel pits in England and France "must have belonged to some peculiar race." Gradually, Worsaae thought, a higher civilization had been introduced "and the transformation from the stone age to the bronze age prepared." This had been followed by the Iron Age, though "the universal diffusion of metals," Worsaae wrote, "could only take place by degrees." In other words, the three ages through which the ancients had passed—the stone, the bronze, and the iron—had occurred at different times in different places as Homo sapiens gradually peopled the earth, an untidy arrangement which would have greatly displeased Dr. Lightfoot.

To the history textbooks which young Arthur would soon

be studying, divided until now into three compartments—ancient, medieval, and modern—a new dimension was being added. In 1865 John Lubbock, a wealthy banker and neighbor of Darwin, wrote a book with a forthright, no-nonsense title, *Prehistoric Times,* in which he coined the words "Palaeolithic" and "Neolithic"—Old Stone Age and New Stone Age—in order to distinguish between the earlier chipped flint tools and the polished ones that had followed. The book was an overnight best-seller. Clearly, not all of the ferment in intellectual circles was on the side of the angels.

The idea of prehistory, meaning prewritten history, was capturing people's minds, along with its corollary: since you couldn't expect to find evidence of man's ancient presence through documents, you had to look for it in the traces he left behind in the earth. Those traces might take the form of everything from rude stone hammers to cave paintings; from fossilized human and animal bones to the remains of seeds and pollen. The earth yields infinitely subtle evidence to modern science, but in John Evans' day the most tangible proof of early man's existence were the tools he made in order to feed and protect himself.

Evans continued to search for flint implements, sometimes taking his son Arthur along on his expeditions. Moreover, being the kind of man he was—self-taught yet of vast learning, insatiably curious but practical, too—he learned how to make flint tools himself, so that he could identify authentic artifacts and expose forgeries made by unscrupulous suppliers of ardent but amateur collectors. He also became adept at drawing the different kinds of implements that had served palaeolithic man. These shapes he had engraved on a large plate. He distributed printed copies both in England and France to men working among gravel pits, building roads or laying beds for railroads. The workmen saved whatever they found for his visits. Evans' own "museum" began to rival that of Boucher de Perthes. Nor was it limited to stone hand axes.

John Evans, a pioneer in discovering man's unwritten history, was also a collector of Roman glass and fibulae, of centuries-old weapons and pottery—that is, of objects fashioned in the remote but *literate* past. For most of his contemporaries that past didn't go very far back. Everybody knew, of course, that the most important ancient civilization was that of Greece, the fountainhead of Western culture. In his monumental *History of Greece,* published in 1846— only five years before Arthur was born—the noted historian George Grote could still flatly declare: "I begin the real history of Greece with the first recorded Olympiad, or 776 B.C." That was a kind of clock-setting no less arbitrary than Dr. Lightfoot's day of creation, and would lead Arthur as a student to express opinions about the ancient-history curriculum which his teachers found highly unsettling.

The fact was that by the mid-nineteenth century many earlier pages had been turned in the written history of mankind. The documents had been there all the time. What had been lacking were the keys to unlock their secrets. In 1822, when a brilliant young Frenchman named Jean-François Champollion succeeded in deciphering Egyptian hieroglyphics from the Rosetta Stone (which was inscribed in three scripts), the people who had built the Sphinx and the pyramids were suddenly no longer silent. Their written records, far older than those of Greece but illegible for fifteen centuries, entered the historical archives. Those of the Assyrians followed when the Englishman Henry Rawlinson deciphered cuneiform writing from an inscription carved in three languages on a rockface in Behistun, Persia.

For John Evans there was still another way of "reading" ancient history: through coins. By the time he was twenty-five he was an expert on gold coinage in Britain before the Roman invasion and had written a paper on the subject. A member of the Numismatic Society and a contributor to the *Numismatic Chronicle,* he was also the author of a remarkable book: *The Coins of the Ancient Britons.* John Evans had inherited his interest in coins from his father, Arthur Benoni Evans, who had started him at an early age on a lifetime of collecting, and he in turn passed on to his son Arthur what became a three-generational passion.

Arthur Benoni Evans was a lively and gifted individual who left his mark not only on his son John but on his grandson Arthur as well; in fact, in traits of personality, more on the latter than the former. He was a Welshman by origin and a man of genial interests, ranging from fossil hunting to folklore, poetry, and especially music. A fine cellist, he was a connoisseur of Handel. Arthur Benoni Evans was a poor country parson by profession, an extravagant antiquarian by preference. He was also a bibliophile and a calligrapher, an aesthete like his grandson and as outspoken as Arthur would prove to be. He considered a newly opened gallery at the British Museum so cluttered and unappealing that he denounced it as "altogether a national blot." He described the ornamental tower near Margate as "Arabesco-Cando-Gothico-thingumbobico, surmounted by an open spandrel lanthorn of iron gingerbread." For a living he composed uplifting sermons, but for his own personal enjoyment and, later that of his grandson, he published a book called *The Cutter,* whose subtitle promised enlightenment "upon the art and practice of cutting friends, acquaintances and relations." Clearly, he was a man of sly humor, and one with little time to waste.

Though Arthur Benoni Evans' means never stretched to include travel, his books and imagination carried him to wild and exotic places. He died when his grandson was only three years old, but it was he who opened the child's first windows onto a world beyond home. To express his joy at Arthur's arrival, Arthur Benoni Evans ransacked his cupboards and portfolios for little engravings and etchings of the faraway places he himself had explored through his literary wanderings. He gathered over 1500 of them, of every imaginable kind, and his wife, Anne, pasted them into two albums covered in bright calico for their new grandson to pore over.

A very young Arthur was already absorbing images of castles on the Rhine and Italian *palazzi,* of Greek statues and the enigmatic Sphinx, of winged lions from Nineveh, of ships in full sail for exotic lands. Later on, when he could read, Arthur came upon his grandfather's favorite travel book and devoured it. Found in a second-hand bookshop by the sedentary but adventurous country parson, the book was called *Overland Tour from Vienna to Constantinople.* The boy born at Nash Mills in Hemel Hempstead, Hertfordshire, on July 8, 1851, would one day satisfy a curiosity instilled by a grandfather he barely remembered. He would travel to that mysterious East with results that Arthur Benoni Evans, alone of the family, would have understood. It was too bad the two of them never knew each other well. They would have gotten along splendidly. In all probability the grandfather would have delighted in those very qualities of flair and imagination, and that adventurous spirit, which sometimes baffled Arthur's father.

Chapter III
Gravel on the Windowpane

"He is a very odd child," his father wrote in describing an incident that occurred when Arthur was eight, "and though I am an Evans myself to a great extent, I cannot quite understand him."

Eight-year-olds before Arthur had buried their broken dolls in the garden. But how many of them equipped the defunct doll with a companion and wardrobe and then placed an inscription over the grave reading: "KING EDWARD SIXTH and the butterfly and their cloths and things"? Was he thinking of the next world, like the ancient Egyptians? Of resurrection? John couldn't help wondering what went on inside the child's finely molded head, so like his own; how he saw the world through the nearsighted eyes he had inherited from his mother. To John Evans, as steady in his seasonal rounds as a farmer, Arthur sometimes seemed as unpredictable as the crops.

Yet they looked much alike. Both were small-boned and wiry, possessed of enormous vigor and stamina. They owed their solid legs, Arthur liked to say, to their Welsh ancestors, who were always going up or coming down mountains. Arthur had his father's short stature, thick black hair, rather sharp cheekbones, an aquiline nose, and the same long-fingered sensitive hands that could pick up a coin or a fragment of ancient glass as though to caress it. His mother, Harriet, loved to see her small son studying the tiniest detail on his father's coins, with that same look of concentration on his face.

His eyes, like hers, were both a handicap and an asset. They were hazel in color, deep-set, and extremely shortsighted. Because he was a reluctant wearer of glasses, he developed a squint when he tried to see things at a distance, a way of carrying his head as though he were peering over somebody's shoulder. But when he brought a small object within inches of his eyes, he had almost microscopic sight.

His grandmother Evans, remembering her own brilliant son (John had finished his Latin grammar by the time he was six), worried that Arthur was "a bit of a dunce," but Harriet assured her he was not. He was a dear loving child— with a little of the "pepper," to be sure, with what his grandfather called the "volcanic" nature and with a tendency to question authority, but quick to understand and very sensitive. Harriet was certain that with such intelligent features, her son Arthur would have good sense; besides, "a great deal can be done by training," she wrote.

She and her son shared a passion for music. Though all of the children—there were two brothers and a sister by the time Arthur was five—loved to hear their mother playing the piano, none listened so intently as Arthur. Watching his absorption, Harriet was filled with love for her first-born, so like his father yet with so much of her own temperament. Like her, he always knew what he wanted. He had her quick temper, her expensive tastes, her love of beautiful things. Having grown up as Harriet Dickinson, the daughter of a rich man, she was accustomed to liveried coachmen and white-aproned parlormaids, and her "ladyisms," as she called them, could border on the imperious. Giving orders would come naturally to Arthur, too. What he never acquired, however, was Harriet's willingness to compromise and her capacity for self-effacement, even self-sacrifice, when others needed her help.

Perhaps he didn't have enough time. Arthur was six and a half years old when his mother fell seriously ill, after bearing her fifth child, a daughter. He and the other children were sent to stay at Abbot's Hill, their grandfather Dickinson's house, but not before Arthur overheard his father and the governess at Nash Mills arranging a signal that left a lasting impression on a sensitive child. For the rest of his life Arthur could recall the sound of gravel thrown lightly against a windowpane. Night after night he tried to stay awake in the strange bed in his grandfather's house, listening fearfully, hoping to will the sound away. But there was no mistaking the light ping on the windowpane during the night of January 1, 1857. It meant that his mother was dead.

Arthur was too young to understand, old enough to remember. He remembered his mother's soft, high-pitched voice, so like his own, and the sound of her laughter as she sat reading *Pickwick Papers* in the garden while he gathered chestnuts that had fallen from the old tree. He saw her dressed for a ball in a satin gown with a long tight bodice and a wide flowing skirt edged with lace. He heard her playing the piano and recalled her mobile face as she read to him when he was in bed with the measles.

When the children were brought home from Abbot's Hill, Arthur was taken to see his mother for the last time. He memorized her features and secured them deep in his mind. But he said little. He asked no questions. Did he try, as the oldest in a Victorian household, to set an example of self-control for his younger siblings? Perhaps he succeeded too well. Or perhaps his father was too immersed in his own bereavement to notice the intense inner suffering of his son. Certainly, had John realized the depth of Arthur's grieving, he would not have written in his diary that the children seemed to be taking their mother's death in stride. Arthur came across the diary more than seventy years later and wrote an indignant "NO!" in the margin.

Outwardly, the boy remained simple and direct in his dealings and deeply attached to his family. But Harriet's death, coming at a crucial period in his childhood, left profound scars. Unconsciously at first, deliberately as he grew older, Arthur tried to avoid deep relationships that might incur future losses. He was a kindhearted and generous friend who went out of his way to help people, but who remained aloof from their problems. Guarding his feelings became such a habit that he built a fence of enigma around himself. It was rarely penetrated, even by those who loved him. Even his sister Alice, the one closest to him because she resembled their mother, would have to admit defeat. Many years later Alice wrote to Arthur's fiancée, "I wish I could tell you more about Arthur, but he is so reserved that I hardly know anything about him."

John Evans, stricken by his wife's death, sought release in work. The paper business had expanded to five mills by now and his increasing responsibilities filled his days. Numismatic studies and the articles he wrote for the *Numismatic Chronicle* helped the long evenings to pass. Meetings of the Geological Society, to which he had been elected shortly after Harriet's death, provided him with intellectual company. He also did his best, despite grief and overwork, to make Nash Mills a happy place for five children ranging in age from six and a half years to two weeks when their mother died. To the same diary in which he had written that the children were taking her death in stride John Evans confided his worries and observations.

The two younger boys, Lewis and Norman, and Alice, who was only seventeen months older than the newborn Harriet, took up little space in the diary. It was Arthur who figured most frequently in his father's thoughts. "Arthur has announced his intention of becoming a poet and an astronomer." "Arthur is taking very diligently to drawing coins and writing letters." Arthur was already "becoming very aristocratic in his tastes and tendencies." The boy continued to peer nearsightedly at flint implements, bronze weapons, and Roman coins. He became absorbed in books. There were the normal games and fights with his two brothers. Indeed, the only thing Nash Mills lacked, during a critical period of loneliness and longing in a six-year-old's life, was a mother.

His father provided the best substitute possible when he married Fanny Phelps about a year and a half after Harriet's death. Fanny, another cousin on the Dickinson side, was then thirty-two years old. She was small, plump, loving, and talented. Like Harriet, she had the same shortsighted hazel eyes that Arthur had inherited and she too played the piano—so well, in fact, that in an age when few women dreamed of a career, she had wanted to be a professional musician. Having lived for many years in Madeira, she spoke

Portuguese fluently and brought something new to Nash Mills—a whiff of the exotic, a relaxed Mediterranean approach to life that somehow she managed to blend with the stern rigors of Victorian propriety and her new husband's scholarly pursuits.

Fanny, who had no children of her own, slowly turned a house into a home for the five she acquired by marriage. Where another woman might have been daunted, she welcomed her new role as stepmother to a large and very young brood. Harriet the baby was still a toddler. Alice was barely three, Norman five and a half, Lewis a year older. To their separate and collective claims for attention—due as often to bruised knees as to a need for affection—she responded with naturalness and love. It was harder to win over Arthur, that odd child who had buried his doll with all its "cloths and things" shortly before he turned eight. His birthday party had preceded the arrival of his new stepmother by exactly two weeks. While John might puzzle over his son's preoccupation with life after death, Fanny was far too sensitive to be unaware of what lay buried along with the doll.

Gently, intuitively, Fanny gained Arthur's trust. Gradually she became to him in his preadolescent years what Harriet had been in his early childhood: an understanding and unfailing source of support. It was she who would assure John, when Arthur's housemaster at school complained of his dirt and untidiness, that there were other merits in a boy who was already cataloguing his own collection of antiquities. Her rosewood piano in the drawing room was a source of pure pleasure. John, indifferent to music, would retire to his library to study flints while the five children clustered around Fanny. To Harriet the youngest, and soon to Lewis, Norman, and Alice as well, she became the only mother they knew. Arthur alone remembered another.

There was a great deal of activity and laughter at Nash Mills, and a surprising informality. The large white stucco house, in which several generations had grown up, stood on spacious grounds shaded by chestnut, cedar, acacia, and walnut trees, with a garden brightened by magnolia, jasmine, and roses. Both Fanny and John were loving enough, and the old house was big enough, to absorb the activities and growing pains of five children plus John's ever-growing collections of antiquities. Each room in Nash Mills played a part in developing Arthur's character. He and his background were woven together like a tapestry.

The dining room, with its bust of Darwin over the door, often had as many as sixteen or eighteen dinner guests around the enormous table. When Arthur was deemed old enough to join them, he was exposed to some of the most stimulating minds of the time. Discussions were always lively, but the one that the twelve-year-old never forgot revolved around his father in the role of detective. John Evans had just exposed a scientific hoax that had provoked heated arguments among many of his colleagues, including his old friend Boucher de Perthes: the discovery of a "palaeolithic human jaw" at Moulin-Quignon in France. Evans proved conclusively that the jawbone in question, however old, had belonged to a man with as little knowledge of his Stone Age forebears as most of Queen Victoria's subjects. It was a clever forgery, planted by a workman in response to an offer of 200 francs to the finder of fossil human bones. This coup won Evans high praise from Edouard Lartet, one of the great French pioneers in palaeontology, who dubbed him "Inspector General of all forgeries on both sides of the Channel." It also delighted his son Arthur, who would one day do a bit of archaeological sleuthing on his own.

If John Evans presided in the dining room, the drawing room at Nash Mills belonged to Fanny. Her mastery of the keyboard turned Arthur from a music lover into a connoisseur. Her cabinet made of exotic wood from Madeira spiced the air and gave him his first sensual contact with a foreign land. Summer brought freshly starched white muslin curtains to the windows. In winter heavy red draperies were drawn to keep in the heat from the fireplace. In spite of too many gold-framed pictures on the wall and an overabundance of chairs covered in cross-stitch embroidery, the room had the same air of dignity as Fanny herself, the same warmth and serenity.

Then there was John's library, lined with bookshelves, filled with treasures: the room where Fanny, like Harriet before her, glowed when she saw Arthur squinting at a coin "like a jackdaw down a marrow bone"; the room where Arthur developed a remarkable visual memory, the most valuable talent of an archaeologist. He learned about the date, use, and typology, or shape, of ancient implements as naturally as other children learned about cricket and farm animals. These hatchets, adzes, and chisels used by primitive men, his father told him, were called celts; and they laughed together at some of the curious folklore and superstitious beliefs people still held about them, like the country folk in the west of England who thought they were weapons that fell originally from the sky as "thunderbolts." No fairy tale spun by the Grimm brothers could have fascinated Arthur more, as he sought to postpone bedtime—and not only because he wanted his father to continue his stories. Going to bed at Nash Mills, especially in winter, required the courage of a stoic. For if the downstairs rooms at Nash Mills were the embodiment of Victorian refinement, the upstairs rooms were no less a reflection of their time.

There were enough bedrooms for the whole family and to accommodate frequent weekend guests. But no fires, unless one were ill. And no bathrooms. It was all very well for Arthur to play the young aristocrat downstairs as he sipped mulled wine and remarked that his baby sister's frilled bonnet looked too "servanty." But some of the Spartan in him was born when he climbed the drafty stairs by candlelight on cold winter nights and broke the ice in his pitcher in order to wash before going to bed. Or took a bath in the tin bathtub into which a maid poured some hot water, with the room temperature near freezing. (Had his Cretan workmen, some forty years later, known this side of their wealthy employer's upbringing, they would have been less astonished at his capacity to ignore physical discomfort while at the same time insisting on French, not local, wine.)

All five of the Evans children grew up in this home filled with beautiful objects, surrounded by relics of hoary antiquity. Yet each, though equally exposed to the past, drew separately from what Nash Mills had to offer for their future. Harriet and Alice both became accomplished musicians and Alice especially never lost the quickness, the vitality she and Arthur had inherited from their mother. Lewis and Norman eventually entered the paper mills—Lewis at twenty on the business side, Norman at thirty-one on the scientific. Each of them had reacted individually to their father's scholarly pursuits and collections. Lewis started his own, very different, collection of old mathematical instruments and eighteenth-century cases of rulers, dividers, and compasses. Norman, for his part, revolted so violently against antiquity that he once threw a stone at his brothers while they were hunting for fossils on a holiday, sending them tumbling down a cliff onto the beach. Arthur was the only one who was as comfortably at home in the past as in the present; sometimes, it seemed to his father, even more comfortable.

Their happiest moments together were spent studying the past. At seven Arthur was already drawing coins and arranging his own incipient collection. At nine he spent his summer holiday helping his father dig ancient pottery out of a cliff at Dunwich. When he was twelve he went along on an archaeological expedition to Reculver, and at fourteen he spent ten glorious days digging with his father, just the two of them, in northern France. It was a splendid holiday, topped off with a performance at the Vaudeville in Paris. The following year John took his son with him to a meeting of the Society of Antiquaries, where "Flint Evans" read a paper to the distinguished assembly on his recent finds in Ireland. Heady stuff for a future archaeologist; a school without walls, an absorption by osmosis. Yet with all of these mutual pleasures of the mind, there was the clash of temperament: the son so imaginative and impulsive, a romantic liberal; the father so deliberate, practical, and conservative.

It was Fanny, not John, who understood Arthur. Fanny made excuses for him, tried to explain him. She sensed Arthur's need, despite his genuine love and respect for his father, to assert himself. It was not so much rebellion as rivalry; or at the very least, the determination to be someone besides "Little Evans, son of John Evans the Great." That very definite "someone" began posting road signs along the path to identity while he was still at Harrow, in his teens.

As secretary of the Scientific Society, the oldest public

school society for natural science in England, Arthur left his first imprint on Harrow. The two papers he read before his fellow members—one on "Mosses" and the other on "The Antiquity of Man"—aroused lively interest, as did the exhibit he arranged of minerals, fossils, and coins from his father's collections, and the neat catalogue he made, with careful ink-drawn "plates," of his own treasures. He also had a keen literary sense, was an avid reader of poetry, especially Elizabethan, and helped to found *The Harrovian*, to which he was a frequent and often satirical contributor. One of the sketches he wrote for it could have come from the pen of his grandfather, author of *The Cutter*, that handbook on the art of cutting people. Arthur Benoni Evans would have recognized himself in his grandson's discourse on "Harrow Animals," including, among others, the bore, the lazy dog, and the toady.

Happily, Arthur 'also wrote prize-winning literary essays and Greek epigrams at Harrow which endeared him to his teachers, since so many of his other activities did not. Arthur tended to rail openly against the classical studies which made schoolboys plod through Homer and Vergil and Cicero to the exclusion of much else. In the Debating Society he invariably took the unpopular side. He already had a well-developed capacity to rebel against conventions and a haughty disdain for the consequences.

Arthur was neither outstandingly brilliant nor particularly popular at Harrow. For one thing, although he was physically strong and active, his eyesight prevented him from playing cricket. During winter months his night blindness was so acute that friends had to guide him to afternoon classes. The only sport he was good at, he said, was jumping to conclusions. In a society where jumping at a ball was what counted, it was an accomplishment to end up a hero, hailed by his classmates for two distinctive contributions to the disruption of routine.

The first was the pet grass snake that he trained to crawl into his jacket through the sleeve and emerge through the collar during math class, to the delight of everyone but the teacher. The second was "The Pen-Viper." He managed to produce just one issue of this irreverent opus before the authorities suppressed it. Along with the other big-brotherly advice it offered new boys was "to be as noisy as you can. That pays more than anything, and if you carry it out well, you are sure to be popular." He also urged them "not to be squeamish about telling a few lies to masters," if the occasion arose and the prospects for getting away with it were good.

"The Pen-Viper" had a brisk sale while it lasted. Arthur left Harrow with a reputation more for wit than for work. His father, thinking of a future successor to himself, offered him a tempting job in the paper mills, but Arthur indignantly refused it. He, go into business? He had expensive tastes, but no interest in the paper mills which financed them. Instead, he applied for admission to Oxford.

Fanny wrote in her diary in March 1868: "Arthur's name is to be put down for New College, but as that requires hard work, it being a competitive exam for entrance, his name is also to be put down for Brasenose, in case he should fail at both Balliol and New College." The precautions were well-taken. Arthur was enrolled at Brasenose.

If he distinguished himself at all at Oxford, it was for independence of mind. He didn't hesitate, for example, to ignore four out of five questions on a history paper because they bored him. He wrote a treatise, however, on the one that interested him—about the Mamelukes. (The Mamelukes, originally turbaned slaves brought to Egypt in the tenth century, became mercenaries and ended up by seizing the sultanate in 1250.) Nor did he take kindly to academic dictates. His heartiest criticism he reserved for the ancient-history curriculum, with its narrow focus on classical Greece and Rome. There was more to man's past than the Parthenon and the Colosseum. More to his present, too, than lectures at Oxford. The adventurer in Arthur was beginning to show. The restless, the insatiably curious traveler. The man whose interests ranged from the remote past to history-in-the-making.

During the Easter vacation in 1871 Arthur made a quick trip to Paris to investigate social and political conditions in the French capital, which was still suffering the effects of the Franco-Prussian War. He provided himself for the occasion—there it was, that penchant for the dramatic—with what he considered the appropriate traveling outfit: a dashing opera cape lined in bright crimson. Jauntily, like a young poet, Arthur wore the cape across the English Channel, its folds billowing in the wind. At the French border, however, he was warned by a friendly customs' official that it made him look more like a spy than a poet. Arthur reluctantly folded the flowing garment into his suitcase, where it remained until he returned home. A few months later, during the long summer vacation, he was off traveling again.

Arthur Benoni Evans would have loved to accompany his grandson on this trip. It was inspired by the book both of them had dog-eared: *Overland Tour from Vienna to Constantinople*. Accompanied by his brother Lewis and a friend, and armed with knapsack and sleeping bag, Arthur set out to satisfy a curiosity that dated from childhood. He was going to explore the Ottoman Empire and the mysterious world of the Balkans.

In 1871 the word Balkans was synonymous with trouble. It covered the vast area extending today from Yugoslavia through Greece to Bulgaria. It was a part of Europe that was smoldering under Turkish dominion and fragmented by religious dissension between Christians and Muslims. It was a world seething with unrest, full of political intrigue, somnolent but volcanic, and totally un-English.

Arthur was enchanted. He was drawn, as he always would be, to the remote, the unfamiliar, and the slightly dangerous. He got around the language barrier by speaking Latin with the priests. He managed to find his way into villages that were almost inaccessible. They seemed untouched by time and impervious to change. By contrast, the city of Konstainiča, where he ended his trip, was like a venerable dowager trying to cling to old habits. Traditional East elbowed pragmatic West in its narrow streets, accentuating the differences between the two worlds. The threat of clash was in the air.

Small, dark and wiry, Arthur was more Mediterranean than English in appearance. Donning the Turkish costume he bought for himself in the pungent, shadowy bazaar of Konstainiča, he looked part of the crowd. The baggy dark-blue trousers suited him. He wound the bright red scarf, four and a half meters long, around his waist with a flourish. His blue sleeveless jacket, richly embroidered in black and gold, was lined in flaming scarlet. Arthur spent what was left of his time and money in the bazaars, sniffing the fragrant spices, listening to the ring of hammer on copper, trying on pointed shoes and fezzes, and storing impressions for the next trip. The veiled women, the mustachioed men, the brightly shuttered houses, the Oriental languor, the dark coffeehouses, even the vague underlying hints of coming violence, all made him sure of one thing: he would be back.

What had started out as an undergraduate's desire for adventure in exotic places became one of Arthur's lifelong interests. The Balkans never lost their fascination for him. It was odd, as his father would have said, for an Evans.

In that same year 1871, shortly after Arthur's return to Oxford, there occurred one of the most stirring archaeological events of the century. A wealthy retired German businessman named Heinrich Schliemann had been insisting for some years—to the derision of professional scholars—that Homer's *Iliad* and *Odyssey*, written in the eighth or ninth century B.C., were based on historical fact. Following the literal texts of the great epic poems, he had been trying to discover the sites Homer wrote about and to learn of the people who had lived there. At last, Schliemann announced, on the mound called Hissarlik overlooking the Dardanelles in Turkey, he had uncovered the ruins of Troy, one of the most famous sites of classical legend.

It was an electrifying announcement. If true (and it was, though the level Schliemann identified as Troy turned out to be the wrong one), it would be a decisive breakthrough into the civilization of prehistoric Greece, or the Aegean Civilization as it was sometimes called. The implications were enormous. If it could be proved that a brilliant and distinctive culture had existed around the Aegean Sea *before* the classical period of Greece (approximately 600 to 300 B.C.), then the Golden Age of classicism had not been created in a vacuum by a few generations of supermen like Pericles, Sophocles, Plato, and Aristotle. And Arthur's own quarrel with Oxford's ancient-history curriculum and the academic classicists was well-founded.

Following Schliemann's discovery Arthur pursued some research of his own. He published his first numismatic paper in 1871, at the age of twenty, "On a Hoard of Coins found at Oxford, with some remarks on Coinage of the first Three Edwards." With this first contribution to learning, together with his own natural talents and his father's generous allowance, he seemed destined for the life of a gentleman-scholar. It was a career highly respected by upper-class Victorians. The road led, at the time, first to Germany for postgraduate study at the University of Göttingen and then to scholarly research.

Arthur duly enrolled at Göttingen. His family could count on him, however, to make a few unorthodox detours along the way. Having heard that there were Roman ruins at Trier, he stopped over to see for himself and to conduct his first, highly impromptu dig. "I secured three men," he wrote home, "one of them extremely intelligent, and we altogether opened out about 20 square yards [16 square meters] of ground in our day's work." The Roman lamps, pottery, and coins they excavated were of little importance (although he sent them home anyway for his father's collections), but he had chalked up his first solo dig.

The intellectual atmosphere at Göttingen was more bracing than that at Oxford, but Arthur soon found that the academic standards at both universities were too formal and prescribed for his tastes. After spending a term at Göttingen he decided to continue the learning process through travel and adventure. He wanted to know more about that part of Europe which had fascinated his grandfather before him. Described in the book *Overland Tour*, it still looked familiar at Vienna but became more and more enigmatic the closer one got to Constantinople.

While still at Oxford he had spent a second summer holiday in the Balkans. He had even, being industrious and ambitious, written an account of his travels which was published in *Frazier's Magazine* under the somewhat flowery title of "Over the Marches of Civilized Europe." But when Arthur left Göttingen in July 1875 for Agram (now called Zagreb, in northern

Yugoslavia), it was with more than a holiday in mind. He intended to become an expert in the politics, archaeology, anthropology, and culture of the Balkans.

If nothing else, it would be one way of distinguishing the name Arthur from that of John when people referred to an Evans.

Chapter IV
On Foot Through the Balkans

On a nineteenth-century map of Europe the Balkan Peninsula was a patchwork of provinces belonging to the Turkish Ottoman Empire. Most of its problems, and much of its fascination for Arthur Evans, derived from its contiguous and captive ethnic mixture of Slavs and Turks, Christians and Muslims, Europeans and Asians, whose only common dimension was the ruling power of the sultan in Constantinople. To a budding archaeologist a region populated since pre-Roman times offered endless exploration into the past. For an incipient anthropologist the complex pluralism of its inhabitants was a laboratory of the present. Evans began his travels in the Balkans intending to investigate both past and present, and ended them as an impassioned champion of Slavic freedom from Turkish domination.

Geographically, the area had served for centuries as a buffer between East and West. Historically, it had been conquered by successive hordes—from Huns to Scythians to Tatars to Turks. Politically, it belonged to Turkey and comprised what was known in the chancelleries of Europe as "the Eastern Question." But if the Great Powers thought that by lumping the problems of the Balkans under one heading they would arrive at solutions, they were mistaken. Each power—England, France, Germany, Austria, Russia—dealt with the Eastern Question according to its own self-interests. They reached consensus only in agreeing with Tsar Alexander II of Russia that Turkey was "the sick man of Europe." What the Eastern Question boiled down to was who would inherit the sick man's property.

The Balkan Peninsula was a land of wild and lavish beauty, a showcase for every natural wonder from savage mountains to translucent seas and lakes, and the people who inhabited it were as full of contrasts as their homeland. There were the straight-backed highland women who climbed craggy slopes with twenty-seven-kilo loads on their heads. There were the sun-tanned fishermen on the Adriatic coast whose reputation as intrepid sailors equaled that of the Illyrian pirates who had ruled the sea in the pre-Roman past. Most of the people were peasants, locked in the slow rhythm of the seasons. Christians outnumbered Muslims by three to one. Slavs writhed under Turks. Arthur Evans, sensing imminent explosion, filled his notebook with facts ranging from land ownership to rug-making. He listened to wandering minstrels singing to the monotonous strains of the *guzla*, or Slavonic lyre. He jotted down long romantic descriptions of mountains, sea, and sky, in a handwriting often so minute that only his nearsighted eyes could read it.

Arthur planned to write a book about the Balkans. Stubbornly refusing to wear spectacles, he provided himself with a walking stick with which he could poke his way through unfamiliar or dark places. For reasons obscure, he called the stick Prodger. It became as much a part of his apparel as the stiff Victorian collars he wore, and contributed to the image people retained of him after the most casual encounter: determined, self-possessed, patrician, for all that he was usually the shortest man present. Accompanied by Prodger, he had traveled by train from the University of Göttingen to Agram, which was in the northern province of Bosnia. He was neither surprised nor sorry to hear, soon after his arrival, that a revolt against Turkish oppression had broken out in the southern province of Herzegovina. (Both provinces are part of Yugoslavia today.)

His brother Lewis joined him in Agram. Different though they were, they made excellent traveling companions. Lewis was more practical than Arthur, less fond of danger, not nearly so romantic. He had already shown his father's good business sense by entering the paper mills, and his future was much more predictable than Arthur's. Warier than his older brother, Lewis was nevertheless content to let Arthur lead the way.

Reports continued to pour into Agram about the revolt in Herzegovina. The two young men in their early twenties, armed with British passports, Bologna sandwiches, and Turkish delight, set off on foot to see for themselves what was happening in the south. They got only as far as Brood (present-day Brod), some 240 kilometers farther down the Save River valley, before being arrested as Russian spies. One could almost sympathize with the police, who must have been mystified by the behavior of an Englishman who jabbed at earthen mounds with his walking stick, stuffed his pocket with arrowheads, and took notes in a handwriting that looked like code. The brothers spent an uncomfortable (though in retrospect exciting) half hour in jail before British passports and moral outrage effected their release. Far from dampening Arthur's zest for adventure, the episode only urged him toward his next goal: Sarajevo, the capital of Bosnia.

He found it a battleground in the making, Turks against Slavs, both nervously awaiting events. Sarajevo, the city from which a World War would be launched in 1914, was already, in 1875, a town of dissensions and passions. There had never been more than an uneasy truce between the mixed population. Everything about them, from their inner beliefs to their outward appearance, outweighed propinquity and exacerbated differences. The red-turbaned Turks and their veiled wives prayed in mosques topped by slender minarets. The Slavs in white tunics or voluminous skirts and embroidered blouses built churches capped by onion-shaped domes. Each group feared and distrusted the other and considered its members infidels. Now the revolt raging to the south of the city had inflamed normal tensions and thinned the crowds in the bazaars.

While merchants closed their shutters, Arthur's buoyant curiosity and unconcern for danger took him into corners of Sarajevo never meant for sightseeing. He wrote long letters home—which his stepmother, Fanny, carefully kept—about ethnological types, religion, eating habits, and marketplaces. His tireless prowling in alleys and bazaars again attracted the eye of the police. The British consul was openly relieved to see the two young men leave Sarajevo and proceed on their way south through Bosnia.

Some days they walked as many as eleven hours. With each turn in the steep mountainous paths the world below and around them changed in color and contour. The Slavic villagers along the way came running from their long narrow huts to greet them, astonished to see two hot and thirsty foreigners—as astonished as Arthur was when his call for water, in English, sent a lad running to the village spring with a small bucket. *"Wada,"* it turned out, was the Slavonic word in that region for water. When a subsequent request for milk produced a pitcher foaming over—the Slavonic word was *"mlieke"*—he made a mental note to do some research. This similarity in words was not accidental, he would later write. It went back to "the primitive forefathers of Slavs and Englishmen," both of them "part of the same agricultural community somewhere in the highlands of Central Asia."

Meanwhile, native tongues grew more voluble with the discovery that the young visitors could speak Slavonic words. Youngsters kept refilling the two brothers' cups. Arthur had already developed the habit of running his hand through his hair, or scratching his left ear with his right hand, whenever he was puzzled, excited, or absorbed in thought, and the villagers responded to him with delight. He asked them questions in Latin or German, essaying an occasional English word, resorting often to pantomime, and wrote down their answers. While Lewis took off his heavy English boots to rest his feet, Arthur made tiny entries in his notebook.

What fascinated him was the way these indomitable highlanders, as poor and rugged as the rocks around them, lived in "family communities," jointly owning their meager property and deciding their affairs in common assembly. For generations they had been sharing both their goods and their dangers in order to survive. He learned their folklore. He traced their origins. He listened to their songs and heard their epics.

"In the South Slavonic lands," he would write, "there is not a glade among the beachwoods [sic] where the fairies do not dance." Indeed, "after considerable wandering among those interesting and primitive Slavonic peoples whose habitation lies in the Illyrian lands between the Danube and the Adriatic," he felt he could safely predict "that it is on the side of sentiment and the imagination, in the fields of poetry and music, that the Slavs are likely to add most to the heirloom of the Ages."

At twenty-four Arthur Evans was a romantic and very confident young man. He was deeply affected by the natural beauty of Bosnia and warmly sympathetic to its inhabitants. The patrician in Evans was more attracted to the Turks, with their air of conquerors, their arrogance of manners, and their haughty reserve. It was Evans the liberal who sided with the Slavs. He who avoided close personal relationships could respond without reservation to people in the mass, if he thought them oppressed. Wholeheartedly he embraced the Slav cause, even though their obtrusive curiosity and effusiveness annoyed him. He would state it frankly in his book:

"In these Illyrian lands I have often been addressed as *brat*, or brother, and the Bosnians are known to call the stranger *shija*, or neighbour. I happen individually not to appreciate this *égalitaire* spirit. I don't choose to be told by every barbarian I meet that he is a man and a brother."

However, having seen for himself how acutely these Slavic "family communities" were threatened by Turkish tyranny, he added with prophetic vision: "It is easy to see how valuable such a spirit of democracy must be amongst a people whose self-respect has been degraded by centuries of oppression. . . . A man must be either blind or a diplomatist not to perceive that in the Slavonic provinces of Turkey the choice ultimately lies between despotism and a democracy almost socialistic."

The destination of the Evans brothers was Ragusa in the southern province of Herzegovina (the city, known today as Dubrovnik, was still called by its Italian name). By the time they reached it Arthur had become an ardent supporter of Pan-Slavic nationalism. Any lingering doubts about where he belonged were dispelled by the overwhelming beauty of the city.

Ragusa, nestled within its walls, lay on the Adriatic coast at the foot of a prodigious pile of rocks which went up in one bound from sea level to 1500 meters. It had been founded centuries before by the Romans, who brought with them their law and order, their strength and enterprise, and their deep-rooted traditions. Though the Slavs had long dominated Ragusa and the mother tongue was Serb, the Roman culture had left its traces both in its imperial ruins and in Latin urbanity. The merchants of Ragusa found it easy to deal with the coastal Italians on the other side of the Adriatic. The city had shared in the great Renaissance led by Italy. Unlike the more primitive Slavic communities, it had produced writers, artists, men of science and of commerce. In Arthur's eyes Ragusa "combined Slavonic fire and Venetian polish in so elegant a fashion" that he was immediately captivated.

The Stradone, the main street which joined the two gates of the walled city, ended in a piazza whose fountain and curious clock tower dated back five hundred years. Narrow little side streets opened out from the Stradone. Walking along them, Arthur caught glimpses through open doors of marble staircases with fine balustrades, leading into drawing rooms with lofty painted ceilings. Old carved chests, damask chairs and sofas yellowed by age, exquisite brass door handles testified to a noble past. Everywhere there was the smell of fruit and flowers. Arthur decided that Ragusa, a city of gray walls and red roofs, of minarets and domes, of sea and mountains and sunshine, was where he wanted to live.

He returned home to Nash Mills and announced to his family that he intended to settle in Ragusa. But first he had to write his book.

In a very practical sense, the book was a family affair. William Longman (whose brother was a partner in John Evans' paper mills) was happy to publish it at the author's expense, which meant that John put up the money for it. And it became Fanny's lot to see the book through the final stages of publication, since by then her overactive stepson had gone off to explore Lapland. Only Arthur, however, could have written *Through Bosnia and the Herzegovina on foot,* with its lengthy explanatory subtitle: "during the Insurrection, August and September 1875, with an historical review of Bosnia and a glimpse at the Croats, Slavonians, and the Ancient

Republic of Ragusa." The impassioned prose, fresh and lively if sometimes pretentious, was all his. So were the minute and telling observations.

The distinguished historian Edward Freeman wrote admiringly: "How you notice everything: things about fiddles and pots, which I would never think of, and things about noses and eyes which I always wish to notice, but don't know how. The more things that are noticed, the better."

The book reviewers were equally enthusiastic. The *Examiner* found Mr. Evans "a describer of no ordinary power. We could not wish for a fuller or more vivid picture of all the externals of Bosnian life, the houses and dresses, the fauna and flora." *The Pall Mall Gazette* praised his "scholarly and lucid style." And the *English Independent* stated forthrightly that "Mr. Evans has published a work which at the present time no intelligent Englishman can overlook."

Many intelligent Englishmen did overlook it, of course, but a surprising number did not. *Through Bosnia and the Herzegovina on foot* appeared at a time when people were increasingly concerned with the Balkans, since the European balance of power might depend on them. In 1876, the year before the book was published, Serbia and Montenegro joined neighboring Bosnia and Herzegovina in their revolt against the sultan. All Europe watched tensely as the fighting spread.

Tsar Alexander II saw in the insurrection a chance to open a Russian path to the Balkans. Emperor Francis Joseph of Austria wavered between fear of Russia and his own designs on Turkish territory. Otto von Bismarck, the chancellor of Germany, stepped in as mediator, invoking the *Dreikaiserbund,* the "League of the Three Emperors," which he himself had created. Bismarck's purpose was not to solve "the Eastern Question" but to insure that if the Ottoman Empire dissolved, it should be by joint agreement of the Great Powers.

British policy, meanwhile, vacillated according to which party and prime minister was in power. Benjamin Disraeli and the Conservatives favored keeping Turkey intact as a buffer against Russian expansionism. William Gladstone and the Liberals were more interested in the sultan's subjects than in "the sick man of Europe," and supported strong national states. Arthur Evans, not one to sit on the sidelines, was actively partisan. He sent Gladstone a copy of his book and was highly pleased to have it quoted in the House of Commons.

"Little Evans, son of John Evans the Great," was making a name for himself at last as an author, an expert on the Balkans, and an ardent Liberal, although his understanding of politics was minimal. His discussions with his father, a lifelong Conservative, were more heated than logical. Arthur never associated politics with questions of economics or trade, of power or spheres of influence. For him, politics was a matter of ideas and causes. He was instrumental in setting up a relief organization for Balkan refugees and served as its secretary, helping to collect food and clothing for the victims of armed struggle. Meanwhile, he anxiously followed events in Eastern Europe.

The Balkan insurgents were no match for the sultan's trained troops. Stories of Turkish massacres and fleeing villagers filled the press. Serbia, the hardest hit of the provinces, was finally forced to seek the intervention of the Great Powers, and the latter sought once more to contain the Eastern Question. They did succeed, at an international congress, in imposing an armistice between Turkey and its rebellious subjects. But in the corridors of the conference hall Russia struck a bargain with Austria. Austria was to have a free hand in Bosnia and Herzegovina, on condition that she remain neutral in the war Russia was planning to wage elsewhere against Turkey. For Arthur Evans the eventual result of this secret and cynical arrangement would be to include Austria with Turkey among the enemies of his beloved Slavs.

With his thoughts concentrated on what was happening in Eastern Europe, Arthur found Victorian life at Nash Mills very dull. He was, in fact, at loose ends. Reviewing other people's books on the Balkans and working for the relief organization could not substitute for direct involvement in a struggle he had adopted as his own. Once again his father, who had agreed to Oxford and Göttingen, who had financed countless trips, and who had little taste for the Balkans, helped his son get what he wanted.

John Evans' friend Joseph Prestwich had a nephew who was the editor of the liberal *Manchester Guardian*. The paper was strongly pro-Gladstone and anti-Turkish. At a salary which covered little more than the cost of telegrams, Arthur was taken on as a special correspondent for the Balkans. By the beginning of 1877 he was on his way back to live in his beloved Ragusa.

Chapter V
From Ochievo to Kulen Vakuf

The future excavator of Knossos, now twenty-six, possessed formidable will and inexhaustible energy. The Slavs were lucky to have him on their side. Arthur Evans returned to the Balkans not as a traveler but as a crusader, determined to awaken the conscience of his countrymen at home to the human struggle taking place on Europe's doorstep.

Within days of his leaving Nash Mills he sent off his first dispatch to *The Manchester Guardian,* describing the plight of Slav refugees—"such a depth of human misery as it has perhaps fallen to the lot of few living men to witness." Crawling out of a cave was "a squalid and half-naked swarm of women, children and old men with faces literally eaten away with hunger and disease." The scene, he wrote, was like "a ghostly medieval picture of the resurrection of the dead."

Evans could be an eloquent advocate. While focusing his own attention on his chosen goals, he had a rare ability to engage that of others. He worked prodigiously hard, with intimidating drive and extraordinary stamina. And always, along with everything else, there was that grand manner in which he accomplished his purposes: the style in which he was accustomed to live, the impact on the people around him of a man used to getting his own way.

He had installed himself in the best hotel in Ragusa. The dark-haired young Englishman with his walking stick became a familiar sight on the Stradone and a welcome guest in some of the marbled salons of the patrician houses hidden behind portals on little side streets. He knew most of the town notables and all of the town's merchants. Word soon got around that he was interested in antiquities, and total strangers approached him, offering to sell artifacts found on one of the nearby Roman sites. The silversmiths knew him. Shopkeepers were deferential. There was something about Arthur Evans even at twenty-six that made people sit up and take notice. Maybe it was his utter disdain for authority and danger.

Whenever he left Ragusa it was for hazardous fact-finding trips to rebel hideouts and sacked villages; to scorched fields where the smoke of battle still hung in the sky. At a later time, had he been reporting from other theaters of action, with more modern means of communication—television, radio—he would have been hailed as one of those fearless war correspondents who risk life to obtain facts. As it was, his dispatches to *The Manchester Guardian* had considerable repercussion.

Evans' dramatic accounts of Balkan struggle and atrocities were beginning to draw sympathetic comment from an appalled public, and to attract the attention of skeptical pro-Turkish officials. Evans, they said, was a Slavophile. He was biased. He exaggerated. Evans' answer to them was an increased flow of well-documented dispatches to his editor. In order to verify his facts he didn't hesitate to climb mountains, explore caverns, and swim rivers. When necessary, and much as he hated traveling by ship—unlike his father, he was a very poor sailor—he took to the sea when there was no other way of reaching his destination.

Reports had reached Ragusa of a Turkish massacre in the village of Ochievo, deep in the mountains of Bosnia. Evans set out to investigate it. A queasy journey by steamer brought him to Zara (now Zadar), a port city located on the Dalmatian coast toward the northern end of the Adriatic Sea. From there he began his arduous climb through wild and rocky wasteland into the interior. He walked with his usual springy, bouncy motion, bending his knees deeply, and poking his way through stubby undergrowth with the aid of Prodger. Even his guides, Bosnian peasants who had grown up on these chaotic slopes, were amazed at the amount of ground he could cover without tiring. Finally they reached the Unnatz River (now the Una River); the village of Ochievo was beyond the ridge on the other side.

They found the usually placid river swollen by rains and melting snow, and overflowing its banks. The icy water boiled and foamed over rocks, carrying tree trunks before it. It was sheer madness, the guides said, to try to swim across. "However, go I must and go I would; so, climbing down the somewhat precipitous rocks to the river, I divested myself of the greater part of my apparel, put a notebook and a few necessaries in my hat, and, leaving clothes, revolver and other impediments to the charge of the astonished Bosniacs, made the fatal plunge."

Fortunately, he was a better swimmer than sailor. He managed to swim across the Unnatz River, made the steep climb—dripping wet, scantily clad, but still hatted—to Ochievo, and verified the results of the Turkish massacre with his own eyes. His report to *The Manchester Guardian* gave a vivid description of the village, where all but two houses had been burned to the ground, and included the names and eyewitness accounts of the survivors. Let the Turkophiles back in England call *that* report exaggerated.

Evans returned to Ragusa with a raging fever, which he ignored. As soon as his legs felt steady enough he took off again, this time on a really foolhardy adventure; it was just as well his family knew nothing about it until it was over. For if the trip to the Slav village of Ochievo had been daring, the one following it was out-and-out perilous. Evans had decided, in the interests of objective reporting, to visit the Turkish village of Kulen Vakuf.

No one from the outside world had penetrated the mountain fortress of Kulen Vakuf in over two years. The village was headquarters for some three thousand Turkish Muslim fanatics who lived by the credo that there could never be peace between themselves and the Christians. "Rather than submit to that," one of the merchants of Kulen Vakuf told Evans, "we will shut ourselves up in our houses, with our wives and children, and with our own hands we will slay our wives and children, and last of all we will cut our own throats."

Evans had prepared for his trip to Kulen Vakuf with unaccustomed caution. He wrote a letter to the village chieftain, whom he addressed as "The Right Hand of the Sultan in Kulen Vakuf," asking for a safe-conduct for the bearer of an English passport stamped with a visa from the Turkish embassy in London. When the reply came back—"to him that cometh in the name of two empires let there be no fear"—he extracted his opera cape, the one he had worn to Paris six years before, from his suitcase. This time he wore it inside out. The bright crimson lining set off his suntanned skin and dark windblown hair. The scarf he wound around his sun helmet made it look like a turban. Thus arrayed, and with his natural bravura, he himself could have passed as the Right Hand of the Sultan.

Evans was met at the outskirts of the village by a Turkish officer who insisted on his mounting a beautiful Arabian horse. Straight-backed and astride, grandly escorted, he rode into Kulen Vakuf in triumph. The entire village turned out to greet him, the first stranger they had seen in over two years. The dignity and proud bearing of his Turkish hosts, and their fierce courage, impressed him as always. Conversation began with the usual Oriental courtesies over tiny cups of thick, sweetened coffee, constantly replenished. The talk soon led, however, to an impasse of ethnic and religious fanaticism. Evans left Kulen Vakuf convinced that the Balkan deadlock would be broken only by force.

The roots of the struggle were deeply embedded in the past. Evans was sensitive to this long history wherever he traveled in the Balkan Peninsula, and was always searching for its roots and remains. He seemed to have a sixth sense for discovering ancient sites and artifacts. "I came upon and explored," he wrote in one of his letters home, "two grand old medieval castles which probably no one outside Bosnia ever heard of; found two old Bosnian inscriptions, the remains of some large Roman building, and a most beautiful bas relief of Mercury. . . . Tell Pa that I have got him a nice flat celt from Topolje on the Dalmatian-Bosnian frontier. I

have also picked up some pretty gems and Roman cameos."
And have acquired, he might have added, a nice nose for
pretty gems that are forgeries. But this story he saved to
tell Pa about later on in person.

It began when he went to visit a private collector near
Belgrade who had a wonderful collection of ancient Eastern
European coins. The coins were truly magnificent. Evans was
full of admiration. The conversation with this fellow numismatist became more and more animated and friendly; it was
a pity Pa was not there to join in. As the two experts,
each armed with the powerful magnifying glass no numismatist
was ever without, examined coin after coin, it occurred to
Arthur to congratulate the other man on his good luck. In
the West, he told him, one had to be constantly on the
alert for imitations and forgeries. This, surely, was no problem
in the East; whereupon the Slav collector burst into laughter
and demonstrated how he had once detected a most ingenious
forgery of an ancient gold coin. He could tell from the ridge
of metal that it had been cast. But under his powerful glass
he could also make out that the handwork had been done
with a tool with a minutely serrated edge. No such tool,
in common use by modern goldsmiths, had existed in antiquity.
"I enquired," Evans' new colleague went on, "and found
out the name of the man who had brought it to me, and
he himself was a jeweler and his name was Alexander Larides."

The sequel to the story, which would have made splendid
dinner conversation at Nash Mills, came months later in a
little church a long way from Belgrade. Evans was examining
an ancient icon when he was told that a young man had
just arrived on horseback to see him. Knowing that word
had gotten around that the Englishman was interested in
antiquities, Evans was not surprised to see the youth pull
a golden crucifix out of his pocket: a very beautiful crucifix,
obviously Byzantine, with what purported to be a Greek inscription on the back. Unfortunately for the young man, however—and for the master who had sent him on his mission—
the Greek letters formed no words whatsoever. Out came
the magnifying glass. Bringing the object within inches of
his myopic eyes, Evans could clearly make out the marks

of a serrated tool. The young man grew increasingly nervous and was happy to gallop off when the Englishman "translated" the inscription: "I, the Holy Cross which cannot lie, was made in the year 1881 by the scoundrelly goldsmith Alexander Larides."

Whether he was searching for authentic relics or exposing false ones, the past was a continuing dimension for Arthur Evans, no matter how caught up he was in the Balkan present. Since his first weeks in Ragusa he had wanted to excavate the large rounded barrow, or tumulus, of stones that dominated a plateau not far from the city. Such mounds usually marked the site of an ancient burial place that could go back to Neolithic times. At the first lull in events he hired fifteen men and began to dig. The workmen, sweating under the bright May sun, were just approaching the center of the barrow when still another Balkan explosion interrupted the work.

On June 4, 1877, war broke out between Turkey and Montenegro, the mountainous principality due south of Herzegovina. Forsaking the long-dead for the embattled living, Evans rushed off to file a report on the situation for *The Manchester Guardian*. In Cetinje, the small village capital of Montenegro, he learned that out of 500 men, 350 were away fighting. He found the women they had left behind "tall and majestic, like the male portion of their race." Every woman carried herself like "a Queen by birthright; every girl a born princess." While he was in Cetinje, news came of the capture of a nearby village from the Turks. "The wild outburst of national delight to which I was a witness must have been seen to be believed," he told his *Manchester Guardian* readers, with a relish somewhat less than objective.

He was still exhilarated when he left Montenegro two weeks later, intending to resume his excavation of the barrow. But this time the dig, already interrupted once, was destined to be abandoned altogether. There were visitors in Ragusa: the historian Edward Freeman and his two daughters, Margaret and Helen. Evans found the company of the Freemans, and especially that of Margaret, the elder daughter, more interesting than anything the burial mound was likely to yield. Peripatetic travel and daredevil exploits had not left Arthur much time until now to cultivate the company of well-brought-up Victorian young ladies, but the desire to do so was not lacking.

The two men already knew each other slightly. Freeman had congratulated Evans on his book about the Balkans and had corresponded with him since about the politics of that troubled region. They were in many ways kindred souls. The short-legged, long-bearded Freeman was also a man who espoused causes, especially desperate ones, and who had a passionate devotion to liberty. An indefatigable traveler, he too was constantly searching for historical origins. Evans, whose discussions with his own father usually revolved around questions of law and order, found Freeman's liberal views and wide-ranging ideas bracing. What attracted him even more than his ideas, however, was his daughter Margaret.

She was short, delicate, and charming, with small hands and feet; pleasing to look at, though no beauty. Her features were neat, her hair smoothly combed, and she carried herself with quiet composure. He sensed the competence and intelligence that lay beneath her unassuming exterior. Margaret, in her long tight-waisted dress, hat, and white gloves, bore up under the strenuous sightseeing trips Arthur led over rutted dirt roads. She complained of neither dust nor fatigue. She responded with delight to the natural beauty of the countryside. Her Greek and Latin were as good as Arthur's, her French and German fluent; she spoke some Italian. Having served for several years as her father's secretary, she not only knew a vast amount of history but had acquired what her father called "a kindly instinct of order"—a quality which Arthur decidedly lacked. Above all, Margaret Freeman had the rare gift of listening. She found it natural to put her own needs in second place, which was where the young man showing such interest in her preferred to put most people's needs.

Margaret was three years older than Arthur. At twenty-nine, well beyond the usual Victorian marrying age, she had perhaps renounced the idea of romance. But she fell in love with this energetic, resourceful young man with a squint, and with the engaging habit of scratching the far corner of his head when he was dubious or quizzical; with this persuasive talker who used his walking stick, Prodger, like an extension of his hand to emphasize a point and who always had a point to make. Who had an impish sense of humor and still made puns as outrageous as those of the schoolboy editor of "The Pen-Viper." But who, as she would soon find out—no matter how much he might love someone—rarely let his feelings interfere with his work.

If Margaret Freeman had hoped for a typical Victorian courtship, with its choreographed graces and gestures, she was doomed to be disappointed. Shortly after the Freemans left Ragusa, "the Eastern Question" was again headline news. War broke out between Russia and Turkey in the provinces to the East: Rumania, Bulgaria, and Serbia. The letters Arthur wrote to Margaret were filled more with Balkan ferment than with love. Nevertheless, their relationship ripened and events moved with the speed Arthur usually generated.

He returned to Nash Mills in November 1877 in order to write his second book about the Balkans, which he entitled, using what he called the "good old term," *Illyrian Letters.* The Illyrian tribes who had preceded the Romans were always part of his historical overview. His fervid prose, wholly lacking in academic neutrality, revealed two things with equal clarity: his partisanship for the Slav present and his acute awareness of their past.

In February of the following year he and Margaret announced their engagement and set an autumn date for the wedding. There was great excitement at Nash Mills and general, if fleeting, relief that Arthur would at last settle down in England. He did, but only long enough to deliver a lecture at Sion College on "The Slavs and European Civilization," in which he strongly pointed out the role played by the Slavs in acting as a breakwater for European civilization against Asiatic barbarians. Six weeks later he left once more for Ragusa, leaving Margaret, Fanny, and his sisters to do whatever women did when they were making preparations for a wedding.

War was still raging between Russia and Turkey. Austria, implementing her secret agreement with the tsar not to interfere in the east in exchange for a free hand in the south, was preparing to move into Bosnia and Herzegovina. Evans owed it to himself and to the readers of *The Manchester Guardian* to report what was happening in his adopted homeland. He did return to Nash Mills in time for his wedding in September, but not before he had fulminated in print over Russia's parceling out of the Balkans, and had rented a house in Ragusa. John Evans was horrified to learn that the lease Arthur signed was for twenty years.

Settle down in England? Leave "these seas that should be valleys, and vales that should be seas? These hills on hills? . . . Where else," he demanded in a letter, "is Earth wedded like this in eternal sympathy to the heavens above?"

He assured Margaret that she would love the house he had rented. True, it needed some "doing over," but the Casa San Lazzaro was a charming old villa on the sea, with a view from its top terrace over the whole of the walled city. After a short honeymoon in England Arthur took his bride— exhausted from buying furniture, packing, and arranging for shipment—to live in Ragusa.

Arthur's sister Alice saw the newlyweds off at the station in London. Alice, warmhearted, spirited, and quick to respond to a need, had done her best to ease Margaret's introduction into the oversized and somewhat intimidating Evans family. The two had become fast friends. In her first letter to her new sister-in-law she wrote: "I have sometimes thought that there were some good points about you, but I never admired you so much as at Charing Cross the other night, when I saw how unworried and unflurried and unhurried you could be under the trying circumstances of no luggage ticket and no spare time. I said in my heart: 'That pair will hunt in couples very well.' "

Chapter VI
Casa San Lazzaro

To get to the Casa San Lazzaro one entered through a gate on the road above, paralleling the sea, and then climbed down 103 steps almost to the beach. It was an unusual and picturesque house and Arthur Evans was having it "done over" from top to bottom with his usual disregard for expense and his very definite ideas about what he wanted. It was Margaret Evans, however, who supervised the work and workmen, who bought supplies, and paid bills. By the time the new dining-room floor had been laid and the upstairs rooms were painted in precisely the dove color Arthur specified, Margaret, not surprisingly, fell ill. Despite her emotional fortitude, she had never been physically strong. Everything in Ragusa was still strange to her—the city itself, the climate, the tradesmen, the language. It was hardly the moment for her new husband to plan to leave her alone with an Italian-speaking maid while he went off to take relief supplies to refugees.

While Arthur was visiting war-ravaged families living in caves and gathering material for *The Manchester Guardian*, Margaret had ample time to think about the man she had married. She already knew that he determined his own priorities, and that these sprang from visions shared by no one. His sister Alice had written to her, "He is so reserved that I hardly know anything about him." Margaret wondered whether she, his wife, would ever succeed in breaking through Arthur's self-protective wall to that inner chamber where he guarded his feelings. That he loved her she didn't doubt. But would she ever take precedence over his self-imposed goals? Would anyone?

Wisely, instead of pursuing the question, the new Mrs. Evans regained her strength and put her house in order. She rented a piano, hired a second maid who, like most Ragusans, spoke only Serb, and began to study the language. She made friends with the butcher, who was happy to reserve for the "Signora Milord Inglese" his choicest and most expensive cuts of meat. Arthur found the house full of flowers when he came home. Bright-colored pillows and draperies brought the spring sunshine indoors. The garden was planted with bulbs about to sprout. For the first time in his life Arthur had a home of his own and discovered that he thoroughly enjoyed it.

The young couple soon became popular members of a very restricted and artificially lively community. They entertained friends at home, went to parties given by the British consul and other diplomats. They were among the few foreigners invited to share some of the inner life that went on in exclusive drawing rooms hung with full-length portraits of ancestors. The gaiety of Ragusan society had the heightened quality of the last dance at the ball. War and destruction were still some distance away, but few people in the city were unaware that ruin was near.

The young Evanses lived grandly. Too grandly, Margaret soon learned to her dismay. Her husband, with his blurred sight combined with untidiness, had the disconcerting habit of stuffing letters he couldn't decipher or was too busy to open into drawers. Sometimes, if they arrived while he was writing or working through a problem, he merely tossed them on the floor. Once her household was organized, Margaret's "kindly instinct of order" led her to sort out the papers in and around Arthur's desk. To her horror, she found that many of them were unpaid bills. Simple arithmetic revealed that the Signora and Milord Inglese were seriously in debt.

Arthur had a simple answer to the problem. He wrote home for money. But it had been a bad year for the paper business, John Evans replied to his son, and the small check he enclosed was all he could manage. Rather than reduce his standard of living, Arthur liquidated some stocks in order to pay off his debts. As a gesture toward economizing he sold his horse, but only dire poverty would part him from his bright-yellow boat with the red cushions. It was christened *Argosy*—the only word in the English language, he explained, which was inherited from the once-mighty merchantmen of Ragusa. The word used to be written *"Ragosie"* and meant a three-masted carrack.

Evans was a remarkable blend of scholar and man of action. His latest project was to write a history of Ragusa from its prehistoric past to the turbulent present. He would sit at his desk late into the night, and one of Margaret's tasks the next day was to remove the candle wax he had dripped onto his clothing. But after a while, he needed action. He himself wrote in a letter, "I cannot stand long sedentary life! You can have no idea how much better I felt during the little walking tour I just made. . . . But if I pore too long over Ragusan history, the good effects will wear off."

One such walking tour, on which he was accompanied only by Prodger and a knapsack, took him into the interior of Bosnia to investigate a report relayed to him by a peasant. It seemed that there were figures of stags drawn—who knew by whom?—directly on a cliff near the peasant's village. Such a report, even if it turned out to be fictitious, required pursuit.

"The place was most romantic: a huge cliff, and a small grotto below," Arthur wrote. "Above this on the apparently inaccessible face of the rock were 'prehistoric frescoes' of extraordinary interest. I climbed up to a difficult ledge overhanging an abyss and was able to copy one of them quite close and the other more or less, but it was rather a risky piece of work."

Even more risky were some of his walking tours in search of articles for *The Manchester Guardian*. They took him into insurgent camps, into villages under Austrian surveillance, through army checkpoints. Austria's "free hand" in Bosnia and Herzegovina, arranged with Russian connivance, had turned into a military and administrative occupation which in Evans' eyes was no less oppressive than Turkish domination. The Austrians, he felt and didn't hesitate to write, treated the Slavs not as a liberated people but as members of an inferior race.

More than he realized, Evans was becoming deeply and dangerously involved in Balkan politics. He openly sided with the Slavs against Turks, Austrians, Russians, or any others— including Englishmen—who refused them their right to self-determination. Any pretense at journalistic impartiality was cast off. His sister Alice wrote Margaret that Arthur, in the last photograph he had sent home to Nash Mills, had even acquired "a slightly insurgent expression."

Margaret, for her part, loyally supported her husband, shared his opinions, kept the Casa San Lazzaro cheerful and bright for his returns home, and worried during his absences. When friends came to tell her that Arthur had had a little "accident" on one of his trips, she was relieved to learn that he had merely been arrested. "As usual," she wrote home, "he had lost his passport, and had been marched for four hours under arrest to Trebinje, where he was recognized and released." When her "much-abused wanderer" returned, as he sometimes did, in the middle of the night, she was prepared to listen to his adventures until dawn. Alice had been right when she predicted, "That pair will hunt in couples very well."

It was a happy marriage marred only by the absence of children, whom both of them adored. While waiting for a child of their own, they made a temporary home for Simo, an orphan whom Arthur brought back from a refugee camp; both for his pleasure and their own they acquired a huge sheep dog puppy named Bruin and a cat named Miss. Margaret helped Simo with his schoolwork and encouraged him to bring friends to the Casa San Lazzaro. The children's party the Evanses gave at Christmas for the offspring of friends and neighbors was one of the liveliest social events in Ragusa. It made Margaret, despite her frail health, more eager than ever to have children of her own. She decided to go to England for medical advice, perhaps even for an operation. She went without Arthur.

Not even his wife during an anxious time, not even a family wedding at Nash Mills, could induce Arthur to leave his work and his refugees. His youngest sister, Harriet, was getting married to Charles Longman, scion of the publishing family who had long been close friends of the Evanses. There was understandable excitement at Nash Mills (though it was a nice insight into Fanny that she could write, "I am only sorry that Harriet is wasted on a rich man, for she would have made such a good poor man's wife"), and considerable pressure on Arthur to return for the festivities. Margaret, of course, planned her trip to arrive in England in time for the wedding. But Arthur remained obdurate. Indeed, with Margaret away, he considered this a good opportunity to take a really long walking tour—all the way to Salonika, due east across the broad peninsula to the Aegean Sea.

He wanted to see conditions for himself, interview Slav leaders and refugees, and gather material for future articles that might muster support for their cause. In answer to Margaret's worried letter about such a long and dangerous trip, he sent a crisp reply. Written by anyone else, the letter might have sounded self-righteous. It might conceivably have betrayed guilt feelings. Written by Arthur, the words revealed Arthur: oblivious to everything but his own lofty purposes.

"Even supposing there was a chance of my being waylaid," he wrote, "if my journey concerns the welfare of people in generations to come—and so far as in me lay it should be so—I do not see that you or my mother or anybody has any right to urge merely personal considerations. They certainly have no weight with me at all and you must know me little if you thought so. I cannot see the wisdom of my mother writing about my 'poor wife' and telling me she is cross at the idea of my going. I cannot help thinking that women more than men are always harping on the personal side of questions."

Nevertheless, it was the personal side Evans missed when he returned to the Casa San Lazzaro. Only now, with Margaret away, did he realize what her presence meant to him and how much warmth and companionship she added to his life. How much comfort and order, too. Papers cluttered his desk again. The child Simo was having trouble in school. The maids quarreled. Indeed, the only good thing that happened while Margaret was in England was that he found a new colleague in the most unlikely of places: the Austrian Army.

Felix von Luschan had come from Vienna expressly to meet Evans. Besides being an army surgeon, Dr. von Luschan was the secretary of the Anthropological Society of Vienna and a serious student of Balkan antiquities. He combined these separate professional disciplines in a specific interest in fossilized skulls found in ancient burials, from which a trained specialist could gather invaluable insight into a people's racial characteristics. His collection of skulls already numbered about nine hundred. The two men quickly became friends.

Together they went cave-exploring for skulls. The strenuous rock-climbing in the cliffs overlooking the sea and the crawling through dark tunnels was good for Evans. The intellectual stimulation was just what he needed. Long afterward he would remember their engrossing discussions about racial skull types and where they came from, when he himself was trying to probe the origins of the long-vanished Minoans. Evans said good-bye to his new friend with genuine regret. The Casa San Lazzaro seemed even more quiet when he returned home alone to Ragusa.

Much livelier were the army barracks in Vienna to which the doctor returned, and where rumors and gossip ran as freely as the beer. The talk Felix von Luschan overheard among his fellow officers back in Vienna prompted him to dispatch an urgent message in code to his new English colleague. He sent Evans a card on·which was drawn "an ancient inscription found at Olympia, 7 May 1880." Transliterated into English, the Greek letters of the inscription spelled out a warning to Evans that the Austrian police were preparing to arrest him as a spy.

Margaret, on her return from England, confirmed that her husband's fiery anti-Austrian articles in *The Manchester Guardian* were causing a sensation. Their Ragusan friends began to hear threats of expulsion. Their servants brought rumors home from the marketplace. Their mail was censored. Margaret began to feel so threatened at the Casa San Lazzaro that she persuaded Arthur to find a safe home for the boy Simo among his own people. But while she worried more than ever during her husband's absences from home, Arthur dismissed all the talk as "very amusing" and merely redoubled his efforts on behalf of Slav freedom.

An insurrection against the harsh Austrian occupation had broken out near Ubli, some 130 kilometers southeast of Ragusa. As the fighting spread, Evans kept his readers informed of every Austrian defeat. In a variety of languages, he corresponded with disaffected politicians and Slavic journalists all over Europe. He hid refugees in his house, received secret messages about troop movements from young boys and old shepherds, and gave shelter to rebels who scratched on his door after dark.

He even visited the rebels themselves at Ubli. It was no easy feat. In order to reach their mountain stronghold he had to bypass an Austrian military guard and scale rock ladders gouged out of sheer cliffs. "Finally," he wrote, "about 3000 feet [900 meters] up, on surmounting a rugged ledge the glen of Ubli itself opened out before me, a huge mountain cauldron girt with one continuous waste of limestone crags. The scanty black earth at the bottom of the glen was scraped together into innumerable small fields, each surrounded with its stone wall, and here and there were scattered the miserable stone hovels that shelter these hardy folk. But for defensive purposes the situation was grand."

"See, here is our citadel," one of the Ubli men told him triumphantly. "Let the troops come and take that!"

From this trip Margaret's intrepid journalist-husband returned feeling very pleased with himself and events. But her joy at his return and his enjoyment of his exploit were short-lived. On March 2, 1882, the Austrians expelled Evans from Ragusa. The wonder, to everybody but Arthur, was that they had waited so long. Evidently the authorities themselves either regretted their delay or had second thoughts about their leniency. Five days later, as Evans was at the port preparing to embark, the police arrested him instead of allowing him to leave.

This time it was not a question of his having lost his passport. He was charged with being "hostile to Austria's interests" and taken under guard to prison.

The cell Evans occupied was in the block marked *Condannati*, condemned. The iron ring fixed in the wall, to which a prisoner could be chained, was intended to discourage resistance. He was denied writing materials and even a candle, lest he try to signal the outside world from his heavily barred window. The view led across a narrow courtyard to a blank wall. Yet Arthur managed to invest even jail with an element of drama, a touch of color.

He contrived to send his first message to Margaret by pricking his arm and writing to her in blood, with a tooth broken from his comb. In his minute handwriting he could write a letter on the scrap of paper he found in his pocket. He was quite comfortable, he assured her, and not ill-treated. He was certain this business would blow over quickly. Still, it would be wise to get a lawyer. The jailer who was delivering this note was a Slav, and could be trusted. Above all, she was not to worry.

Margaret, however, after sending clean bedding, fresh clothes, and a warm meal to her "much-abused wanderer" in his medieval cell, worried very much and with reason. Seven policemen were engaged in turning the Casa San Lazzaro inside out in their search for incriminating evidence. They began with Arthur's desk. The pile of papers grew: clippings from *The Manchester Guardian;* correspondence with pro-Slavic politicians; the key to a "code"; a map, carefully hand-drawn and mysteriously annotated. It was his map of prehistoric sites in the Balkans, crammed along with everything else into a desk drawer.

Had he been present, Arthur would have savored the official puzzling over his verbatim notes of peasant stories about dragons and vampires, written in Serbian; his cryptic jottings about coins and inscriptions; the stray half sheets of paper with archaic words scribbled on them, and the column of figures testifying not—as the police thought—to sums paid out to insurgents, but merely to an attempt to balance his checkbook. To anyone who knew Arthur, the papers were a cross-section of the man. To the police they confirmed old suspicions and aroused new ones. They would be back tomorrow, they assured Margaret. And the day after. What

Arthur had referred to as "this business" would not blow over so quickly.

Margaret's first visit to her husband took place in the prison office in the presence of two wardens and on condition that she speak Italian. No one had forbidden her, however, to bring Bruin the sheep dog along. In the confusion that ensued while the overlarge animal greeted his master with wild puppy joy and affection, she managed to slip Arthur a note. Then, in her best Italian, she addressed herself to the wardens. She made a point of declaring that the family at Nash Mills, the readers of *The Manchester Guardian*, and indeed Her Majesty Queen Victoria's entire government were highly agitated at what had happened. The officials were not impressed. Austria, too, was an imperial government.

How, the examining magistrates wanted to know, did Evans explain his relations with the insurgents? The notes on Austrian army camps on the back of his passport? His trip to Ubli? Who was Gopčevič? (Spiridion Gopčevič was a flaming rebel who managed to keep in touch with Evans even in jail, through the prison cook who was a Slav. Messages arrived in freshly baked bread.) Why did shepherds come down from the hills to visit the Casa San Lazzaro? Who was Miljan? (He was another insurgent.)

From Nash Mills came frantic letters. "The poor father," Fanny wrote to Margaret, "has been to the Foreign Office every day since the news came, except once when I went instead." Lewis was too busy at the mills, but Arthur's other brother, Norman, and his sister Alice were on their way to Ragusa to help her. John had spoken to several members of Parliament. (Fanny didn't add that they considered Arthur to have been "imprudent," at the very least.) Letters from outraged readers were pouring into *The Manchester Guardian*. Was Arthur getting proper food? How was he, who so loved freedom and fresh air, able to endure confinement?

Margaret did her best, in letters tailored for the censor, to reassure Fanny and John. She had visited Arthur in jail. "I made him elegant with a flower from his own garden." He looked well and skipped around the room as they talked. He was his usual "chirpy" self. They were allowing him books and light, and his meals were sent from home. She even managed to add, "I think this rest and quiet are good for him, he has been so much on the rush lately."

After Norman and Alice arrived in Ragusa, armed with a code for communicating with Nash Mills, it was easier to transmit facts about the sobering realities. The letter Norman took back with him to England (Alice stayed in Ragusa to help Margaret) painted a somber picture of the situation. The lawyer Margaret had engaged was very pessimistic about the outcome of the case if it were to be brought to trial. He felt that the authorities would not acquit Arthur and that he faced a minimum of ten years, a maximum of twenty years in prison. The lawyer was convinced that their only hope lay in getting Vienna to stop proceedings. There were even rumors that Margaret would be arrested next. "Indeed," she wrote, "they are engaged in reading through all my letters; you can imagine how I hated it the first day."

Should she leave Ragusa? Should she pack up their belongings? To go where? "How long the waiting seems, three weeks today," Margaret wrote her husband. "How I long to have you once again all to myself. . . . Ragusa has become odious to me." On the thinnest possible half sheets of paper, hidden in snapdragons from the garden or smuggled in with his meals, they managed to communicate with each other. Arthur answered Margaret that she should sell as many things as possible, pack the rest, and go to England with Alice. He assured her, with his customary optimism, that he would join her there shortly.

While Arthur devoured novels in prison—Thackeray's *The Virginians,* Brontë's *Jane Eyre,* Hawthorne's *The Scarlet Letter*—Margaret and Alice began packing coins and other collections for the long journey by sea from Ragusa to Nash Mills. The happy days at Casa San Lazzaro were over.

By now Arthur knew every crack in the paved court, with the potted lemon tree in the center, where he took his daily exercises. Even he was beginning to get discouraged. Most disheartening of all was the news that arrived with his bread, via the Slav cook, that the insurrection of his valiant friends at Ubli had been crushed. He shuddered to contemplate their fate, though it was probably their defeat that bought him his freedom.

With the Balkans once more firmly in hand, the authorities in Vienna decided to rid themselves of their troublesome Englishman. On April 23, 1882, a decree of release from prison and expulsion from Ragusa was signed. After six weeks in prison, Arthur was a free man again. As his wife and sister had emptied the Casa San Lazzaro, had packed the household goods, and made all the arrangements, he had nothing left to do but board the ship with Margaret and Alice for Venice. From there, they returned to England.

"How beautifully the persistent energy of his two ladies has answered its purpose," his grandmother Evans tartly remarked. To which his great-aunt Ann Grover on the Dickinson side added the hope that he "has had a lesson which will keep him at home."

Chapter VII
A Closet of Rarities

"Arthur has been capering in and out of the house all day, bearing Prodger and visiting the raspberries," Alice reported. It seemed to his long-suffering family that he had really learned his lesson and was content to stay at Nash Mills. At the celebration of Alice's engagement to William Minet, an old friend of Arthur's from Harrow and Oxford, the newly released jailbird danced until dawn with his wife. Margaret, so recently wrestling with bills of lading and packing cases, looked radiant in her new ball gown. Her father, Edward Freeman, was relieved to see his daughter looking happy again. John Evans looked forward to evenings in his library with his son, and Fanny was delighted to have all the bedrooms at Nash Mills occupied.

Arthur, however, who was now accustomed to having a home of his own, could hardly wait to move out. The young couple rented a house on Broad Street in Oxford, which Margaret did her best to decorate in Mediterranean colors, and Arthur plunged into work—on behalf of his beloved Slavs, naturally; if he couldn't be with them physically, he could at least write about them. His wife was soon removing candle wax from his clothes again; it was one chore she never complained about. So long as her husband was engrossed in writing about the Balkans, she hoped that the itinerant Evanses might be able to settle down in Oxford.

Arthur, the author of two books on the Balkans and fresh from a Ragusa jail, was considered an authority on the history, both ancient and current, of that troubled part of the world. For the learned and prestigious periodical *Archaeologia* he wrote an article on "Antiquarian Researches of Illyricum." He also continued to work on his history of Ragusa. In his spare time, like his father, he pored over coins and engraved gems. He was becoming an expert on Greek and Roman coins, on which his microscopic sight enabled him to detect artists' signatures and other minute details of style invisible to the normal eye. But the time came, even sooner than Margaret had feared, when her hopes for a moderately protracted home life were ended.

Such intense but sedentary occupations might have satisfied a less energetic man. For Arthur, they only intensified his need for brighter skies and adventure. Less than a year after he had left the cell block marked *Condannati* he was on the move again. With Fanny pleading that he should not get into trouble—he had already given his father gray hairs— Arthur and Margaret left for Greece. It was a trip that was to have momentous impact on his future.

The highlight of their stay in Athens was a visit to the renowned German archaeologist Heinrich Schliemann and his beautiful young Greek wife, Sophia. Schliemann was sixty-one years old by now—almost twice Arthur's age—and world-famous: no longer the fool and visionary people had considered him before 1871, when he announced that he had found Homer's Troy. Until then scholars had dismissed the poet's *Iliad* and *Odyssey* as pure myths, a kind of classical fairyland, though the study of Homer was an obligatory part of one's education.

There was hardly a schoolchild in England who didn't know about Paris, son of King Priam of Troy. Paris had stolen the lovely Helen from her husband, Menelaus of Sparta. The outraged Menelaus, together with his brother Agamemnon, king of Mycenae, had led the army of the Achaeans—Homer's Greeks—to the gates of Troy and laid siege to it for ten years. Who hadn't read of the Wooden Horse devised by the cunning Odysseus as a stratagem to penetrate the city walls? Who didn't know about the Greek hero Achilles and Hector the great Trojan?

Margaret and Arthur listened with fascination as Heinrich Schliemann described the dramatic closing days of his early excavations. The year was 1873. Schliemann and his twenty-year-old bride, Sophia, had been digging for three years and were weary, although satisfied that they had found Homer's Troy. (They were wrong. Later research placed it not at stratum II but at stratum VII-A of the dig.) The time had come to cease their efforts. And then suddenly, on June 14—one day before the dig was due to end—Schliemann's eye had caught the gleam of gold. They had brought forth from the earth what they thought were the treasures of the Palace of Priam, king of Troy.

Margaret watched Sophia's glowing face as she took up the story. As Heinrich had pried the objects out of the hard-packed dirt, Sophia had carefully wrapped them in her red shawl. There were two magnificent gold diadems. Sophia showed the Evanses a photograph of herself wearing the re-stored headbands adorned with long fringes that fell to her shoulders. There were also a golden goblet and countless gold earrings, finger rings, buttons, and other precious objects.

From Troy Schliemann had gone on to excavate Mycenae, where Agamemnon King of Men had reigned. Again, he told Margaret and Arthur, he had "proved Homer right." He had found, as he expected to, the great *tholos*, or beehive tomb, which the Greek traveler and geographer Pausanias, also re-lying on Homer, had seen and described in the second century A.D. But this was only the prelude to more spectacular dis-coveries.

Within the walls of the citadel of Mycenae, guarded by the famous Lion Gate, which was still standing, Schliemann had unearthed five shaft graves varying in depth from ap-proximately one meter to five (later a sixth was discovered). In one of these shaft graves, buried together with priceless treasures of gold for the next world, lay the body of a man—wonderfully preserved under its massive gold mask. It could only be, Schliemann was convinced, the body of Mycenae's great ruler who had led the Achaean hosts against Troy.

Exhilarated, he sent off a triumphant wire to the king of Greece: "I have gazed on the face of Agamemnon."

The face of Agamemnon! Evans was an undergraduate at Oxford at the time, but he still remembered the thrill with which scholars and laymen alike had received the news. It was *still* thrilling, even though Schliemann's own brilliant assistant Wilhelm Dörpfeld had since proved the master wrong. Agamemnon, assuming that he was a historical personage, would have had to live around 1200 B.C. to take part in the Trojan War. The shaft graves, archaeologists now knew, had been constructed much earlier, roughly between 1600 and 1500 B.C., during the Middle Bronze Age. But it was exactly *that* which excited Evans: the fact that a thousand years before the Classical Greek flowering, a brilliant and distinctive civilization had flourished on Greek soil.

Evans was slightly amused by Schliemann's ardent desire to "prove Homer right." Many years later, when he himself was an old man, he would write in an introduction to Emil Ludwig's biography of Schliemann that the German pioneer's "excavations were the outcome of this literal belief in the records of Homer and of other ancient authors. It was a form of belief comparable to that of a 'Bible Christian,' and there is something disarming about his simple faith." Nevertheless, Evans was highly impressed with Schliemann's finds. He examined the magnificent gold objects from Mycenae with rapt interest. What intrigued him was not only their beauty, but the fact that they were so different from Classical Greek art. He peered even more closely at the tiny engraved bead-seals and signet rings. Curiously, they reminded him in some ways of Assyrian or Egyptian gems. But the mystery really deepened when his phenomenal eyes made out designs which included the octopus, a puzzling indication of Aegean influence. How did the octopus of the Aegean Sea islands get to the Greek mainland?

Arthur set out with Margaret to see for himself what Schliemann's spade had uncovered. They went not only to Mycenae but also to Orchomenos, where Schliemann had found a *tholos* similar to the one at Mycenae; and then to the city Homer had called "Tiryns of the Great Walls." The mighty fortress, in its days of glory around 1200 B.C., had been girdled by walls varying in width from seven and a half to fifteen meters. It was possible to estimate that some of the Cyclopean blocks of rough-hewn stone weighed up to ten tons.

Evans was struck by the vast differences in the architecture of this Middle Bronze Age civilization—which Schliemann called Mycenaean after its principal city—and the architecture of Classical Greece. Nothing could offer more startling contrasts than the Lion Gate of Mycenae, constructed around 1250 B.C., and the Parthenon of Athens, built in the fifth century B.C.: the former with its big square portal and monolithic lintel stone surmounted by two rampant lions within a triangle; the latter with its pure rows of perfectly proportioned columns.

Only a technologically advanced society, Evans reasoned, could have produced the shaft graves and the *tholoi* that looked like gigantic beehives. Only an artistic people could have fashioned the treasures buried within them. This must have been a flourishing civilization. Whether or not one looked to Homer for confirmation of the archaeological remains, there was no doubt that mighty city-states had preceded the hegemony of Classical Athens by a thousand years.

What, if anything, had preceded Mycenae? Where had the inspiration come for this art, so fine in workmanship? These burial offerings that recalled Egyptian traditions? These sealstones engraved with the Aegean octopus? (Sealstones were small objects made of a hard substance, usually stone, and bearing a carved device which could be transferred to soft clay or wax. Although sometimes used as charms or amulets, their usual purpose was to mark ownership of some object.) Was it not probable that a people with such a high civilization had also known how to write? Surely, Evans surmised, their rulers must have needed to keep records of some sort, if only inventories of their goods and supplies. Why were there no traces?

Schliemann, the great pioneer, had unknowingly produced his successor in a new field of archaeology when he and Sophia entertained the young Evanses in Athens. From that moment on Arthur's attention was riveted on the Mycenaean culture of the Greek Bronze Age. He and Margaret spent five months in Greece, visiting archaeological sites all over

the mainland. Now, however, Arthur studied ruins and excavations with heightened perception, seeking solutions to
the problems already formulated in his mind. He was far
less interested in the classical civilization which had ripened
long after the Mycenaean than in whatever culture—if any—
had preceded it. "If any": the very words goaded the imagination. Could the Mycenaeans indeed have been heirs to an
earlier society? This was still a daring question in the year
1883, rarely asked. Most scholars were having too much
trouble trying to digest the implications of Schliemann's discoveries, and adjust their historical calendars accordingly, to
take on the imponderable as well.

It was a very reluctant Arthur who left Greece after five
months of mind-tingling experiences; five months of the sparkling light, sea, and mountains that reminded both him and
Margaret of Ragusa. Nash Mills, when they returned to it,
promised little of interest. Arthur's future was as hazy as
the sky. It was a stroke of good fortune, no doubt assisted
by family connections and his own sprouting reputation, when
new horizons suddenly opened.

Shortly after the young couple's return, the long-ailing
Keeper (curator) of the Ashmolean Museum in Oxford, whose
name was John Henry Parker, decided to retire. It came
as a great relief to the family when Arthur was offered and
accepted the post. Fanny and John, who had celebrated their
silver wedding anniversary while their roving son was in
Greece, saw it as a chance to anchor him in England. Margaret
was delighted to be living near her father, who had recently
been appointed professor of modern history at the university.
Arthur saw it as an opportunity to effect much-needed changes
in the museum and give wider expression to his expanding
vision of the past.

The new Keeper, aged thirty-three, entitled his inaugural
address "The Ashmolean Museum as a Home of Archaeology
in Oxford." He didn't hesitate to tell his audience that "Our
theme is History—the history of the rise and succession of
human Arts, Institutions and Beliefs in our historic portion
of the globe. There are some periods—like the 'Paper Age'
in which we live—in which Archaeology may appear as the
humble handmaiden of a book-written History; but there are

earlier Ages in which our Science reigns supreme. The unwritten History of Mankind precedes the written, the lore of monuments precedes the lore of books."

The Ashmolean Museum, world-famous today, was more like a historical sideshow in 1884, when Evans became its Keeper. The "Closet of Rarities" collected in the seventeenth century by John Tradescant, naturalist and gardener to the king, formed its nucleus. This collection included—according to *Museum Tradescantianum*, a book of 179 pages published in 1656—birds, quadrupeds, fish, shells, insects, minerals, fruits, war instruments, habits, and utensils. In addition Tradescant provided a catalogue in English and Latin of the botany, herbs, and "physics" garden surrounding his home, known locally as "Tradescant's Ark." It was altogether fitting that such treasures should have passed from one genial eccentric to another. The Closet of Rarities was acquired in 1659 by Elias Ashmole, "the greatest virtuoso and curioso that ever was known or read about in England before his time."

Ashmole had studied everything from astrology and botany to Hebrew, engraving, and heraldry. He had amassed everything from coins and medals to stuffed birds. In 1675 he offered his own collection, together with that of Tradescant—whose "rarities" alone filled twelve wagons—to the University of Oxford on condition that a suitable repository be built. In 1683 the Ashmolean Museum, the first public museum in Great Britain, opened its doors to students and visitors.

It contained antiquities, coins, specimens of natural history, and such oddities as "flea-chains" and "chirurgeon's instruments framed upon the points of needles." New acquisitions since then had ranged from classical sculptures to relics of the South Sea Islands brought back by Captain Cook. There was little direction and no focus. By the year 1884, when its new Keeper took over, the museum seemed to be as fossilized as some of its own exhibits.

Evans was determined to resuscitate the Ashmolean. "This Museum," he declared in his inaugural address, "is not to sink into an 'Old Curiosity Shop,' a dingy receptacle for the odds and ends of Antiquity." The Ashmolean must become a center for the study of Archaeology in its broadest sense. "I feel it wholly impossible," he said, "to confine my interests or studies to one period, or even to recognize barriers when they are pointed out to me." One of the barriers he refused to accept was that imposed between archaeology and anthropology. For him no boundary existed between the two; they overlapped. "The same object—to illustrate the laws of Evolution as applied to human Arts—is largely shared by both." Nor would he limit himself to the period favored by classical scholars, for whom the glories of the past were synonymous with Greece and Rome.

"Consider for a moment," Evans said, "the services rendered within quite recent years by what has been called Prehistoric Archaeology, but which in truth was never more Historic, in widening the horizon of our Past. It has drawn aside the curtain and revealed the Dawn." Eloquently, a true son of his father, he sketched a picture of those distant times when "Man was already in existence here," in this very valley in which Oxford was located, "fashioning his flint weapons to aid him in his struggle against the sabretoothed Tiger, or the woolly haired Rhinoceros." He deplored the fact that "we have yet too little in our Museum to illustrate these early chapters in the history of human arts."

Then Evans went on to more practical matters. It was time to bring technology to the rescue of the Muses. "To gain complete security from fire, and to check the damp which at present literally oozes up through our basement floor, I have proposed, in place of the existing fireplaces, to heat the Museum with hot-water pipes."

This proposal in itself was alarmingly revolutionary. Not all of the Visitors of the Museum (the governing body) were pleased with their young Keeper's frontal assault on inertia and tradition. Their meetings with his elderly predecessor had been far less upsetting. One knew where one stood, even if it meant standing still. Evans soon realized that to combat years of lethargy and chronic lack of funds would be a different kind of fight from the one he had waged with the Austrian authorities in Ragusa, but he warmed to it with the same enthusiasm and persistence.

Since a museum was only as valuable as the objects contained within it, he proceeded—with his talent for choosing the right thing and with his contacts with archaeological workers at home and abroad—to expand the Ashmolean's collections as rapidly as possible. Within three years he informed the astonished Visitors in his Annual Report that he had added over two thousand new acquisitions. Within five years he had almost doubled the collections. Indeed, he worked so fast that in 1892, eight years after he took office as Keeper, the original building was no longer adequate to house its treasures. They included by then a splendid collection of Phoenician and Hittite seals as well as generous gifts from his own and his father's collections of coins and Stone Age artifacts, and would soon be enriched by fresh finds from his friend John Myres's excavations in Cyprus and his friend Flinders Petrie's work in Egypt.

That the old Ashmolean might outgrow itself came as no shock to Evans. He himself had invited expansion by negotiating, early in his Keepership, to acquire the Fortnum Collection. Charles Drury Edward Fortnum was an antiquary friend of John Evans whom Arthur had met through his father. Fortnum was both wealthy and generous, and owned some of the finest examples of classical and medieval art in England. He offered his collection to the Ashmolean on loan, with the promise of an eventual bequest and endowment, on condition that Evans get the university to do its part by properly housing and displaying it.

The funds Evans would have to secure to implement Fortnum's gift were not insignificant. Characteristically, he launched the project in elegant style—by giving a party in the museum for two hundred carefully chosen guests. He floodlighted an upper gallery, filled it with photographs of Fortnum's collection, and lined it with borrowed cases and borrowed objects from Nash Mills and elsewhere. Having thus dazzled the Visitors and benefactors of the museum collectively with this glimpse into an obtainable future, he proceeded to seek out each Visitor separately to outline his plans for the Fortnum Collection.

Patience, tact, diplomacy—these were not Evans' strong points. Nor did he have any stomach for university politics or any aptitude for budgeting. The Ashmolean's finances were so deplorable, Evans wrote his father, that "for months now I have had to advance my assistant's pay out of my own funds." Administrative work bored him. Nevertheless, the plans for a new and bigger Ashmolean Museum of Archaeology and Art went forward, and would eventually result in the handsome new building which was inaugurated at the end of 1894, only ten and a half years after Evans had become Keeper. He had, in effect, re-founded the Museum.

Evans was the guiding spirit and presiding angel of the Ashmolean for almost a quarter of a century, and he remained Honorary Keeper until his death. There were very few weeks when, if he was in Oxford, he did not revisit and enhance his creation. Unflagging to the end, he insisted that the Ashmolean, in addition to being a museum, must be a first-class medium of teaching and research. He, more than anyone else, helped to make it that by setting the pattern during his first ten years as Keeper.

For Evans, those ten years were immensely productive professionally. To them belong a series of lectures at the university, articles in the journals of learned societies, the systematic search for choice ancient coins and engraved gems, and the excavation of a Roman villa at Frilford near Oxford. His discovery of a Late Celtic Urnfield at Aylesford in Kent was a truly significant contribution to prehistory. (An urnfield is a cemetery of individual cremation graves with the ashes of the dead placed in pottery vessels or funerary urns.) In an article published in *Archaeologia* in 1890 he identified the Aylesford people with the Belgic tribes who, he believed, invaded southeast Britain in about 100 B.C. In so doing he was the first scholar to recognize a separate culture within the Iron Age.

Evans also gave a course on "British Prehistoric Antiquities" at a Summer Meeting of the Oxford University Extension. This, for him, was a labor less of love than of duty, as were the public lectures expected of the Keeper of the Ashmolean Museum. He disliked both teaching and public speaking. He could raise his normally soft, high-pitched voice in anger, and did so on more than one shattering occasion, but he never mastered the technique of popular or illustrated lecturing. No matter how lucid or trenchant Evans could be with his pen, his spoken remarks were punctuated by too many "eh's" and "er's" to hold the attention of an audience, and his habit of running his hand through his hair could be very distracting, especially to a group of Oxford students or an unselected assembly of lay people.

Fortunately, though his duties as the Ashmolean's Keeper included occasional public addresses, there were other perquisites to the position which suited Evans admirably. One was travel. The Keeper, he was told 'when he accepted the post, was not only permitted but even expected to engage in frequent travel. How frequent wasn't specified; and the rare sallies of Evans' ailing predecessor could hardly have prepared the Visitors of the Museum for the peregrinations of their present Keeper. If Margaret's wanderer was no longer "much abused," he was still a wanderer.

A solitary trip to the Crimea took him from Sebastopol to Tiflis, where he roamed with the old fascination through the carpet bazaar and the streets of the silversmiths. A strenuous journey on which Margaret accompanied him began in Calabria and ended in Macedonia: tantalizingly close to Ragusa. Margaret managed to make a quick visit to their former home. Arthur, denied permission to enter by the Austrian authorities, exploded in indignation. That he had been first incarcerated in a Ragusan jail and then banished from the region; that he had continued writing denunciatory letters to the editor of *The Manchester Guardian* ever since—these he considered paltry reasons for being refused a visa. A fuming Arthur had to content himself with second-hand reports about the garden at Casa San Lazzaro, the butcher who still remembered the Signora Milord Inglese, and the unchanging beauty of Ragusa in an area where everything else was in flux.

This trip was followed soon after by a tour of Sicily with his father-in-law, Edward Freeman, who was writing a monumental history of the island. It resulted in three masterful studies for the *Numismatic Chronicle*: "The Horsemen of Tarentum," "Syracusan Medallions," and "New Artists' Signatures on Sicilian Coins." (Freeman, in a letter home, wrote that he "found new interest in looking at things through

Arthur's eyes." He hadn't realized it before, but "in this island one gets numismatical and geological.") Indeed, so numerous were Arthur's absences from Oxford that his assistant, Edward Evans (no relation), hard put to keep track of his employer's whereabouts, took to answering queries with a vague, "The Keeper, sir, is somewhere in Bohemia."

By comparison, life in Oxford proceeded along safe and predictable paths, dull and unexciting, even though the scholar in Evans found increasing outlets. He renewed his boyhood interest in ancient British archaeology and Romano-British coins, with particular attention to their relation to parallel cultural elements in southern Europe. The articles on Sicilian coins and medallions established his solid reputation as a numismatist. They, together with his research into the ancient history of the Balkans, earned him recognition from "Classical" archaeologists. These days, when Arthur Evans attended meetings of the Society of Antiquaries, with John Evans in the chair, no one present thought of them as "little Evans" or "great Evans," but as colleagues.

Nevertheless, despite his own growing reputation and that of the Ashmolean Museum, Evans threatened more than once to resign during his first ten years as Keeper. No amount of professional satisfaction and recognition could reconcile him to the climate and the way of life of Oxford. Margaret was acutely aware of the many times when her husband would gladly have exchanged his title and position for a visa enabling him to return to Ragusa.

Chapter VIII
Through Troublous Times

John Evans once remarked, while sitting in a café in Bari in southern Italy, that the place looked full of Arthurs. Arthur not only looked more Mediterranean than English, he was also temperamentally more suited to Southern expansiveness than to British understatement—so long, that is, as the former made no inroads on his privacy or privileges. The man who did not wish to be called *brat*, or "brother," by Slav peasants, nevertheless preferred Slavic exuberance to English restraint. He also preferred an active life under bright skies to dull meetings in boardrooms. After Ragusa, Oxford was gray and leaden. His sparring with tradition-bound academics seemed polite and peripheral compared to direct involvement in Balkan struggle. Acquiring antiquities for a museum was not nearly so satisfying as discovering them. Though he spent as much time as possible outside Oxford, he was increasingly unhappy when he came home.

The Evanses had rented a new and larger house at 33 Holywell Street, and Margaret tried to convert it, against all odds, into a second Casa San Lazzaro. From the glowing Slavic embroidery and hangings she had brought back from Ragusa she made pillows and curtains to offset rainy skies. The pictures on the walls recalled sea and mountains, and the carpets on the floors came from Balkan bazaars. Arthur's devoted wife kept an orderly house that was filled with guests whenever the master was in residence. He loved to entertain and was warmly hospitable to the people he liked. There was much visiting back and forth among the family: his sisters Alice Minet and Harriet Longman, his brothers Lewis and Norman, and of course John and Fanny. The Keeper of the Ashmolean Museum would look back on those years in retrospect as an interlude of normality and stability.

Arthur was away from home, as usual, when tragedy struck the Evans family. Though he generally traveled not for pleasure but to learn and explore, this time it was one of those rare occasions when he and Margaret had gone away solely for a holiday. They were in Sicily in March 1887, sunning and relaxing, when they were recalled to Nash Mills by grievous news. His sister Alice, only thirty-one years old, had died after an illness of a few days, leaving a small daughter of three. It seemed only yesterday that they had all danced at her wedding.

It was a cruel loss for Arthur, to whom Alice, of all the family, had always been the closest. It was an almost equal blow for Margaret, who had found in her sister-in-law a warm friend and a buttress, and who would never forget her cheerful and supportive presence during those tense weeks when Arthur paced a cell in Ragusa. The whole family was stricken. Alice, Fanny wrote, had been "the center of our lives, the bond of union." Without her laughter and high spirits, her quick wit, Nash Mills grew silent and strained.

Three years later Fanny herself was mortally ill, after an operation which revealed that nothing could save her. How long she had known the nature of her illness the family could only surmise. Fanny, with her customary concern for others, and especially for her husband, had through long months of her own suffering tried to alleviate that of John. Now it was no longer possible.

Margaret went to Nash Mills to be with Fanny. On September 18, 1890, she wrote to Arthur in Oxford: "Twelve years tomorrow since we started in double harness! This year the uppermost thought in my mind is that that day gave me my second mother who has always been so dear and good to me—love and gentleness that I feel can only be repaid by devotion to him to whom her loss will be so great."

Arthur joined Margaret three days later. The next day Fanny died and Nash Mills was plunged into deep mourning. With her going, the comfortable old-fashioned house, with its two generations of memories, ceased to be a family anchorage.

Fanny, not John, had been the magnet. It was through her that common joys had been celebrated and sorrows shared. With Fanny gone, John Evans' children realized how central their stepmother had been to Nash Mills; what a unifying thread running through the fabric of their separate lives. Their father, inconsolable, found himself as much alone with his collections as when his first wife had died thirty-three years before.

The problem of how to keep Nash Mills running became acute. First Margaret would spend a few weeks there, then Harriet would come. There was a succession of housekeepers. Finally Arthur wrote his father suggesting that he and Margaret give up their home in Oxford and come to live with him at Nash Mills. "I know that however much all the members of the family may do for you by turns, some continuity is needed in a household, and I could not bear to think that you should ever be without some of your own about you."

John was deeply touched. He was grateful for the help Margaret had given him and for Arthur's offer. But, he wrote his son, "I do not like having myself and my house taken possession of." What he didn't add was that he found Margaret's orderliness a bit wearing. He hated having solicitous friends suggest "outlets"—even the faithful Joseph Prestwich, with whom he had made that memorable trip to Abbeville over forty years before, couldn't rekindle his interest in geology. Being fussed over by well-meaning housekeepers only irritated him. Fanny's death had not deprived John Evans of his independence. He needed a home of his own and only a wife of his own could provide it. He set about finding one.

Two years after Fanny's death, in June 1892, John Evans was made a Knight Commander of the Order of the Bath by Queen Victoria for his distinguished contributions to geology and prehistory. One month later he surprised everyone by marrying Maria Lathbury, a lecturer in Greek art, who was in her mid-thirties. Any questions the marriage might have raised were offset by relief, and by general agreement with the sentiments expressed by Joseph Prestwich in his letter of congratulations: "There may be some disparity of years, but you may well take twelve or thirteen off yours, seeing how vigorous you are in mind and body. Besides, the disparity disappears before a parity in taste and thoughts." As though to bear out his friend's words, Sir John was seventy years old and vigorously delighted when his daughter Joan was born the following year.

This new addition to the Evans family amounted to a third generation: Arthur was forty-two years older than his new half sister. Her arrival in June 1893 was warmly welcomed by Sir John's grown children. Unfortunately, celebration was followed by mourning when their brother Norman died only six months later. Norman had barely turned forty; like Alice, he had been taken from them prematurely. Though Arthur had never felt the same degree of affection for the brother as for the sister, he was nevertheless deeply affected by still another death, coming as it did at a time when he was beset with heartaches and worry.

Indeed, John Evans' newfound happiness seemed to coincide with one tragedy after another in his son's life. In the very same year in which John had been both knighted and married, Margaret's father died suddenly, bringing grief not only to her but to Arthur. Edward Freeman had been more valued friend than father-in-law. The two men had shared political views and adventures, had fought for and against the same principles with equal unconcern for the consequences. Almost until the day of his death the doughty historian had been working on his history of Sicily, for which he and his son-in-law had gathered material together during their visit to the island. As a measure of respect for Freeman's memory, Evans undertook to complete the last volume with his wife as a willing assistant. No one could have been more suited than Margaret to the role of collaborator.

Margaret was familiar with her father's handwriting from her years as his secretary, and helped to decipher his notes and arrange papers. She worked hard and meticulously. Yet Arthur, usually oblivious to everything else when he was concentrating, was more and more conscious of her labored breathing. Looking up from his desk, he would find her face pale and drawn. Frequently, in the midst of checking a footnote or verifying a source, she had to lie down to rest. She had never been robust. She had always tired easily. But this was more than fatigue.

Evans either could not or would not accept the specialists' diagnosis: a tubercular infection. Margaret's illness, he kept insisting, was due to the shock of her father's death. The climate of Oxford was unhealthy for her. All she needed was a change of air, some warm Mediterranean sunshine and the smell of the sea. Was it his habitual defense against deprivation that made him turn from the facts? That early trauma of his mother's death, never wholly absorbed, now augmented by the loss of so many others? Or was it sheer dread of the possible?

Evans took his wife to Torre del Greco, on the rocky Italian coast, where she spent many hours resting on the beach. At Taormina, Sicily, despite the walks along the seashore and the siestas on the terrace of their hotel, Margaret felt feverish and weak. They tried the sea air of the Italian Riviera. When Margaret was still no better on their return to Oxford, Arthur determined to move out of the house on Holywell Street to a healthier location.

Twenty years before, as an undergraduate at the university, he had spent all his free hours exploring Boars Hill, a wild and heavily wooded elevation a few miles from Oxford. Even then he had succumbed to its beauty; had dreamed of building himself a home there. Now the dream became an obsession and a race against time. In the pure air of Boars Hill, where the wind came over the sea and over the downs from the south and east, and blew fresh and soft, Margaret would get well again. On Boars Hill, away from the damp cold of Oxford, he and Margaret would have a home worthy to succeed the Casa San Lazzaro. Boars Hill was near enough to the city for him to keep his eye on the Ashmolean, whose new building, for which he had so long agitated, was finally under construction. Arthur began roaming the hill, looking for a spot on which to build his home.

Except for the tiny hamlet of Boars Hill, containing a

few farms and the simple dwellings of a few tenant farmers or market gardeners, the mount was uninhabited and covered with trees, wild heather, and yellow furze. There were no fences or hedges to mutilate the unbroken surface, nothing to obstruct the incomparable view from the crest. The few old-timers living in the small cottages liked to recall the tradition of how Boars Hill got its name. They told of the Oxford scholar, absentmindedly climbing to the brow of the hill while reading a great thick book. Suddenly a wild boar charged at him and would have killed him, but for his presence of mind. He pushed Thucydides' *History of the Peloponnesian War* into the beast's mouth and choked him to death.

It was as likely a story as any other and pleasing, too, since it associated Boars Hill with both the age-old conception of a scholar and a chronicler of age-old events. Evans had already noted traces of an earlier period on the hill, undoubtedly Roman. He made a mental note to investigate them when he came to live there, but right now he was engaged in choosing the site. He found it without difficulty: on the far northern edge of the hill near the summit. The property he had set his heart on, necessary for the house and landscaping he had in mind, was sixty acres. Arthur saw no logic to his father's objections that so enormous an estate would be expensive to maintain.

By the end of the year 1892, with his father's financial help, Evans had bought the land and had had a small house built on it where he and Margaret could live while their new home was being constructed. He chose a lovely spot among fir trees; had the tops of the fir trees cut off, leaving the stumps; and upon the stumps built a summerhouse of pine logs. It had a veranda all around, reached by a flight of stairs about four and a half meters from the ground. Margaret's view, as she sat on the veranda high above the treetops, breathing in the pure fresh air, would stretch all the way to the distant Berkshire hills. Here she would recover while their new home neared completion. He had already chosen its name: Youlbury, from the ancient name of the heath below. But there was no time left for Margaret either to see Youlbury or to live in the treehouse. Her health was failing fast.

Still desperately clinging to his faith in a change of air, Arthur took his wife once more to the Italian Riviera and there, in Alassio, she died on March 11, 1893. Her death was a crushing blow—how great, "I cannot yet fully realize," he wrote to his father. "I do not think anyone can ever know what Margaret has been to me. All seems very dark and without consolation." During their fifteen years of marriage Arthur had come to depend on his wife for the kind of love and companionship he never again sought from a fellow being. For the rest of his life he wrote on black-edged paper; even his scribbled notes were bordered in black. It was his way of keeping Margaret's place in his heart and of warding off any future claimant.

Evans was not a man given to introspection. He had no gift for psychological insight. Yet the epitaph he composed for his wife's tombstone revealed unexpected depths of tenderness and an awareness of his own exigencies. In it he commemorated both Margaret, "within a year gathered to her Father," and Edward Freeman as well: "To him, in his library at Somerleaze, she had once been as a right hand; to her husband—in wild travel, through troublous times, and in quiet study—she was a helpmate such as few have known. Her bright energetic spirit, undaunted by suffering to the last, and ever working for the welfare of those around her, made a short life long."

Without Margaret he could not return to the old house on Holywell Street. From the house built on the stumps of fir trees on Boars Hill he guided his two grandiose projects to completion: Youlbury, his future home, and the new Ashmolean Museum, which was finally opened to the public in 1894. Both were a reflection of the man, if only in their suitability for their purposes. The Ashmolean was built to be not only a repository of fine arts but a center for archaeological research. Youlbury grew into an extension of Evans. In Youlbury he was destined to entertain two generations of friends and scholars, who would look upon his home as an important addition to their own lives and work.

"In wild travel, through troublous times, and in quiet study": those words, engraved on his wife's tomb, were a summation of the first half of Arthur Evans' life. The second half was about to begin. Ahead of him lay one of the most stunning archaeological discoveries ever made.

Studiously, he had been mapping his path to the site for ten years, ever since he and Margaret had visited Schliemann's excavations. The extraordinary gold treasures from Troy, which Sophia had wrapped in her red shawl, had never ceased to mystify him: the diadems, the signet rings, the goblets, and other treasures, but especially the tiny bead-seals like those at Mycenae, engraved—so unexpectedly—with the octopus design common to the Aegean. He puzzled over some of the objects found at Mycenae: for example, a silver rhyton, or vase, used for pouring libations to a god, in the form of a bull's head, with golden horns. The Lion Gate of Mycenae, the Cyclopean walls of Tiryns, the shaft graves and the beehive tombs—so different from classical architecture—were still vivid in his memory. That they belonged to a Bronze Age civilization dating back to perhaps 1600 B.C. he never doubted. What perplexed him was something else. The questions kept reverberating in his mind.

Who were these people? Where lay their cultural roots? Who or what had inspired their art, with its provocative hints of "foreign" derivation—quasi-Egyptian, vaguely Assyrian? Above all, Aegean? The more he thought about it the more convinced he was that the wellspring of the Mycenaean civilization lay outside the Greek mainland and that it belonged to an even older, more advanced society. A society, moreover, that had devised a system of writing. If, as he himself had seen, an ancient race had scratched primitive pictographs on a cliff of the Alpes Maritimes and on the troll-drums of Lapland, then surely the people who built the citadel of Mycenae had had a written means of communication. Furthermore, they had left behind a myriad of clues.

These clues—for example, the so-called "island-stone" in the Ashmolean Museum with its strange markings, and the traces of mysterious designs on stones, on a piece of an ancient vase—kept nagging at him; kept drawing him to the Aegean Sea and especially to Crete, the largest of the Aegean islands. These clues plus intuition.

The questions that had been simmering for ten years and

the hypotheses taking form in his mind coalesced at a time of personal crisis in his life. He would undoubtedly have found his way to Crete sooner or later, but two momentous trips he made shortly before Margaret's death—and the void she left behind her—sharply advanced his encounter with the Minoans.

The first trip was to Rome.

Chapter IX
There Lies a Land Called Crete

Evans' meeting with the archaeologist Federico Halbherr in Rome on February 3, 1892, was the beginning of a long and fruitful relationship for both men. Though the one was an aristocratic Englishman and the other a devout Italian of Alpine origin, they found common ground immediately. They even had the same physical makeup. Like Evans, Halbherr was slight of frame but had tremendous stamina. He too moved quickly, impatiently, and liked to get to wherever he was going in the fastest possible way. But the strongest bond between them was the island in the Aegean that Evans had come to talk about.

Halbherr had long had what was still for Evans an awakening passion: the exploration of Crete. He had already investigated several sites dating back to Greek and Roman times; but, he told Evans, the island was impregnated with much earlier remains, still unexplored, still unexplained. He was certain that these remains emanated from dim prehistoric times, but only the spade could prove it. Halbherr's words echoed in Evans' ears long after he had returned to England.

One year later he was in Athens, where he met John Linton Myres. Myres was then a handsome, black-bearded, blue-eyed youth of twenty-four, rather sedate and reflective, but with a lively twinkle in his eye. He was not yet the famous prehistorian he would become. Already, however, he was a thorough explorer "who is combining," Evans wrote home, "geology and archaeology in a useful way." The two men became and remained fast friends. The almost twenty years' difference in their ages was forgotten in the interests they shared and in their matched vigor and enthusiasm. "Yesterday," Evans reported in his letter, "I was grubbing with him below the 'Pelasgian' wall of the Acropolis and picking out fragments of pre-Mycenaean vases which nobody here seems to have heeded before." Myres agreed, when Evans pointed them out, that certain signs scratched on the clay were very curious indeed.

Evans, poking around in antiquity shops in Shoe Lane in Athens, saw things nobody else noticed. When he brought tiny objects close to his shortsighted eyes, he could make out details with extraordinary clarity, even though everything else was a vague blur. Among the clutter of dusty wares on wooden trays he spotted some curious three- and four-sided sealstones engraved with symbols. He examined them with the focused concentration of a laboratory researcher. If the symbols were what he thought they were—hieroglyphs, a kind of picture-writing—then the theory taking shape in his mind was right. He asked the antique dealers where the sealstones came from. The answer was Crete.

Now Evans remembered other things: the sealstones in his own collection, engraved with devices which seemed to be symbolic; reports from the Berlin Museum of seals with similar markings; the "scratches" found by the Greek archaeologist Chrestos Tsountas on two vases at Mycenae, which Tsountas ruled out as "writing" but Evans did not. With that gift of his for being able to deduce historical truths from a bare minimum of long-buried facts—with that burst of illumination which so often accompanies genius—he was ready by the autumn of 1893 to announce to the Hellenic Society that he had "a clue to the existence of a system of picture-writing in the Greek lands." Furthermore, he was convinced that this "pre-historical system of writing" was to be found somewhere on the island of Crete. Determined to find it, he made his first trip to Crete in the spring of

1894. It was a rough sea voyage from Athens, but he was on deck long before the ship anchored to catch his first glimpse of land.

The island sat athwart the Aegean Sea in the Mediterranean almost equidistant from three continents: Europe, Asia, and Africa. It was flanked by the Libyan promontory to the south and was linked by smaller island stepping-stones to the Peloponnesus, in southernmost Greece, and the Turkish mainland. It was a curiously shaped island, looking somewhat like a horned lizard, with its elongated body stretching 249.6 kilometers from east to west; its narrow girth, only 57.6 kilometers at the widest point from north to south; and its spiny hump of mountains running down the middle from tip to tip, hardly interrupted except for two fair-sized breaks. Much of the year found Mount Ida, the highest peak, covered with snow, even when the figs and grapes were at their most bountiful in the lowlands. It was a lovely island. An island with a long, long past and a very troubled present.

In approximately the ninth century B.C. Homer had called Crete "a ravisher of eyes." In the sixteenth century A.D. a Venetian nobleman wrote passionately from Candia, the island's principal city, that Crete "deserves to become the capital of the world." In the twentieth century one of the island's most famous native sons, Nikos Kazantzakis, would describe his homeland in words of stark beauty: "The face of Crete is stern and weathered. Truly Crete has about her something primeval and holy, bitter and proud." Almost thirty centuries separated the three men. That the island they all loved could be at once so stern and weathered, yet so primeval and holy, bespoke a singular history.

Even in Homer's time Crete was old. Its sailors had been sailing the Mediterranean for a thousand years and more. Because their island was so strategically placed, they could set their single square-rigged sail for Europe, Africa, or Asia and return home safely in their frail craft, manned by no more than fifteen oarsmen on each side. The rich cargoes they carried—produce of a generous soil, products of a gifted people—fostered curiosity as well as commerce. By Homer's day the sagas told about the sea people already seemed fabulous.

Unlike Schliemann, Evans was not interested in "proving Homer right." Nevertheless, like archaeologists before and after him, he looked upon the Homeric epics, as well as the Greek and Roman historians and traditional mythology, as valuable historical clues. Like most educated Englishmen in the time of Her Majesty Queen Victoria he knew his *Iliad* and *Odyssey* almost by heart.

"Out in the dark blue sea there lies a land called Crete, a rich and lovely land, washed by the waves on every side, densely peopled and boasting ninety cities. . . . One of the ninety towns is a great city called Knossos, and there, for nine years, King Minos ruled and enjoyed the friendship of almighty Zeus."

So had the Greek poet written. King Minos was a legendary figure among the ancients. He had been priest-king of Knossos, ruler over a maritime empire, and suppressor of piracy on the high seas. His fame had echoed down the corridors of prehistory. Thucydides, the Greek historian who lived in Athens in the fifth century B.C., wrote about him in his *History of the Peloponnesian War*: "Minos is the earliest ruler we know of who possessed a fleet, and controlled most of what are now Greek waters. He ruled the Cyclades, and was the first colonizer of most of them, installing his own sons as governors. In all probability he cleared the sea of pirates, so far as he could, to secure his own revenues."

In order to safeguard his gains and protect his home island, with its long coastline and isolated island valleys, King Minos had recourse to one of the wonders of the ancient world: a bronze giant called Talos. According to one legend, Hephaestus, god of fire and forge, invented this mechanical colossus; a second legend credited Minos's great architect Daedalus with the feat. Whoever his creator, the bronze robot struck fear into any stranger daring to approach the House of Minos. Three times a day Talos patrolled the Cretan waters, hurling firebrands and stones at enemy or pirate ships. He spouted fire from his mouth and made a thundering clang with each of his great strides. But when he wasn't guarding the sea, he peaceably strode the land, warding off not enemies but injustice. In his huge metallic hands he displayed the bronze tablets of the law for all Cretans to see.

For Minos was more than just conqueror. He also had a fabled reputation as lawgiver. The Cretans lived under such enlightened rule, wrote the great Aristotle himself, that they accorded their slaves the same institutions as themselves, withholding from them only the rights to practice gymnastics and to bear arms. Such prohibitions were eminently reasonable on the part of a ruler whose empire extended far beyond his own safe waters. To maintain that empire King Minos called again upon the ingenuity of wily Daedalus.

Underneath the Palace at Knossos, so went the story, Daedalus built the Labyrinth where the dread Minotaur—a hybrid monster with the body of a bull and the head of a man— exacted his yearly tribute from subjected Athens. Seven handsome youths and seven beautiful maidens, fourteen of Athens' noblest youth drawn by lot, were sent each twelfth month, in a ship fitted out with black sails, from the Greek mainland to Knossos on the isle of Crete. There they were cast into the Labyrinth to grapple with the Minotaur and to die— until the year when Theseus, son of Athens' King Aegeus, sailed to Knossos with the group.

Ariadne, King Minos's daughter, fell in love with Theseus. She gave him a ball of thread to unwind as he groped his way through the tortuous maze to encounter the Minotaur. Theseus felled the monstrous creature and then, following Ariadne's thread, retraced his steps through the Labyrinth to sunlight and freedom. It was a stirring tale—but with a sad ending.

King Aegeus had arranged with his son Theseus that, should the brave youth succeed in killing the Minotaur, he would change the black sail on his ship for one of purest white on his return to Athens. Alas, Theseus in his excitement forgot. His father, overcome with grief at seeing the black sail near the shore, threw himself into the sea. To this day that part of the Mediterranean which separates Greece from Turkey bears his name: the Aegean Sea.

To Daedalus also befell a sad fate. It was he who had given Ariadne the ball of thread for Theseus. Furious when he learned about it, King Minos threw both Daedalus and his son Icarus into the very Labyrinth from which Theseus had escaped. The cunning architect, however, knew his way around the maze. On wings of wax which he fashioned for himself and Icarus the prisoners fled from Knossos to a safer home. But Icarus was young, and drunk with the power of locomotion. He flew too close to the sun, whose bright rays melted the wax of his wings, and he plunged into the sea below.

King Minos, then, was a lawgiver not only just but stern. He was all-powerful and enjoyed, Homer had written, the friendship of the almighty Zeus. In Evans' day the country folk of Crete still pointed out the cave on Mount Dicte where Zeus, King of Gods, was born to his mother Rhea. His tomb, they said, was on Mount Juktas, the isolated peak overlooking Candia. In the right light, from certain directions, they said, one could make out the bearded face of the recumbent Zeus in the silhouette of the mountain.

Homer was in the back of Evans' mind on that spring day in 1894 when the ship carrying him to Crete made its choppy way through the surging sea. When he landed at Candia, the island's largest city, he felt almost as though he were landing at Ragusa. (He called the city Candia all his life, even after its old Italian name was changed to present-day Herakleion.) He was immediately at home. The same lustrous light bathed both cities in jewel colors. The same architectural silhouettes—Venetian walls and palaces, Turkish minarets and Christian domes—were outlined against the blue sky. There was the same sound of the sea, and the changing contours of the mountains. Unfortunately, even the political situation was familiar. Though Evans had come to investigate Crete's past, its present made first claims on his attention.

Crete, like the Balkans, was struggling to gain independence from the crumbling but still oppressive Ottoman Empire. Although bright-kerchiefed housewives still shopped together with veiled women in the old bazaars, an experienced observer like Evans had no difficulty in recognizing the tensions between the Christian majority and the Muslim minority. Within two years of his first visit there would be tragic civil war, followed by open revolt against Turkish rule. But by then Evans would have learned Crete's rivers and mountains and seas. He would know its caves and its grottoes, its people and their legends. From the moment he first set foot on its soil, his whole life would become bound up with both the past and the present of Crete.

With three mules and a muleteer, and speaking only halting Greek, Evans set out from Candia in 1894 to explore an island far more ancient than its present inhabitants could imagine. He went to Phaistos, Kamáres, Gortyna, Zakro, and other storied sites. He stopped over in Gortyna only long enough for a quick look at the famous Classical Greek inscription which his friend Halbherr had discovered ten years before. It was impressive, but not nearly so interesting as the strange markings on more ancient relics. In one place he came upon an inscribed fragment of a pottery vase, in another some engraved gems. He even detected mysterious traces of a "linear" script—a writing not pictographic but almost alphabetic—on some stones and clay vessels, on a bronze axe. By the time Evans returned to Candia, where Halbherr was coming from Rome to meet him, he was convinced that proof existed of not one but two systems of writing on the island, the first pictorial and hieroglyphic, the second linear and quasi-alphabetic.

As usual, he was so sure of himself that he wrote an article for the *Journal of Hellenic Studies* in which he declared that "In the absence of abiding monuments, the fact has too generally been lost sight of that throughout what is now the civilized European area there must once have existed systems of picture-writing such as still survive among the more primitive races of mankind." He also began working on a book entitled *Cretan Pictographs and Pre-Phoenician Script*—all this before he had yet begun to excavate. But he already knew exactly where he would dig when the time came. Tradition going back many generations had given the site its name: Knossos. "Broad Knossos," Homer had called it. It was not far from Candia where his friend Halbherr had already arrived from Rome and was waiting for him.

Halbherr introduced Evans to a Cretan antiquarian whose name came naturally to the tongue on an island saturated with legend: Minos Kalokairinos. Sixteen years earlier this latter-day Minos had dug up some enormous ancient storage jars, or *pithoi* (singular *pithos*), on a hilltop about six and a half kilometers from Candia. Ever since, the local people had called the site *sta pithára*, "place of the jars." Its actual name was Kephála, "Squire's Knoll"—called thus because it was owned by the family of a Turkish bey who had built his country house near the stream below. However, in tradition and folk memory the name Knossos was the one attached to the spot.

Kephála was a large, rounded mound that mingled with the surrounding terrain on two sides but fell steeply downward into deep gullies on the south and east, where the Kairatos stream ran. When Evans first saw it, parts of the site looked untouched even by a plow. There was nothing visible above the ground except for some minor relics and the tumbled remains of a wall above the southern slope. Nothing, that is, but the superstitions, even mysticism, that had grown up through the centuries about the mound to which the name Knossos clung.

Other archaeologists before Evans, including Halbherr and the great Schliemann, had wanted to excavate Kephála. As early as 1888, long before Evans' first visit to the island, Schliemann had written in a letter, "I would like to end my life's labours with one great work—the prehistoric palace of the Kings of Knossos in Crete." Schliemann had actually secured an excavation grant from the Turkish authorities, after overcoming enormous difficulties, but was then unable to reach financial agreement with the owner of the land. Two years later Schliemann died. "Nor can I pretend to be sorry that he did not dig at Knossos," Evans blandly admitted some forty years later, in his introduction to Emil Ludwig's *Schliemann of Troy*. "The complicated nature of the task in the great palace was little adapted to his summary methods."

Indeed, there was even doubt in Evans' mind that Schliemann had planned to attack the correct site. The one the German archaeologist described contained farms and valuable olive groves and was marshy, whereas "the hill of Kephála, where the remains of the House of Minos lie . . . had neither farms nor olive-trees and, owing to its elevation, was decidedly dry." Evans fully understood, however, "that Schliemann should have been put off by the Turkish obstruction," since he himself had to struggle with it arduously.

In the year 1894, the Turkish authorities were far more preoccupied with disturbances on the island of Crete than with its past glories. They would have little interest, Evans shrewdly surmised, in handing out excavation grants to a myopic Englishman who might cause further trouble. He decided that the only way to excavate the site where he was sure Knossos lay buried was first to buy it. This he proceeded to do—with no less difficulty than Schliemann had encountered but with more stubbornness and experience.

Evans knew his Turkish pashas. He was long familiar with Turkish pride. Many were the bazaars he had haggled in. Conversations over small cups of sweetened coffee, drawn out by diversionary pleasantries, were not new to him. Nevertheless, he had nearly met his match in these Muslim proprietors of Kephála, "to whose almost inexhaustible powers of obstruction," he wrote his father, "I can pay the highest tribute." But in the end sheer persistence won out.

Evans emerged from the negotiations as the owner of a quarter-share of Kephála under Ottoman law, thus acquiring a veto on excavation by anyone else and the right legally to compel sale on the rest of the site. He planned, he announced, to raise money for the entire purchase in England through the "Cretan Exploration Fund"—nonexistent as yet except in his own mind. Meanwhile, his colleague Federico Halbherr would act for this still-to-be-created Cretan Exploration Fund as epigraphic explorer, continuing the search for written records of the past.

Evans returned to Youlbury on Boars Hill with a vested interest in the still-unknown people who slumbered under his quarter-share of Kephála. He spent the rest of the year 1894 in England, attending to his duties as Keeper of the Ashmolean and continuing to write *Cretan Pictographs and Pre-Phoenician Script.* In April 1895 he was back in Crete, accompanied this time by his friend John Myres.

The mound of Kephála beckoned invitingly under the warm spring sun, but there was no question of looking for Knossos beneath its surface. Not yet. The Turks were still in harsh control of Crete in 1895. The purpose of Evans' and Myres's trip was to explore as much of the island as they had time

for, and in particular to track down archaeological evidence
that betrayed ancient sites. They found their way into odd
corners rarely penetrated by foreigners.

"I remember my father commenting on what a tricky business travelling with Evans in remote places could be," wrote
John Myres's son many years later. The son, John Nowell
Linton Myres, was by then himself a distinguished historian
and archaeologist. But though his memories of Evans went
back to his childhood, they were still vivid. Evans was not
the kind of man one easily forgot. His letter continued:

> Though extremely short-sighted, Evans had an uncanny
> sense for antiquities, almost like a dog's sense of smell. They
> would be sitting over coffee in a village street in some far
> away place, and Evans would suddenly spring to his feet
> and dart off, saying "Excuse me a minute. I think that woman
> over there has something." Nothing more might be heard
> of him for hours, but as often as not he would eventually
> return in triumph with a Greek gem or a Mycenaean seal.
> Needless to say, this sort of thing could give rise to mis-
> understandings, especially with the ladies' friends and re-
> lations, and it sometimes fell to my father to bail Evans
> out of the local police station or some military *oubliette* [dun-
> geon].

Rescued from the hands of the law, Evans would triumphantly display to his friend Myres, still recovering from
the negotiations over bail, a *galopetra*, a "milkstone." Prized
as amulets by villagers ignorant of their own past, they were
ancient gems and sealstones carved with signs or scenes of
extraordinary beauty. Peasants found them while plowing their
fields. A donkey's hoof on a rutted path kicked them up
from the earth. Cretan mothers wore them around their necks
as charms to insure an adequate supply of milk for their
babies. Sometimes even Evans, that "child-like lover of children," as John Myres described him, wasn't able to persuade
a mother that no harm would come to her infant if she
parted with her "milkstone." In that case, Evans asked permission to make an impression of its engraving. Then, after
thanking the still-dubious mother, the "crazy Englishmen"
continued their explorations.

The two of them—the quiet, bearded Myres and Evans with his walking stick, Prodger—traveled on foot and by mule to the farthest corners of central and eastern Crete. Wherever they found clay potsherds that had been fired millennia ago, they knew that here lay a town which had existed long before the Greeks and Romans reached Crete. At Goulas, one such site, they stopped long enough for some digging. As the spade turned over the earth, Evans could identify from the rough and weathered stones the gates, stairways, shrine, and palace of a thriving trading town going back to Mycenaean times. It made him all the more eager to enlarge his quarter-share in Kephála and begin excavating the city Homer had called "broad Knossos."

Despite the political troubles brewing on the island, despite his co-owners' obduracy, Evans was already thinking ahead. Picnicking with Myres on a sunny April day in an open field overlooking the ancient mound, he suddenly told his friend, "This is where I shall live when I come to dig up Knossos." Just as he had selected the site of Youlbury when he was still an undergraduate at Oxford, so Evans decided that someday he would build his Cretan home on this very spot. And so he did, eleven years later.

His return to Youlbury not long after the picnic lunch with Myres set a pattern of travel between Crete and England that would continue for many years. But whichever of the two islands he was on, Evans' life revolved around a people he still hadn't discovered. In an article published in June 1896 in *Academy*, a literary review highly respected for its scholarly character, he called them Minoans for the first time, after their great King Minos. This was four years before he had begun to dig at Knossos. Nevertheless, he wrote with remarkable prescience that "The great days of Crete were those of which we still find a reflection in the Homeric poems—the period of the Mycenaean culture, to which here at least we would fain attach the name 'Minoan.'"

He went on to explain why. "Nothing more continually strikes the archaeological explorer of [Crete's] ancient remains than the comparative paucity and unimportance of the historic period." By historic period he meant that of Greece, which the historian George Grote had so categorically stated began in 776 B.C. with the first recorded Olympiad. Evans continued with his thesis: "The Golden Age of Crete lies far beyond the limits of the historical period; its culture not only displays within the three seas an uniformity never afterwards attained, but is practically identical with that of the Peloponnese and a large part of the Aegean world."

Once again Evans had formulated, from a minimum amount of evidence, a hypothesis so clear that for him it had the weight of a theory. All that remained was to prove it, and for this he relied on the dig. Unfortunately, politics and war delayed his impatient spade. While King Minos still slept undisturbed at Knossos, the roar of the Minotaur was heard in the land. The island reverberated to the sounds of violence.

Chapter X
A Throne Room, a "Saint"

Muslim against Christian, neighbor against neighbor: the conflict raging in Crete was not only insurrection against the Turks but civil war. The tensions had finally boiled over. From Youlbury Evans followed the lurid reports of massacres on both sides. It was like reliving his experience in the Balkans. In 1897, Prince George of Greece, yielding to the nationalist clamor of the Christians, sent a small expeditionary force to Crete. In return the sultan of the Ottoman Empire declared war. What had been conflict became carnage.

Within a month, the far superior Turkish troops had so decimated the unprepared and ill-equipped Greek force that Prince George had to appeal to the Great Powers to bring about an armistice. While fighting kept flaring out on the island, negotiations dragged on in the chancelleries of Europe and resulted in an arrangement euphemistically called a peace agreement in September 1897. This arrangement did little more than to provide a breathing spell for renewed violence, triggered by inflamed nationalism and fanaticism.

As the year 1898 began, six Ottoman peasants committed the rash act of murdering the British consul at Candia. This finally ended the dallying of the powers. A settlement was imposed. Though it failed to fulfill Cretan hopes for a union with Greece—that would not come until 1913—it did provide a fairly satisfactory half-measure. Crete was granted autonomy, with Prince George acting as high commissioner under the protection of Great Britain, Russia, Italy, and France. Each of these "great Christian Powers" was to occupy a portion of the island until order was restored.

Evans returned to Crete with John Myres in March 1898 as the settlement was beginning to be implemented. They were joined by David Hogarth, who was then director of the British School of Archaeology at Athens. Hogarth, eleven years younger than Evans and a descendant of the famous eighteenth-century artist, was the only one of the three who was already an experienced excavator. He had done fieldwork in Cyprus, Ephesus, and Carchemish after having excavated in Egypt, where, he wrote, "largely through becoming known" to the great Egyptologist Flinders Petrie, "and living with men who had served apprenticeship to him, I had learned to dig." His help to Evans would be invaluable.

The three men found Candia a desolate place, still governed by the Turkish pasha, despite the presence of British troops. No sounds of goatherds piping to their goats came down from the hills to break the silence. Most of the inns, cookshops, and coffeehouses were either burned or closed down. Houses were shuttered, the medieval streets were deserted, and the rank smell of burning oil from vats stored in flaming houses filled the air.

To Evans the plight of desperate men, anguished women, and children with swollen bellies was a familiar call to action. Unhesitatingly, the archaeologist once again became journalist and relief worker. His long days began with the first rays of the sun and ended only when his night blindness forced a halt. Gesticulating with Prodger, he speeded up relief supplies. He even boarded a gunboat of Her Majesty's Royal Navy to help distribute food and grain himself along the coast. For someone as prone to seasickness as he was, this was an act of pure devotion.

A tour of the island quickly revealed the extent of the damage. What he saw, the readers of *The Manchester Guardian* would soon learn. His dispatches were indignant and explicit. Sometimes, when power politics ignored human needs, Evans felt the same self-involvement and fury that had landed him in a Balkan jail. Although it was not he but his muleteer,

Herakles, who fell into the hands of the authorities, Evans' scathing protest reached the halls of Parliament.

He was returning to Candia from a fact-finding trip through eastern Crete, he informed the readers of *The Manchester Guardian*. With him was Herakles, a Christian, "a jovial little elderly man" with a talent for hunting out antiquities; a combination muleteer, guide, cook, and general servant. Herakles had no formal pass to enter the city, but there was no cause for worry. The British commandant of Candia had told Evans to have Herakles report to the Turkish police on arrival and say that he, Colonel Chermside, had sent him. Instead, the old man was arrested at the gates of the city and "thrown into a noisome den, used by the Turks as a privy, foul with ordure."

Evans was furious. He sent an urgent note to Colonel Chermside on his visiting card: "The plea is that he had no regular pass—but are such obtainable in the mountains?"

Chermside's reply was crisp and damning: "I am here to cooperate with the Turks."

Now wild with indignation, Evans demanded to see the Turkish pasha, whose "shrinking glance, sour expression, and long, narrow face, sallow and wrinkled as a last year's pippin" could still terrorize Candia despite the presence of Her Majesty's troops. No pasha, however, could terrorize Evans. He traded sour expressions in kind until the unfortunate Herakles was released from his noisome den.

Before returning to England, Evans sent a crackling report to *The Manchester Guardian* summing up the situation: "We are here to cooperate with the Turks. Our system is diametrically opposite to that followed by other European powers on Crete. The French and Russians especially try to prepare the population for a new order of things.... Instead, every action of the British in Candia is calculated to keep Moslems in their fool's paradise." Evans' angry outburst hardly endeared him to the Conservative Party in England, but it set him apart in Cretan eyes as a warm friend and advocate. The Cretans would never forget him and would seize every opportunity to express their gratitude.

The last of the Turkish troops finally left the island on November 14, 1898. The following spring Evans was back with David Hogarth. Hogarth described their visit in his book *Accidents of an Antiquary's Life*: "We journeyed all around the eastern half of the island, pegging out claims for future digging. Known to the islanders as we both were (though I the less), we were made gladly welcome everywhere. The land still showed ghastly wounds of its late long fight. Many villages lay gaunt skeletons of ruin; and where olive groves had been, blackened stumps and pits bore witness to the ethnicidal fury of religious war in the Near East."

This trip was but a prelude to what was ahead. The Minoans were still waiting for Evans. But with Crete now free and autonomous the hour of encounter was not far off. Hogarth wrote:

> Arthur Evans had long laid his plans, and with the fore-thought of genius, had cast his bread on troubled waters by buying a Bey's part share of the site of the Palace of Minos. . . . When others, who coveted Knossos, put forward moral rights, he alone could urge the convincing claim of sacrifice, and the Cretans, for whom he had done much in their hour of danger, upheld his cause in the hour of freedom.
>
> For us, then, and no others, in the following year (1900) Minos was waiting when we rode out from Candia. Over the very site of his buried throne a desolate donkey drooped, the one living thing in view. He was driven off and the digging of Knossos began.

Arthur Evans began probing for a buried civilization on March 23, 1900, when the first pickaxe penetrated the *tell*, or mound, of Kephála. *Tell* was the Arabic word for an artificial mound formed by human occupation over a long period of time. Such a mound was composed of layer upon layer of houses, towns, temples, tombs, or palaces resting on the ruins of their predecessors. It was the accumulation of each later generation's floors on top of the previous in-habitants' caved-in roofs; of the stones and rubbish and tum-bled walls of succeeding lifetimes, used as building materials by descendants or conquerors. The earliest occupants of a *tell* might have lived on the ground level of a surrounding plain. The latest could have built their dwellings twenty or more meters above the plain, with no notion that they owed their "hill" to generations of forebears. But to an archaeologist a *tell*, with its many strata of human occupation, was like a cross-section of history.

Evans, one of the pioneers in archaeology, was unfamiliar with all the modern skills of excavation. He did not know today's accepted techniques of making a deep cut through all the strata down to virgin soil. Of clearing stratum by stratum horizontally. Of leaving standing sections at frequent intervals from the surface down, to serve as "control points" whereby one could relate structures or disturbances to their proper strata. Nevertheless, the principle of stratigraphy— of distinguishing one deposit from another by its color, texture, or contents—is one of the major tools of archaeology. It was adopted from geology, a science in which the son of Sir John Evans had been trained from childhood. He was unlikely to make the mistakes of his great predecessor Heinrich Schliemann who, in his desire to "get to the bottom" and find Homer's Troy, had driven a great trench across the site of Hissarlik, thus not only mutilating and confusing the finds but ending up with the wrong Troy.

To Evans' educated eyes each layer of a *tell* looked different from the one above or below it. Each could be identified by a change of color, consistency, or texture in the soil and by the objects embedded in it; by the remains of buildings and the man-made artifacts that betrayed a human presence, no matter how far back. As far back as the Stone Age. Evans uncovered traces, when he reached the level of virgin rock, of a Neolithic people who might have lived at Knossos, he thought, as early as 8000 B.C. (Modern archaeologists, using radioactive carbon 14 dating, place the date at 6100 B.C.) But he didn't have to dig that far down for surprises. The mound of Knossos had more immediate revelations to offer only thirty-three centimeters beneath its flowering topsoil.

Evans knew from the day the dig started that under the ground he walked on lay a labyrinth of buildings. As early as the second day his workmen came upon the remains of an ancient house, with fragments of frescoes. The third day revealed walls blackened by smoke from a great conflagration, and large quantities of pottery, most of it broken. Rims of huge storage jars, or *pithoi*, began to appear. Bits of frescoes turned up—part of a large fish, a fragment with a graceful spray of leaves. By the fifth day Evans was ready to enter in his notebook a fundamental discovery: "The extraordinary phenomenon: nothing Greek—nothing Roman—perhaps one single fragment of late black varnished ware among tens of thousands. . . . Nay, its great period goes at least well back to a pre-Mycenaean period." And then came the final justification for all his years of preparation, all the theories he had expounded, articles written, lectures delivered.

Exactly one week after he began excavating, Arthur Evans found what he was looking for: evidence of a prehistoric writing system. His entry in his notebook on March 30 described the most remarkable discovery so far: "a kind of baked clay bar rather like a stone chisel in shape, though broken at one end, with script on it and what appears to be numerals. It at once recalled a clay tablet of unknown age that I had copied at Candia, also found at Knossos. Also broken. There is something like cursive writing about these."

Within days the workmen had turned up a hundred tablets and more. By the end of the first season's dig there were over a thousand. He had discovered "a hoard," Evans triumphantly announced in *The Times*, a hoard of written records in an unknown tongue. They were the memoranda of a literate society still awaiting rescue by his spade. They were the oldest documents yet found on the doorstep of Europe.

Most of the tablets were from five to twenty centimeters long and from one and a half to seven and a half centimeters wide. Others were rectangular in shape and large enough to carry several lines of inscription. Evans deduced that "these inscriptions engraved on the wet clay are evidently the work of practised scribes." Holding the larger tablets close to his eyes, he could detect the faint horizontal markings used by the scribes as guidelines. Most of the characters, carefully incised in straight rows, were linear and of two kinds, which he promptly called Linear A and Linear B. However, a few of the characters were pictographic, "showing what the subject of the documents was. Thus in one chamber occurred a series with chariots and horses' heads on them, others show vases. . . ."

Were they an inventory? Palace records? The archives of commerce? Studying certain repeated arrangements of vertical and diagonal strokes, broken by dots and check marks, Evans could distinguish a system of numbers based on the decimal system. But a really thorough study of the tablets would have to wait. There was almost daily excitement on the *tell* of Knossos.

Turning over the earth in the early days of April, one of the workmen let out a piercing cry which brought Evans running to the spot. There on the floor level of what appeared to be a hall or a corridor lay two large pieces of fresco. Dirt-spattered though they were, their bright colors seemed almost freshly painted. One of the fragments represented the head and forehead, the other the waist and part of the skirt— it seemed to be a skirt—of a life-size figure holding in its right hand a rhyton, or high funnel-shaped vase. It was, Evans wrote dramatically, "by far the most remarkable figure of the Mycenaean Age that has yet come to light."

He used the word Mycenaean instead of Minoan. Nevertheless, he had crossed the threshold into a long-forgotten world and come face-to-face with the inventors of the writing system on the tablets. It was an unforgettable moment which he wanted to share first of all with his father. "Have found frescoes and script love Arthur," he cabled. Sir John was so carried away when he heard the news that he immediately sent his son a check for £500.

Lifting the frescoes from the earth was a long and delicate process, requiring time and great patience. Some one would have to stand guard over the precious fragments at night, and for this duty Evans appointed Manolis, one of his most trusted workmen. Like the other simple and devout Cretan diggers, old Manoli, as everyone called him, had been awe-struck at finding a painting buried in the earth. It could only be the icon of a saint. Dozing off during his nighttime vigil, Manoli saw the face of the saint in his troubled dreams. He awoke with a start, "conscious of a mysterious presence; the animals around began to low and neigh, and there were visions about. . . . He said in summing up his experiences next morning, 'the whole place spooks!' "

And indeed, it did seem as though supernatural powers

were at work. A few days after the discovery of the fresco there was another outcry from a group of workmen. They had sunk their spades barely half a meter below the surface into what was evidently a chamber. Already a wall, with some remains of painted plaster stuck to the rubble, stood revealed. As they continued to dig they uncovered first the curved top, then the arched back, the hollowed-out seat, and finally the whole of what turned out to be a finely carved chair. It was made of gypsum, an attractive soft-veined stone resembling alabaster, quarried from the hill of Gypsades just south of Knossos. Soon, on each side of this high-backed chair, two gypsum benches emerged from their long burial, and alongside and above them appeared further remains of wall painting.

The men continued clearing away the debris that filled the room. Opposite the chair they came upon a balustrade, also of gypsum, and flanked by a similar low bench. Behind the bench Evans could clearly make out three sockets, still bearing the imprints of the columns which had been fitted into them. The columns themselves had been made of wood. Their fragile carbonized remains crumbled into dust at a finger's touch.

Digging beyond the balustrade, the workmen reached a flight of gypsum stairs leading down to a sunken room. With increasing excitement they removed the dirt that filled the area. There was a small gypsum fount, or basin, in the center. A high-pedestaled stone lamp stood nearby. One alabaster oil vessel was still upright and the marks of five others, now scattered near the entrance to the room, were plainly marked out on the floor. A large clay oil jar lay overturned on its side. Smoke stains from a fearful conflagration were plainly visible on the walls, which were covered with fine plaster painted in Venetian red. Amid this gloom and destruction the white alabaster-like basin had a ghostly gleam.

Evans thought at first that it was a bath chamber. But as his eager Cretan helpers continued their work, more and more elements of the original construction came to light. It was obvious that the three columns, placed in the still-visible sockets, had supported a gallery above the room with the chair. This gallery—perhaps intended for spectators—had overlooked the sunken basin, like a loge at the theater. It could not have been a bath chamber, then, as he had thought at first. The basin was a lustral basin, the sunken chamber a lustral area—that is, a place with religious significance, used for ceremonial purification and ritual anointing.

Now additional bits of colored plaster were sifted from the dirt. From these fragments emerged a pattern of great wingless griffins with elaborate crests of peacock feathers that had covered one of the frescoed walls. From adjoining walls came bits and pieces of a painted landscape of hills, a river, and flowering sedges. The stone chair itself had been stuccoed and brightly painted. Its high back, made of a single piece of gypsum, had an undulating leaflike pattern, and the whole chair was elevated on a square base with a curious molding.

Whoever had sat on its seat, so artfully hollowed out, would tower majestically over the people sitting on the side benches. Evans estimated that there could have been as many as twenty spectators—councillors? worshippers?—in the room. Clearly, he concluded, "The elaborate decoration, the stately aloofness, superior size and elevation of the gypsum seat sufficiently declare it to be a throne-room." On this very throne, "the oldest throne in Europe"—only yesterday still buried in the earth—the mighty priest-king himself might have presided over the anointment ceremony taking place in the lustral area below.

Had he needed confirmation, the Throne Room provided it: Evans had discovered the Palace of Knossos, "the realm of the legendary Minos, the great conqueror and law-giver." Minos had ruled over a civilization far, far older than that of Classical Greece; far older even than that of Homer's Trojans and Mycenaeans. Everything pointed to this conclusion. The test pits Evans had sunk deep into the ground revealed evidence of almost continuous human settlement since Neolithic times. The figure on the fresco old Manoli had called a saint was unlike any in ancient art heretofore discovered. Pottery decorated with marine creatures—octopus, starfish, sea urchin—bore out Thucydides' assertions, written in the fifth century B.C., that on Crete had lived a sea-people ruled by Minos, controller of Greek waters and first colonizer of the Greek islands.

In his vivid prose, which injected poetry into scholarship, Evans announced his epochal discovery in an article in *The Times*:

> Crete was in remote times the home of a highly developed culture which vanished before the dawn of history . . . among the prehistoric cities of Crete, Knossos, the capital of Minos, is indicated by legend as holding the foremost place. Here the great law-giver promulgated his famous institutions . . . here was established a . . . maritime empire, suppressing piracy, conquering the islands of the Archipelago, and imposing a tribute on subjected Athens. Here Daedalos constructed the Labyrinth, the den of the Minotaur, and fashioned the wings— perhaps the sails—with which he and Icarus took flight over the Aegean.

Londoners, reading *The Times* over breakfast, were startled by this clarion evocation of the past. They would soon become accustomed to scanning the paper eagerly for the latest account from Crete. While Evans the archaeologist continued digging at Knossos, Evans the publicist kept both the scholarly and lay worlds informed of his progress. His pen could soar, along with his imagination, to heights as dramatic as Homer's own. The crowning discovery of the first season's dig, *The Times'* readers would learn on August 10, 1900, came "when the remains of a painted stucco bull, a marvellously realistic work, were brought to light in the north-east propylaea. . . . Here we have, perhaps, the effigy of the beautiful animal which won the heart of Pasiphaë, or of the equally famous quadruped that transported Europa to Crete." There was little doubt, in the opinion of *The Times* correspondent, that the results of Mr. Evans' explorations would "equal, if they do not surpass, in importance the discoveries of Schliemann at Tiryns and Mycenae." Soon, newspapers everywhere were spreading the news.

"Are we, at the opening of the twentieth century," asked *The New York Times*, "to see an ancient figure drawn out of mythology into authenticity? Are we to catch a glimpse of a Homeric god as he lived in the flesh?" A distinguished body of "Oxford explorers," under the leadership of Professor

Evans, the paper went on to say, had reason to believe that the answer was yes.

But no matter how great the fervor of the public or the excitement at Nash Mills, it was nothing compared to the exhilaration at Knossos. Evans had little realized, when he began penetrating the ancient *tell*, that the hoary mound, so barren in its outward form, had once teemed with life within; that the civilization created by generations of gifted people would turn out to be unique among their contemporaries in antiquity.

Chapter XI
A Man Called User

The 50 workmen Evans employed in March 1900, selected with the help of David Hogarth, had increased to 180 by June 2 when the dig ended. They included Muslims and Christians of both sexes, a risky experiment which turned out unexpectedly well. Only a few months earlier the two communities had been sworn enemies, sacking each other's homes and burning villages. Now they found common ground through the spade and celebrated a holiday by dancing the Cretan *Choros* together on the site of their ancient forebears.

The men were grateful for the work, after the ravages of war, and worked hard. They filled the iron wheelbarrows (imported from England) with rubble and wheeled them over and over again to the dump heap. The women were kept busy washing pottery and small objects. "It is always well," Hogarth observed shrewdly, "to have a few women among your diggers. The men labour better in their company, and with a vivacity which is of no small value where boredom spells failure. The day, which also might drag its slow length along, goes merrily in chatter and laughter, and the task is sought cheerfully at dawn and not willingly left at eve."

Hogarth spent only a few weeks with Evans before going off to conduct his own dig at Psychro in eastern Crete, but he returned to Knossos from time to time to see how the work was progressing. He was not unaware of his own contribution. "I did something to help my colleague to start, for in digging, as in most ventures, the first steps are the most difficult; and I did more in the following months to define the limits of his vast field, of which much still awaits the spade." He also knew the importance of teaching workers how to dig within a defined area and how to keep careful watch for any objects found therein. No task, he felt, should take priority over the training of even the humblest member of the field crew.

"The common labourer's eyes and hands and purpose," Hogarth wrote, "must be extensions of one's own. If an excavator, deaf to the first and greatest commandment of his calling, take no care to make his labourers better than unskilled navvies, what should he find except the things that a navvy could not miss in the dark?"

At the end of each week the workers were paid extra for any objects they had found, as a reward for vigilance and an inducement to honesty. Pocketing a potsherd might be overlooked, but deviation from what Evans called "the permissible limit of peculation" was severely punished. Aristides, Evans' first foreman, lost his job when inscribed tablets from Knossos turned up on the Athens market and were traced to him. But there were remarkably few such cases. Gradually, unskilled workers became keen and devoted members of a team.

They learned to remove the earth in layers from the surface so that pieces of fresco, otherwise ruined by the pick, would remain intact. Then they sifted the earth through large sieves set in wooden stands, sometimes two and even three times, in order to trap any small objects embedded in it. This procedure, commonplace today, was such an innovation then that a correspondent for *The Times* cabled London about the great advance in methods since Schliemann's day. "The methods have become more minute, precise and scientific," he wrote. "The use of the sieve, for instance, has rescued hundreds of seal-impressions and other objects hitherto liable to be overlooked."

Evans, with his bouncy step and his walking stick, Prodger, seemed to be everywhere at once. Without looking up from their spades, the workmen felt his presence as he examined the waste heaps after each sifting, finding incredibly tiny relics and drawing from them, with his visionary intuition, conclusions which might have eluded a less imaginative man. One particularly interesting object trapped by the sieve he noted in his Notebook on April 10. It was "... the clay impression of a Mycenaean signet. It bore a bold but somewhat imperfectly executed design of a lion in a contracted position, with a star-like object on the foreshoulder.... The clay impression had broken off showing a hollow where the string had passed through, some small strands of which, spirally woven, were visible. Near were found four small bronze hinges, which evidently had belonged to the box which it had sealed. There was also found a piece of charred wood with carving, probably a part of the coffer itself."

Not even minute strands of string escaped his notice; not even carving on a bit of charred wood. His Cretan workmen were acutely aware of him as he studied almost invisible inscriptions. Truth to tell, they stood in awe of Evans. Their employer was kind and generous but aloof; always the aristocrat who, for all his espousal of oppressed masses, remained a Victorian imperialist. They felt much more at ease with Evans' assistant Duncan Mackenzie, whose modest origins in the highlands of Scotland were closer to their own.

On a modern dig Mackenzie would be called the site supervisor. Educated in Vienna and Edinburgh, he had come to Knossos after many years of field experience with the British School of Archaeology at Athens. Beginning as a staff member, he had ended up in charge of the dig at Phylakopi, a deeply stratified and complex site on the island of Melos. Phylakopi, whose excavation had begun in 1895, was the first stratified site to be explored in the Aegean. It produced important results by offering a standard sequence of periods and ceramic styles and by bringing the evidence from Cycladic tombs in other islands into perspective. While he was working there, Mackenzie had perfected techniques of his own, especially in the correlation of pottery with the architectural remains found in a given stratum. It was his misfortune that the full report of the dig was not published until 1904, by which time the discoveries at Knossos far outshone those at Phylakopi. Hired as an assistant, Mackenzie was destined to remain in second place. Evans towered over him, despite the enormous difference in their size.

They made quite a pair. Evans was not much more than five feet two inches tall. Mackenzie, close to six feet three inches in his stocking feet, was a giant, though a gentle giant, by comparison. He wore a big mustache, had a thatch of red hair, and spoke in an almost inaudible voice. A fluent linguist, he was quick to pick up regional idioms and accents and this, together with his disarming simplicity, endeared him to the Cretan workmen. No villager thought of inviting Evans to a wedding, baptism, or wake; yet no ceremony was complete without Mackenzie. The red-headed Scotsman had a quick temper but never bore grudges. Normally reticent, he loosened up over a glass of raki, the favorite local drink made of fermented raisins. He made genial toasts in the Cretan dialect of modern Greek. His soft voice joined in the "table songs" his hosts sang, songs about love, friendship, war, and freedom. He could eat as much *koukiá*—the special Cretan dish of boiled beans mashed down with olive oil— as anyone at the table. Mackenzie, brought up on Scottish reels, could spontaneously join hands in a native dance on holidays, yet command utmost respect during work hours.

Off and on for thirty years, the Scotsman was Evans' as- sistant, a relationship from which, one could imagine, he might occasionally welcome relief at a Cretan wedding. To his credit, Evans exercised sound judgment in choosing his staff. Nevertheless, with his terrifying energy and his autocratic ways, he was a difficult man to work with. One did not freely disagree with the master or question his authority. Since Mackenzie could be testy in his own way, there were inevitably times when tempers were buried as treasures were unearthed.

On such occasions Mackenzie would seek relief over a bottle of raki, a beverage which Evans scorned. He preferred champagne or French wines. Or perhaps the two of them dispelled rancor with a toast at dinner to the success of their common labors. The Scotsman was an able excavator and a loyal collaborator. His complete devotion to his work, coupled with his inner understanding of his workmen, made him a valuable asset to Evans.

One of Mackenzie's responsibilities was to keep the Day Books. Evans filled his notebooks with particular points that interested him, but he depended on his assistant for a precise and thorough record of each day's excavations. Every evening Mackenzie carefully noted the pottery and other objects found, the levels reached, the progress of the dig. He drew neat sketches of half-exposed plans and made detailed entries of the main findings. These Day Books, reflecting fresh impressions of work in progress, were more an excavator's running diary than an archaeologist's conclusions, since tomorrow's dig might alter today's hypothesis. Neither Evans nor Mackenzie could have imagined that half a century later the Day Books would spark a scientific, but nevertheless savage, controversy among scholars questioning some of Evans' theories.

Very likely, arguments over entries in the Day Books would have left Evans unperturbed. He pursued his goals in his own way, serenely recognizing that others in addition to Mackenzie might find his methods high-handed. No one could deny, however, that they were imaginative.

Evans was one of the first archaeologists to employ an architect on the site at all times. He brought over Theodore Fyfe from the British School of Archaeology at Athens when it became apparent how vast Knossos was, both in breadth and in depth, and how exceedingly complex in its layout. Fyfe drew the conclusions of a professional architect from imprints of doorjambs, from evidence of columns, from floor levels and ceilings, and the remains of staircases. His plans, sections, and drawings visualized on paper what were ruins to the eyes. By the end of the first season's dig he was able to draw up a general plan of the Palace of Knossos. Though many details were still lacking, it was already clear that the great building was a mystifying complex of chambers, courts, and corridors: if not a labyrinth, at least labyrinthine.

It was no wonder, Evans thought, picturing how much more of the structure must have been exposed in the time of Homer's Greeks, that the ancients had equated Knossos's twists and turns with Daedalus's maze. However, he noted, it was more likely that the fabled labyrinth got its name from the word *labrys,* or double axe, the symbolic weapon of the Minoan Mother Goddess. She manifested herself in many forms: as nature goddess, huntress, queen of animals, sea goddess, earth goddess. Her visible presence was often indicated by doves or by birds of ravenlike appearance; by lions and leopards. As Lady of the Underworld her emblem was the spotted snake. But the special and most frequent representation of the Mother Goddess was the double axe. Evans found the sacred symbol carved everywhere, outnumbering all the other marks on the palace walls put together. It was woven into the very fabric of the palace history—an exceedingly long history indeed.

For Knossos had been lived in since Stone Age days. The site predated the reign of even the first King Minos ("or whatever historic personage is covered by that name," Evans wrote. He took Minos to be a dynastic title, similar to the Egyptian pharaoh.) Under the oldest palace level he found the stone implements, clay spindle whorls, bone needles, and shuttles of a Neolithic folk who had developed a surprisingly advanced civilization. They had lived in flat mud-brick houses and sowed seeds of wild grasses which were the earliest strains of wheat and barley. Their men domesticated sheep, goats, cattle, and pigs, and cleared land for cultivation. Their women played a remarkable role in inventing major technical resources. They ground and cooked grain, spun and wove cloth, made clothes and pottery.

Evans thought that around 2800 B.C.—opinions still differ as to the exact date—the indigenous Neolithic settlers of Crete were joined by new migrants from Asia Minor and, based on certain traits he considered common to both regions, from Libya. These newcomers put an end to the Neolithic way of life in Crete. They introduced bronze. They learned to fuse copper with tin. The metal thus created could be cast and forged. It was hard and durable and handsome. From it one could make far superior tools and weapons, and objects of great beauty and utility.

These metalworkers inherited the achievements of the stoneworkers and richly extended them. Isolated mud houses became villages; villages became towns and eventually kingdoms. By the beginning of the third millennium Crete was

already heavily populated and its horizons lay beyond the
sea. Even the earliest Minoans had been good sailors, and
why not? Their island, wrote the Greek historian Diodorus
in the first century B.C., "lay in a most favorable position
for travel to all parts of the world."

During the first season's dig Evans was still only groping
toward dates. Even in the early months of 1900, however,
the spade turned up certain findings which he could pinpoint
on· the calendar of prehistory. He knew already, from the
archaeological evidence, that the original palace itself had
been built and destroyed, rebuilt and again destroyed several
times over during the centuries. He could clearly distinguish
the different floor levels and pottery that marked different
epochs. And then came one of those moments when history,
helping to unravel itself, drops a clue.

In the stratum immediately above the Neolithic level—
the stratum which was probably, therefore, the "first palace
level"—Evans found pottery of a very distinctive style, which
had been puzzling scholars for ten years. This pottery was
called Kamáres ware, from the name of the cave sanctuary
in central Crete, on the southern slope of Mount Ida, where
the first samples were discovered. Doubtlessly, the vases found
at Kamáres had originally been filled with foods and liquids
offered to the divinity worshipped in the cave. But who had
fired them and when? And how had similar vases made their
way to Egypt, where Flinders Petrie, in excavating a town
called Kahun in 1890, had discovered them mixed in with
the other relics?

The painted Kamáres sherds found at Kahun were so unmistakably different from the other objects buried with them
that Petrie had immediately identified them as Aegean. Three
years later Evans' friend Myres had recognized the identical
pottery in the Candia Museum. Now, when it showed up
in a well-defined stratum at Knossos, the mystery was solved,
both as to the provenance of Kamáres ware and the date
its potters had produced it. For the town called Kahun, which
Petrie had excavated, was one of those sites an archaeologist
dreams of finding. It and everything in it could be absolutely
dated. Kahun had been built to house the workmen and
officials engaged in constructing a pyramid for Sesostris II,

one of the great pharaohs of the Twelfth Dynasty, who reigned from approximately 1906 B.C. to 1888 B.C. Some time just before or during those years Minoan ships must have carried these colorful jugs and vases to Egypt. On the return voyage the same ships had brought imports made in Egypt and elsewhere back to Crete.

Boats had left Cretan harbors loaded with fine pottery, textiles, and timber, and with the purple dye extracted from the sea snail, murex. The jars they carried in the hold were filled with the products of a bountiful soil: olive oil and honey, aromatic and medicinal herbs, raisins and wine. The same boats had returned from Libya, Egypt, and the Cycladic islands with cargoes of precious stones, ivory, and gold; and maybe, included among the costly treasures, even with beans. Evans found a small *pithos* filled with burned beans in one of the workshops excavated at Knossos. His workmen immediately recognized them as Egyptian beans, a dwarf variety still imported into Crete from Alexandria. The thread of history could be spun of homely stuff. Sometimes, even, by one man, who unwittingly left his name on the calendar buried in the earth.

As though to synchronize historic timepieces, Evans' workmen—still excavating at the same first palace level—turned up an Egyptian diorite figure carved with the name User, perhaps a merchant or even an ambassador to the court of Knossos. The date of this figure could be approximately fixed at 2000 B.C. The man called User, who had no other claim to fame, earned immortality by thus adding his own testimony to that of the potters who had produced the beautiful Kamáres ware.

Something momentous, then, had happened in Crete around 2000 B.C. For the first time buildings large enough to be called palaces were erected, the largest at Knossos but elsewhere on Crete, too: at Phaistos, where Evans' friend Halbherr was digging, and at Mallia. All three of these palaces were located in the most fertile plains of the island. Their princely rulers had lacked neither the foodstuffs nor the niceties of life. They could drink from cups of gold or silver. Their cooks had copper cauldrons large enough to boil a whole sheep or goat. (Mackenzie, invited to a Cretan feast, found similar cauldrons still in use.) One of the "kitchen" vessels rescued from the earth was a clay "grater," perhaps for cheese. Another still had fishbones in it, indication of a balanced and varied diet. Moreover, the *pithoi* in which these early Minoans stored their wine, the jugs from which they poured it, the cups from which they drank it—all were beautiful.

The potter's wheel had found its way to Crete. With it these gifted craftsmen had produced a marvelous variety of shapes which they then coated with black paint, ready to be decorated in varying tones of white and red. This light-on-dark decoration was the hallmark of the Kamáres potter; this and his endless artistic inventions of spirals, rosettes, circles, stripes, flowers, and fish, alone or in combinations. There were seldom two pieces alike. Each was a work of art, designed for daily use.

At Phaistos, Halbherr found a vase with a strainer and a feeding spout; a baby, or a person sick in bed could want for nothing better today. At Knossos, Evans found a footed fruit stand and cups with walls as thin as eggshell. They were "as light and spontaneous as a bubble," he wrote. The miracle of discovery kept renewing itself. Each turning over of the earth by one of his workmen revealed new works of art. Slowly, as they dug and his knowledge grew, he began piecing the story together—from this potsherd or that fresco fragment, from this sealstone or that metal vase, this column, that balustrade.

It was like unfolding a road map into the past.

Chapter XII
"But They Are Parisians!"

The southwind called the *nótos,* the scourge of the Cretan spring, blew over Knossos. It was the familiar khamsin of Egypt, a hot dry gust coming fresh from the Libyan desert, searing the land and raising blinding clouds of dust. Often the *nótos* raged for three days at a time with no letup in intensity. It attained its maximum force in March. It was this same dread *nótos,* blowing with gale-strength, Evans surmised, that must have fanned the blaze which had left smoke stains still visible on the walls of the Throne Room. He could only approximate the year of the catastrophe—somewhere around 1400 B.C., he thought—but he was already certain of the month.

During that fateful, long-ago March the heavens must have looked as baleful as they did in March 1900. Desert sands carried by the wind gave the sky a lurid, evil color. The dump heaps of the palace excavations took on a rusted look. Reddish dust covered the housetops of Candia. In the Turkish house that Evans shared with Hogarth, when the latter wasn't digging at Psychro, the floors were gritty with sand.

It was an old house, situated in the valley below Knossos and much too close to the malaria-breeding Kairatos stream to be healthy. Despite a drastic disinfecting and whitewashing, the rooms were dank and smelled of mildew. The thatched roof leaked. It offered no more protection than a sieve, as

Evans discovered to his dismay when a sudden spring rain turned overnight into a tropical deluge. That day he had carefully cut out four inscribed tablets, together with the hardened earth that kept them intact, and brought them home for temporary shelter. During the night a violent cloudburst poured water through the rotten thatch, inundating the tray that held the tablets. The next morning they were a pulpy mass.

·Sometimes the workmen stood in pits half-filled with water and waded through mud to empty their heavy loads of sodden earth on the dump. At other times either the swirling dust clouds or the torrential rains brought on by shifting gales interrupted the work entirely. On such days Evans, confined to his soggy quarters, had to content himself with studying the relics already unearthed. At the slightest improvement in the weather he was back at Knossos, digging for new ones. Dressed as usual in shirt and tie, wearing a hat, Prodger in hand, the only concession he made to the elements was the mud-splattered and battered raincoat that reached halfway down his calves and gave him what his sister Alice had once described as an "intrepid" look, the look of an explorer braving hardships and dangers in search of his quarry.

The finds of that first season were indeed marvelous: exquisite pottery, sealstones, jewelry, carved ivories, copper and stone vessels. But above all, the Minoans had transmitted their feeling for beauty and their joy of living in the frescoes they had painted to adorn their palace. Parts of these frescoes still clung to remaining walls. Far more, however, were broken into sparkling bits of colored plaster and were retrieved by the sieve. If they were not to crumble into dust, they required prompt cleaning and repair. From repairing them to restoring them was a small step for Evans to take. To him, the brightly painted fragments of plaster were like the pieces of a jigsaw puzzle awaiting completion. He could not only picture the walls as they had once been but conceived the idea of revivifying them insofar as possible with replicas of their original paintings.

To begin the process of restoring the frescoes Evans commissioned a Swiss artist named Emile Gilliéron from Athens, where he worked mostly for the French Institute of Archaeology. Neither of them foresaw, at their first meeting, a generation of collaboration. Monsieur Gilliéron became one of the dig's regulars. For the next quarter of a century either he or his equally gifted son Edouard was in residence during the season at Knossos. Where the Minoans were concerned, Gilliéron and Evans saw eye to eye, though the only outward attribute they shared was their age. They were born within two months of each other in the same year. What Emile Gilliéron from Villeneuve in Switzerland, the son of a high-school teacher, and Arthur Evans from Nash Mills, son of Sir John Evans, had in common was an uncommonly rich historical imagination.

Gilliéron was a talented painter with an ardent interest in archaeology. After studying art in Basel, Munich, and Paris, he had made his way to Athens early in his career, at the age of twenty-six, and had remained there ever since, specializing in archaeological drawings. His work appeared regularly in the learned publications not only of the French Institute but of the German, Italian, Austrian, English, and American as well. In addition to everything else, he served as professor of drawing to the princes and princesses of the Greek court and even found the time—and obviously had the ability— to run a business which turned ancient masterpieces into tangible profits.

The illustrated catalogue of Gilliéron's wares was entitled *Galvanoplastic Copies of MYCENAEAN AND CRETAN (MINOAN) ANTIQUITIES.* They were executed and sold by the Württembergische Metallwarenfabrik in Württemberg, but could also be ordered direct from E. Gilliéron and Son at Rue Skoufa 43, Athens. In the Introduction to the Catalogue, written by Professor Dr. Paul Wolters, director of the Royal Glyptothek at Munich and formerly secretary of the Imperial German Institute at Athens, the prospective buyer was assured of a superior product. Gilliéron's metal copies of ancient bronze, silver, and gold cups, goblets, jugs, vases, bowls, swords, diadems, and pendants were produced "with the help of exact mouldings," Professor Dr. Wolters affirmed. Furthermore, they "have been made by galvanoplastic process, in order to obtain models which give the original form as

well as the color and brilliancy of the metals." Nor was
that all. The objects "as now presented to us are not in
the bent, crushed or broken condition in which they were
found, but have been reset in their original forms so far
as these could be ascertained with certainty. Even the needful
restorations are throughout founded on reliable traces, or trust-
worthy analogy."

A man capable of executing such faithful reproductions
of timeworn originals was just what Evans needed. Moreover,
the fact that Gilliéron found the time to put his talents to
such profitable use bore testimony to exceptional energy. Evans
harnessed both the talents and the energy, enriched by Gilliéron's genuine feeling for the past, in the service of the
Minoans, adding his own considerable imagination to the re-
storer's skills.

The pieces of colored stucco turned up by the spade were
true frescoes, painted on fresh plaster. Evans could easily
make out the parallel lines drawn by fine cords across wet
surfaces to guide the artists' hands. Putting the pieces together,
however, was painstaking work, requiring the infinite patience
and the years of experience which Gilliéron brought to the
task. There were literally hundreds of tiny fragments, ran-
domly scattered, to be assembled, cleaned, and restored. Sometimes it took the united ingenuity of both Evans and artist
to solve the puzzle. Often the work was carried out "in accordance with my own suggestions," Evans admitted. He insisted, however, that "as regards the main features of the
composition there are, at any rate, good analogies for the
restorations supplied." The arms, legs, faces, and backgrounds
which replaced those that were missing did not come entirely
from either his or Gilliéron's imagination. The artist always
had something to guide him, either in parts of the picture
being reconstructed or in the evidence drawn from similar
pictures found at Knossos or elsewhere in Crete.

So Evans insisted. Later archaeologists would hotly dispute
the sufficiency of his evidence and analogies, and would apply
adjectives like "lavish" and "daring" to his reproductive
imagination. Even tourists studying the restored frescoes in
the Candia (now Herakleion) Museum would marvel at what

Gilliéron was able to project from the scanty guidelines of the original fragments. Sometimes Evans in his ingenious interpretation of the findings did go astray, and carried Gilliéron with him on an enthusiastic detour from the facts, but the instances were amazingly few. The most famous one involved the fresco he called the "Saffron Gatherer."

Eight pieces of this fresco showed up, depicting the figure (but not the head) of what Evans took to be a young boy. The youth was naked except for a girdle and seemed to be gathering saffron crocuses and setting them into a bowl in a rocky field. True, it puzzled Evans that the figure was painted blue, and not the conventional red for male figures; he thought it possible that it might be a young girl rather than a boy. But whatever the sex of the Saffron Gatherer, Evans was enchanted with the naturalism in the drawing of the flowers. They highlighted, he pointed out, the importance to the Minoans of the saffron crocus, from which they obtained and even exported the yellow dye that colored so many of their costumes. And the lithe movement expressed in the figure was remarkable.

To Evans' contemporaries also, since he had so proclaimed it, the Saffron Gatherer remained a boy. It did seem strange to Ronald W. Burrows, a professor of Greek in the University College at Cardiff, that the "Little Boy Blue," as he called him in his book entitled *The Discoveries in Crete*, should have blue flesh and not red; nor was he "an anatomically correct figure." Nevertheless, Burrows found "a refinement in the idea" that he should be plucking flowers to arrange them in a vase. Only much later, when a blue *tail* turned up, did the boy turn out to be a monkey, itself so delightful as to detract nothing from the refinement of the fresco.

Indeed, no one could question the endearing charm of Evans' Minoans as they emerged from Gilliéron's atelier. Pieced together from additional fragments found near the first two, Manoli's icon of a saint proved to be the life-size figure of a youth with long curling hair and a noble profile, a constricted waist, slender legs. He was wearing an embroidered loincloth (not a skirt, as Evans had first thought) and a handsome belt and frontlet of silver. On his feet were sandals, on his wrist a bracelet. He was carrying a conical rhyton, used for pouring libations to a god, and it was quite clear that he was only one of an immense fresco procession of such youths—over five hundred of them, Evans estimated.

A replica of the "Cup-bearer," for so Evans dubbed him, eventually took his place along with several companions in the hall which was restored and appropriately named the "Corridor of the Cup-bearer." Gilliéron had executed the copies "with his usual mastery of the Minoan spirit," Evans wrote. "The result has been to present to the spectator, at least in a fractional degree, the brilliant effect which these processional figures, one ranged above the other, must once have presented in this inner entrance hall."

The frescoed portraits went from Saint to Devil. Hassan, one of Evans' best workmen, shouted out in terror when he came upon a fairly large piece of stucco whose painted image seemed to breathe fire and brimstone. The "Devil" proved to be a magnificent painted plaster relief of a charging bull, life-size or even larger, with a woolly-haired head, red-rimmed truculent eyes, and horns of a brilliant blue. The modeling was superb. The creature seemed to be straining with all his vigor and bellowing, either in anger or agony. It was a reminder, lest anyone forget, of the dread Minotaur stalking the Labyrinth.

The bull, which was then regarded as the king of animals, seemed to pervade Knossos. "What a part these creatures play here!" Evans exclaimed. He found them everywhere— on frescoes and reliefs, as the chief design on seals, on a soapstone vase. The somewhat stylized representation of bulls' horns was one of the most ubiquitous of all Minoan symbols, used to indicate the sanctity of a place. These "horns of consecration," as Evans called them, appeared almost as frequently as the sacred double axe on the palace site.

The most famous bull scene of all was depicted on the fresco, restored by Gilliéron, which Evans named the "Toreador Fresco." The animal portrayed in it seemed to be galloping headlong into the arms of a girl acrobat. The scene dramatized by the Minoan artist took one's breath away. There were one male and two female performers, distinguished by their red skin and white skin, an artistic convention also used by the Egyptians. Each "toreador" was clad only in a loincloth, a very narrow metallic girdle, striped socks, and moccasins. Each was executing a feat of incredible daring. The boy was in midair, having just taken a flying backward somersault over the bull's back. His feet were already coming down toward the ground, where one of the girl acrobats was waiting to catch or steady him. The other girl acrobat, standing in front of the coursing bull, was preparing to seize his horns and do a back somersault in her turn.

This bull-leaping sport seemed so dangerous, so improbable, that Evans pondered long over its meaning. To try to determine whether it was a forerunner of modern bullfighting, he went to Madrid to see what happened if the matador was caught by the bull; whether he'd be thrown over the bull's horns. The cruelty of the Spanish sport revolted him, and he noted that even Francisco Goya had written *"Bárbara diversión!"* under one of the copper-plate etchings in his famous series entitled "Tauromachia." Evans could detect no similarity between the techniques used by the matador and those of the Minoans. He speculated, nevertheless, that "The sports of the amphitheatre, which have never lost their hold on the Mediterranean world, may thus in Crete at least be traced back to prehistoric times. It may well be that, long before the days when enslaved barbarians were 'butchered to make a Roman holiday,' captives, perhaps of gentle blood, shared the same fate within sight of the 'House of Minos,' and that the legends of Athenian prisoners devoured by the Minotaur preserve a real tradition of these cruel sports."

Evans acknowledged his debt to Professor Baldwin Brown, who showed the Toreador Fresco to a veteran steer-wrestler from America's Far West to learn whether the bull-leaping feat could be done. "There is no chance," the professor was told, "of a human person being able to obtain a balance when the bull is charging full against him." Yet Evans found the same sport depicted on sealstones, on the engraving of a gold signet ring, and in a bronze figurine of a bull and an acrobat. "All that can be said," he concluded, "is that the performance as featured by the Minoan artist seems to be of a kind pronounced impossible by modern champions of the sport."

Moreover, there was good reason to believe that the Minoans had engaged in other bull-sports that were equally astonishing. In 1889 the Greek archaeologist Chrestos Tsountas had published his discovery of two magnificent gold cups found together in a tholos tomb at Vapheio, near Sparta. Each was decorated in relief with three scenes depicting the hunting and capture of wild or semi-wild bulls. No one doubted their Cretan origin: cups of similar shape and with the same distinctive handles had turned up at Knossos and other sites. As he pondered the meaning of the Toreador Fresco, Evans was remembering the Vapheio cups and drawing parallels.

The first cup told a story of danger and suspense. Slim-waisted Minoan "cowboys" and "cowgirls," gathered in a wooded glen to demonstrate their grappling skill, were trying to drive a herd of bulls toward a net slung between two olive trees. One beast had escaped the ambush and was shown galloping off to the right. A second, less adroit, was caught in the net cradle and entangled in it. The third animal had managed to fling one bull-grappler to the ground, where he lay with his arms thrown behind him, while another—this one a "cowgirl"—locked both arms and legs around the monster's horns in a desperate attempt to fell it. The three scenes, compressed onto a restricted curved surface, were charged with sheer drama.

The narrative engraved on the second gold cup was less sensational but more subtle and witty. It had eluded interpretation until Evans trained his eyes on it, after procuring two of Gilliéron's facsimiles of the Vapheio treasures for the Ashmolean Museum. Until then archaeologists had assumed that both of the animals shown were bulls. It took Evans to detect the raised tail by which one of them betrayed both its sex and the role assigned to it in the story. It was a decoy-cow, artfully identified, as Evans delicately put it, by the "physical sign of sexual inclination regularly shown by the cow in such cases." Having solved the riddle of the second Vapheio cup, he went on to describe the three scenes engraved on it. "In the first scene the bull is depicted nosing the cow's tail; in the second his treacherous companion engaged him in amorous converse, of which her raised tail shows the sexual reaction. . . . In the third scene the herdsman takes advantage of this dalliance to lasso the mighty beast by his hind leg."

What kind of people *were* these Minoans, who not only grappled with bulls and leaped over their horns, but also hunted them with such wily cunning? As though in answer to the question, the earth produced other frescoes, miniature in size, which told an animated story of habits and events in a style without parallel in ancient art. One such fresco was little over a meter in width. Its human figures seldom measured more than a couple of centimeters. Yet within such narrow confines the artist had contrived to paint a crowd of approximately eight hundred persons gathered in tiers on either side of a shrine, watching whatever spectacle was taking place.

Evans called it the "Temple Fresco." Elaborately dressed ladies were seated in the front row and in some sort of balcony around a shrine or temple. All around them were hundreds of other spectators, portrayed by a sort of artistic shorthand in which only heads were shown—in swathes of terra-cotta color for the men, white for the women. Yet the female heads in the back rows seemed as gay and curled and bejeweled as those of the elegant court ladies up front. These ladies wore long, gaily colored skirts with bands of flouncing. Their breasts were bared beneath tight-fitting jackets with puffed sleeves. While the rest of the crowd concentrated on the performance, they turned and twisted in their seats, indulging in lively chitchat among themselves.

Introduced to the Minoans in such large numbers, Evans could restrain neither his fancy nor his pen. He marveled at the ancient craftsmen who, working in only two dimensions, had achieved such remarkable naturalism through the language of gesticulation. One lady "raises her head in amazement. 'You don't say so!'" Another does the same "in deprecation of her sharp-tongued neighbor." "May we venture to suppose," he mused, "that we have here a mother giving social advice to a debutante daughter?" Altogether, he summed up, "these scenes of feminine confidences, of tittle-tattle and society scandals, take us far away from the productions of Classical Art in any Age. Such lively *genre* and the *rococo* atmosphere bring us nearer indeed to quite modern times."

That was what was so astonishing: the feeling that these ancients could almost be one's contemporaries. *Genre* painting by definition portrays scenes of everyday life. *Rococo* art is distinguished by its smallness of size, delicacy of color, freedom of brushwork, gay and playful subjects. Nothing remotely like such naturalism had ever been seen in ancient art—certainly not in the pure, perfectly proportioned, godlike statues of classical Greece, nor the stiff conventional figures of Egypt. In contrast, the people in these miniature frescoes from Knossos seemed infused with life.

There was the "Camp-stool Fresco," which also owed its felicitous title to Evans' gift for nomenclature. Gilliéron was able to restore twelve of the original male and female figures and found them seated, to his and everyone else's surprise, on folding chairs with slim metal legs. One careless youth had dropped his glove and there it was—complete with thumb and four fingers—caught in the intersection of the legs of his stool. The other glove was still tucked in his belt where it belonged, and where its reddish brown color contrasted smartly with the blue-green and yellow of his garment. A French scholar, watching Gilliéron restoring the Camp-stool Fresco, paid a spontaneous Gallic tribute to the women's beauty and fashion. *"Mais ce sont des Parisiennes!"* he exclaimed. "But they are Parisians!"

Indeed, "La Parisienne" is what generations of tourists have called the figure seated in the front row: the beautiful and sophisticated young woman whose portrait is today to the Herakleion Museum what the Mona Lisa is to the Louvre. "La Parisienne" had dark almond-shaped eyes, long black hair curling over her shoulder, and bright red lips. The bodice of her dress was made of a thin transparent material. A scarf of the same gauzy fabric was gathered at the back of her neck into a large and filmy knot with fringed ends. Though her fetching coiffure and scarlet lips seemed to point to an active social life, the scarf indicated her office as a priestess. The knot was a "sacral knot," Evans explained, a kind of ceremonial badge with ritual significance which he had found on other paintings and carvings showing the Minoan goddess attended by her votaries.

The spade, then, had turned up a priestess dressed in the latest Paris fashion. What next?

"What next?" was the question being asked all over Crete. The island, freed from Ottoman domination and at last accessible, had become an open invitation to archaeologists. The Italians, directed by the energetic Halbherr, were digging at Phaistos in the Messara lowlands to the south, and uncovering a palace that would rival Knossos in all but artistic splendor. The French would later begin excavating a smaller palace at Mallia on the northern coast. Near the village of Psychro, David Hogarth was exploring the cave on Mount Dicte, where Zeus was said to have been born, and finding offerings, he reported, at the rate of one a minute: bronze blades, pins, tweezers, brooches, rings, needles. John Myres, no longer bailing Evans out of jail, was uncovering the votive sanctuary at Petsofa. There was even, among these pioneer excavators, a young woman from America.

Harriet Boyd later married Charles Henry Hawkes, and together they wrote a book entitled *Crete: The Forerunner of Greece*. In 1900 she was a student in her twenties at the American School of Classical Studies in Athens. Tightly corseted, in ankle-length dress and wide-brimmed hat, she traveled all over Crete accompanied by a native muleteer, with his mother as chaperone. On the mid-April afternoon of her visit to Knossos she found 140 men at work. "Mr. Evans has bought up the site of Knossos and in a few weeks he has discovered the palace of Minos." She could not hope to equal such a feat, but she was determined to add her chapter to the unfolding Cretan story.

There were few roads in Crete in 1900, only mule tracks. Sitting sideways on a wooden saddle and carrying the simplest possible equipment, Harriet Boyd went by mule from village to village, seeking clues to a likely place to dig. The following year she returned to excavate hilly Gournia, an "industrial town," whose inhabitants had been fishermen, weavers, bronze

casters, stonemasons, and potters. The cobbled alleys they
had climbed were still so well preserved, more than three
thousand years later, that it seemed as though the town's
craftsmen had only recently departed.

Evans kept in close touch with his colleagues digging elsewhere on the island, and particularly with Halbherr. Halbherr
would gallop over on his swift horse to see Evans' latest
finds. He could reach Knossos from Phaistos in little over
five hours. Evans, more slowly on his mule, would ride over
to Phaistos to compare notes with his Italian friend. Perhaps
a fresco from Phaistos would corroborate his intuition about
a missing fragment at Knossos. He visited Myres to examine
the findings at Petsofa. The stone he purchased from a shep-
herd boy sent from Psychro by Hogarth became part of the
written record left behind by the Minoans. It had letters
on it, the boy said, that not even the priest could read.
So the evidence grew. So the story was unraveled.

By the end of the first season more than two acres of
the Palace of Knossos lay exposed. The overall architectural
plan was now clear. Its dominating and central feature was
an immense paved court, covering an area 57 meters long
by 27 meters wide. To the west of this Central Court were
the Throne Room, the halls of state, the ceremonial rooms,
and the shrines. To the east of it, where the ground sloped
steeply down to the valley, was what Evans already called
the Domestic Quarter, though he had not yet begun to excavate it.

There were long underground corridors lined with rows
and rows of huge storage jars. At one time there must have
been over four hundred of them, capable of holding some
16,000 gallons (over 60,000 liters) of olive oil, Evans estimated. The sheer size of the jars was staggering. Some
were large enough for a man to stand in (the giant of them
all measured 2.17 meters), and had three or even four handles
placed horizontally around the circumference at different levels
or "zones" from top to bottom. Thus, depending on the weight
of the contents, as many men as were required could take
a firm handhold in order to move a jar or tip it over when
the need arose. The spaces between the "zones" formed by
the handles were decorated with medallions, with herringbone

bands, with rope-work, or with painted motifs of plants. Evans found twenty such *pithoi* in a single storeroom, many still in position and undamaged. One could easily imagine them still filled with wine or oil for the priest-king's household.

One of Evans' frequent pleasures at Knossos was to climb to the top of the view-tower he had had built. It was four stories high and proudly flew the Union Jack from its summit. From this great height he could oversee the whole expanse of the excavations under way. Looking out over the relic-strewn mound, he could transform wheelbarrows, pickaxes, and trenches in his mind's eye into rooms, staircases, and terraces. Gradually Knossos for him became peopled again. The palace and its surroundings throbbed and hummed with the easily evoked noises and bustle of habitation. He could close his eyes and hear Minoan farmers singing lustily (for the grapes of Crete made fine wine) on their way home from the day's harvesting. He could feel the fishermen straining under the weight of their baskets filled with murex. When he found vases of elegant form with a hole in their base for drainage, just like modern flowerpots, he saw them filled with iris or anemone, gracing the queen's table. His imagination reproduced life in the great palace.

The inner life of the palace had radiated around the Central Court. The sounds of potters' wheels and stonemasons' hammers had come from workshops. Women had chattered on their way to their looms. Water carriers, cooks, and maid-servants had crisscrossed the great courtyard, as little aware of their own predecessors—buried under the stones they trod and going back to the Stone Age—as Evans' diggers had been aware of the Minoans.

Now that he had rescued Minos's palace from oblivion, Evans had no intention of letting storms, winds, sand, and earth cover it up again. He had a temporary shelter built over the Throne Room and all precious objects removed to the museum in Candia. But he was not content with merely preserving what he found. He started from the beginning to invest Knossos with as much of its former beauty as possible. While the architect Fyfe reconstructed walls, Gilliéron continued to restore frescoes and make copies of the most important scenes. Evans felt a passionate need to return the frescoes, or at least their modern replicas, to the walls they belonged to, in order "to conserve something of the inner life of the old palace-sanctuary."

Did he, then, allow his conclusions to go beyond evidence? Was his imagination given too much scope? These are fascinating questions. Archaeologists have been debating them, pro and con, for half a century. But J. N. L. Myres, the son of Evans' closest friend, raised a more startling question by recalling an incident told him by his father. It must have taken place at a time when donkeys still grazed on the mound of Knossos and the Minoans lay undiscovered beneath the topsoil; perhaps while Myres and Evans were sitting in a café in some remote Cretan village, or after Myres had bailed his overadventurous companion out of the local jail.

"My father used to say," wrote the younger Myres, "that at one point they tossed a coin to determine which should concentrate on Crete and which on Cyprus. Evans took Crete, with what results we all know. My father did a lot of work in Cyprus, but even if the coin had fallen the other way, the results would have been quite different, for my father never had either the financial resources or the taste for publicity that made Evans' operations in Crete so extensive and spectacular."

This glimpse into one man's impact on events is as dazzling as the Minoans themselves. It allows speculation a free hand. What if Myres and not Evans had won the toss? How would the excavated palace look today? But Myres lost: and it may well be that the Minoans owe at least some of their irresistibility and much of their visibility to the man who won the toss.

Certainly, in 1900, Evans had "the taste for publicity" that was making Londoners reach eagerly for *The Times* to find out what was happening in Crete. What he didn't have, yet, were the financial resources that would make his operations so extensive and spectacular. He already knew that even with his father's generous help he would soon be obliged to appeal for public funds—in other words, to launch that hypothetical "Cretan Exploration Fund" he had so blithely conjured up when he bought his first quarter-share of the mound of Kephála. But more than money, his immediate concern was the Cretan climate.

The clammy Turkish abode Evans had rented in the valley, with its leaking roof and damp walls, turned out to be decidedly unhealthy. By the end of May the swarms of malaria-carrying mosquitoes that bred in the Kairatos stream had infected him, Mackenzie, and a growing number of workers with the disease. Alternating fevers and chills slowed the work, until the increasing prevalence of malaria made it impossible to continue.

On June 3, 1900, Evans' Cretan helpers downed their spades and pickaxes and put on their finest clothing. The master gave a huge *glendi*, a party, for the workers and their families to celebrate the rescue of the Minoans and the end of the first season's excavations. Then he returned to England to begin writing up the discoveries which would add a new chapter to the textbooks. But first, back in Oxford, the Keeper of the Ashmolean Museum had to meet priority demands on his time.

Though he now had a new and younger assistant, Charles Bell, who was proving well able to cope with daily routines, there were nevertheless certain problems, and above all personalities, that clamored for Evans' attention. Some of the Visitors of the Museum had little sympathy for their Keeper's prolonged absences and would have less as time went on. Evans had to divide his time between Oxford and Boars Hill where, often late at night, he worked on his first report to the scholarly world on the excavations at Knossos. He also published a paper on "Writing in Prehistoric Greece."

John Evans was understandably proud when his son's paper was discussed at a meeting of the British Association for the Advancement of Science in 1900. However, Sir John could not refrain from expressing his "personal satisfaction in finding that theories which he had suggested some 20 or 30 years before, had thus been supported by his son." The competition between father and son, it appeared—however friendly and generous—was not all one-sided.

Evans estimated that his work at Knossos was barely half

completed. He was mistaken. Five more years of extensive digging would follow, then twenty-five years of interrupted digging, before his work at Knossos would be over. During much of that time, when he wasn't reconstructing King Minos's Palace at Knossos, he was building his own home at Youlbury.

Chapter XIII
The Oxford
Labyrinth

Youlbury, like the Casa San Lazzaro before it, was both an extension and a reflection of the man Evans. In 1900 he had ample time ahead in which to enlarge, remodel, and refurbish it, and so impregnate it with his own personality that to understand Evans one had to see him in his own home. The man presiding over the dinner table, wearing a yellow rose in his lapel, was very different from the one chairing a scientific conference or dealing with the Visitors of the Ashmolean. His Cretan workmen, too awed by their lordly and aloof master to invite him to a wedding, would have been stunned to see him in the role of host. Two entire floors were given over for guest rooms in his home on Boars Hill.

Like the Palace at Knossos, Youlbury dominated its surroundings, and its sixty acres of hilly ground afforded the horticulturist in Evans broad scope for expression. Certain parts of the estate suggested that its proprietor was trying to make his piece of England look as much as possible like a transplanted Ragusa. Winding paths—he never built straight paths—led to gardens in every direction, planted so experimentally and successfully over the years that fuchsias and camellias grew over two meters high, mimosa more than six. The grounds sheltered a Japanese lemon tree and a loquat, hydrangeas that could survive an English winter, lofty arbutus trees, rhododendrons up to four and a half meters high, and a towering bamboo grove. There were beautiful orchards full of peaches and nectarines and gooseberries—the big "eating" kind which Evans loved—and vines heavy with grapes. Almost lost among the fruit, flowers, and trees, yet the central piece, was the artificial lake he created at the bottom of the slope, where the rippling natural spring on the Youlbury property could empty into it.

To build the lake Evans had to dredge out a huge old sand pit, measuring two to three acres, and line it on all sides with cement. In some places the water was almost twelve meters deep. When the rays of the sun were reflected over its smooth surface, breaking it up into thousands of pieces of shimmering color like the patina on old Roman glass, the lake was a luminous sight to look down on from the windows of the house high above.

As for the house itself, Evans' friends variously described Youlbury as "shocking" or "fantastic," depending on their tolerance for sheer bulk. It defied all architectural principles of proportion or uniformity of style. Vast to begin with, it grew monstrously large as it rambled without reason and sprouted additions to accommodate this fantasy or that whim of its owner. As a result, recalled J. N. L. Myres, "its geography became so complex that people in Oxford called it the Cretan labyrinth"—an allusion corroborated for the visitor as soon as he entered the front door. The floor of the huge entrance hall was laid out in black-and-white marble like a labyrinth, with the Minotaur in the center. Facsimiles of Minoan columns and two mahogany replicas of the throne of Minos brought other echoes of Knossos to Oxford. Surrounded by these reminders of ancient glories, multiplied a thousandfold by the priceless treasures in glass cases, in drawers, and in exquisite cabinets, Arthur Evans lived in Victorian opulence.

In addition to the servants' wing built over the kitchen, Youlbury had a magnificent drawing room, a large dining room, a ballroom-size library, a morning room, and an "octagonal" room from whose window seats one could look out over the lake while taking after-dinner coffee. At the top of the house there was a "solar" room, but Evans—like

Icarus—found even this not close enough to the sun. He had a special room built on top of the house, reached by circular iron steps from the gallery on the second floor which overlooked the great entrance hall. He furnished his lofty nest with comfortable chairs and a bed. From it, one could step out onto the flat roof, climb another wrought-iron staircase to a "lookout" perch, and see all the way to the distant Berkshire downs.

There were three staircases in the house, twenty-eight bedrooms, and nine baths. One of the latter was a blue-tiled Roman bath, two steps down and wide enough for a young guest to swim two breaststrokes in any direction. Many young guests did. Even without the gentle but efficient Margaret to supervise it, Youlbury became the kind of home that Nash Mills had been when Fanny was alive. Although John Evans still lived in the old family homestead with his new wife and young daughter, festive occasions were celebrated at Youlbury. It was nothing for Evans to take in his brother Lewis's tribe of five for the summer holidays. Or fill the house over weekends with their friends.

Evans also shared his home and its gardens, generously though not indiscriminately, with his friends and neighbors in the vicinity of Boars Hill. Among the outstanding events of the Oxford countryside was the annual flower show at Youlbury. It ended with a spirited tug-of-war between the neighboring villages of Wootton and Suningwell, and was followed by refreshments for the perspiring opponents and their partisans. On one such occasion Evans noticed a small boy of five standing at the edge of the crowd, clutching his mother's skirt and looking distinctly unhappy as he tried to peer through the legs of taller onlookers. Evans recognized the child's mother, the wife of a tenant farmer on Boars Hill. He asked Mrs. Candy if her son would like to watch the tug-of-war, and then stooped down so that she could hoist him onto his shoulders.

This was James Candy's first contact with the man he would describe as "the kindest man I've ever known." The child had no way of knowing, then, that this chance meeting would change the course of his life; or that one day he would live on the other side of the front door through which a constant stream of visitors entered Youlbury. The guests ranged from the very young, invited for a picnic on the grounds, to the very learned, eager to discuss Minoan Linear A and Linear B script with their discoverer.

The interest in this still-unidentified writing was intense. Inquiries poured in from scholars everywhere. Evans assured his colleagues that he would spare no effort (and no expense) "to publish the whole collected material at the earliest possible moment. The Oxford University Press has undertaken the publication . . . and has already set in hand the preliminary work, including a 'Mycenaean Fount.'" Always the optimist, he ordered this prehistoric script not in one, but in two sizes of type—and this in 1901, barely a year after the first inscribed tablet had been found at Knossos. In an article published in March 1901 in *The Monthly Review* he acknowledged that it would take considerable study and comparison "for the elucidation of these materials." But he went on to say, with a prophetic insight he himself would come to doubt, that "If, as may well be the case, the language in which they were written was some primitive form of Greek, we need not despair of the final decipherment of these Knossian archives. . . ."

The article in *The Monthly Review* brought the Palace of Minos alive for the nonscholarly world as well as for the experts. Not since Schliemann's discoveries, wrote Professor Ronald Burrows, had there been anything in archaeology that made such a vivid impression on the popular imagination. "Nor is the impression solely due to the nature of the material; it is largely due to Mr. Evans himself. . . . Mr. Evans naturally does not see things in a dry light. He has the dramatic instinct, and he impresses it on all he touches." His "gift of clear and attractive writing" made King Minos, the Minotaur, and the Labyrinth seem more than myth.

This gift, and what John Myres's son called his "taste for publicity," now helped to create the Cretan Exploration Fund, no longer an abstract source of future support but an immediate and practical necessity. With public excitement actively aroused and with Prince George of Athens as its royal patron, the Cretan Exploration Fund got off to an encouraging start. The British School of Archaeology at Athens was associated with it in the person of David Hogarth, its director. The delightful Minoans themselves provided the appeal, ably abetted by their discoverer. For the frontispiece of his first report to the fund, Evans used a photograph showing the excavation of the Throne Room in progress. In the foreground four diggers were bent over their work. In the background were the plank-ways, the baskets of dug-out earth, the sieves. And there, occupying full center, was the still half-buried throne of the ancient king. Only its carved back was fully visible, untouched and unchipped, unmoved from the spot where it had lain for over thirty centuries. What could be more dramatic?

Subscriptions began pouring in. Evans could look ahead. He was still in England when Queen Victoria died on January 22, 1901, ending one of the longest reigns in European history. She was succeeded by her son King Edward VII, who was already almost sixty years old. Evans inaugurated the Edwardian era by buying equipment and laying in supplies—which included a gross of nailbrushes and a gross of bottles of Eno's Fruit Salts—for the next season's dig. By early February he was back in Crete. He bought the remaining part of the site of Kephála. Now it was all his.

It had rained off and on since February 27, the day the work started. But the same late-winter rains which so often muddied the buried secrets of Knossos could also expose them to an observant eye. Evans was quick to notice, after a heavy downpour, a flat block of stone bearing the impression—clearly brought out in black by the moisture—of two round columns standing side by side. The black color indicated that the columns had been made of wood and destroyed by fire. Their size and position showed that they had supported considerable weight. They confirmed what Evans had never doubted: that the palace had been more than one story high. And then came that moment when "the course of the excavation on the Palace site of Knossos took its most dramatic turn."

Digging southward in the Domestic Quarter, on the eastern side of the Central Court, the workmen came unexpectedly upon a blocked doorway. As they cautiously probed their way through it, they opened up a prospect whose vastness not even Evans could yet perceive. He, together with his assistant Mackenzie and the architect Fyfe, had assumed they were on the ground level of this part of the building. Instead, when the workers had chipped away the clogging debris, the doorway led not to another corridor or an adjoining room but to an ascending flight of stairs. In the stone wall flanking the staircase were the clear outlines of socketed bases for the wooden columns which had supported the floor below.

But the disclosures had only begun. A few steps to the right of the staircase the paved surface, instead of remaining level, suddenly began to descend to what was obviously another story below. Perhaps to more than one story below. Who could tell? How to proceed? Evans and his co-workers realized the enormity of the task facing them. One false move downward risked tumbling the entire superstructure. One false move upward could destroy what lay underneath. Each probe of the pickaxe into the debris loosened dirt and set stones in motion. Yet it was this very debris, transformed by moisture over the millennia into a solid mass, which held everything together—both the staircase itself and the walls, floors, and ceilings of the rooms above and below.

The excavator had only two choices. He could continue to dig, at the risk of reburying as much evidence as he uncovered and leaving behind "what would largely have been an unintelligible mass of crumbling ruins." Or he could try to preserve what he found as he went along, through a painstaking and expensive process of propping up ceilings, shoring up walls, replacing fallen columns and beams, and reconstructing balustrades and landings. Evans opted for the second choice, even though it "involved a risk such as never before probably has confronted excavators."

Luckily, two of his diggers turned out to be experienced miners. They had worked in the Laurion mines on the Greek mainland (the silver mined there since antiquity had helped to make Athens prosperous). Even for them it was a perilous venture. It took them eight anxious days, using wooden props every few feet to support what lay overhead, to tunnel down through the earth from the first flight of steps to a second landing; from this landing down twelve more steps; then, descending at right angles, to still another, lower flight; and finally, after long and arduous digging, to the open colonnaded court which had provided light for the whole staircase. By the time the work of "recompacting" it would be completed, the Grand Staircase would rise in four magnificent flights, with fifty-two massive stone steps—thirty-eight of them preserved from the Minoan originals—plus a landing block found *in situ* where a fifth flight had once existed.

Cautiously, Evans, Mackenzie, and Fyfe burrowed through the miners' tunneling down three flights of stairs. Fearful yet hoping, they reached the lowest floor in the Domestic Quarter. They found it virtually intact, undoubtedly helped by the fact that it had been built into a great cutting in the hillside and had received a good deal of lateral support. In places where the rubble had been loosened, they could make out pavements, even doorjambs. It was nothing short of miraculous; yet they scarcely dared to explore farther. Right over their heads hung the remains of the upper stories, precariously suspended in air, with nothing but a concretion of clay and debris to keep them from crashing to earth. The wooden columns which had supported roofs, the wooden beams of ceilings, the timber-framed walls—all had long since crumbled in the Cretan dampness or been carbonized by fire. The masonry they had supported had collapsed in interlocking wedges. Exposed after 3500 years, this part of King Minos's Palace, the part where everyday life had been lived, seemed to be dangling in space. To anchor this long-decayed past to the solid present was a challenge too compelling to resist.

Evans formed a team of his best, most careful workers, with the architect Fyfe playing a key role. As the men dug, Fyfe followed in their spade-tracks, as it were, so that excavation and reconstruction could proceed simultaneously. For carbonized posts and beams Fyfe substituted new ones made of seasoned wood. Stumps of wooden columns still remaining in their bases were replaced with new columns of the same shape and size. (A good architect can determine height and proportion through careful surveying and by a comparative study of other architectural remains on a site.) Fallen masonry was removed block by block and returned to its original level. Every fragment of stone that could be recovered was kept and used, so that the reconstructed Domestic Quarter would contain as much of the original masonry as possible.

Thus they gradually emerged: walls, doorways, stairs, balustrades, light wells, forming a vast and complicated series of rooms where an ancient people had lived, worked, played, slept, cooked, mourned, rejoiced, and died. The means used to reconstruct the Domestic Quarter were based not on conjecture but on the actual remains found on the spot at the moment of excavation. In those early days of the Knossos dig, Evans and his colleagues had to work quickly against time and the elements. The methods and materials they employed to safeguard crumbling ruins were necessarily provisional. But the important goal had been achieved. The Grand Staircase and the Domestic Quarter had been saved.

Among the many highlights of the 1901 season was a visit from John Evans and his wife, Maria. Since the age of fourteen Arthur had accompanied his father on archaeological trips. Now the roles were reversed. This time the father, on his first visit to Knossos, accompanied the son.

Sir John was seventy-seven years old that spring, a ripe age for adventure. But nothing daunted him. Each morning at dawn he and Arthur rode out on mules, over a very rough road, from the temporary house Arthur had rented in Candia to the excavations eight kilometers away. They spent days together on the site, "on which," Sir John wrote to his daughter Harriet, "there are nearly 100 men at work." (How different from his own explorations, with perhaps a learned colleague or two for company, an occasional hand hired to dig.) At the time of Sir John's visit they were opening out another of the great underground storerooms. Fragments of gold turned up, and large pots in a state of perfect preservation. They found "a good early gem," the letter went on, "and a small stone hatchet in a stratum lower than the Palace." Arthur led the way with Prodger, which he used alternately to negotiate a difficult passage or point out an exceptional find. He saw to it that Sir John missed nothing. Never had father and son been so close.

They set out together on an expedition across Crete to Gortyna, where Evans' Italian colleague Federico Halbherr was waiting to receive them. It was an eight-hour trip by mule. The track, for it could hardly be called a road, led over the main range of mountains that formed the spine of the island. Above them presided Mount Ida, mantled in snow. The dazzling blue of the Mediterranean ringed the distance. But underfoot the going was rugged. Hour after hour the mules picked their way through underbrush, over rocks, up steps sliced out of sheer cliffs, along narrow paths. They arrived bone-weary at their destination and went to sleep on beds made of planks set on trestles, with a thin mattress between them and the hard wood.

The next day Halbherr took them on an archaeological tour of Gortyna, which Arthur had briefly visited on his first trip to Crete. The Minoan habitation of the site was still largely buried. Close to the surface, however, and in excellent condition was the famous Law Code of Gortyna, dating from the sixth–fifth century B.C. Halbherr had discovered it in 1884, and took justifiable pride in explaining that it was the longest ancient Greek Code in existence. It contained more than seventeen thousand letters, and regulated everything from property rights and inheritance to moral offenses, the dissolution of marriages, relations between parents and children, and conflicts between villagers over domestic animals. The two Englishmen examined it minutely. The day after, they got back on their mules for the trip back to Candia. Sir John had ridden some eighty miles in three days. Not many men of his age could have undertaken such a trip and felt more exhilarated than tired when it was over.

The visit brought Nash Mills much closer to Knossos. From his library Sir John could now pinpoint his son's progress on the dig as a general follows battles on a map. Not far from where they had been excavating the storerooms, Arthur wrote him, they had found a stone vase so large that it took several men with poles and ropes to remove it from the site. Soon, even this find was overshadowed.

Once again shouts had brought Evans and Mackenzie on the run. The workmen had spotted some fragments of crystal and ivory glittering in the earth thrown up by their spades. Careful probing in the loosened dirt revealed others. They belonged, Evans saw, to a kind of inlaid gaming board still lying where it had toppled, perhaps from the priest-king's own table. Where the pick had disturbed it, the framework was bent, but many of the parts were still in position. The problem was how to raise these friable remains from the earth without watching them crumble into dust.

It would take infinite skill. Evans turned the job over to Kyrios Papadakis, his trained *formatore* (mender and re-storer). This all-patient man began by surrounding the outer margins of the board with a wooden framing. Then he carefully secured the surface of the board by filling in gaps with plaster. Once he felt certain that the whole could be moved in one piece, he slowly introduced strips of plastered wood under-neath the entire frame and thus raised it to ground level. It took him three days, but the gaming board emerged with its intricate inlaid designs in position, just as they had been found.

Some parts were missing, others had disintegrated or were crushed. These Fyfe replaced, "in accordance with my sug-gestions," Evans wrote, either with the fragments found scat-tered about or with replicas. When completed, the royal gaming board, for it was indeed fit for a king, measured about a meter long and fifty centimeters wide. It was made of ivory, gold, silver, and rock crystal. A pattern of crystal daisies set on a gold background formed its outer borders. Four large medallions of ivory, still flaked with their original gold plating, were set out at the top of the board. Ten small discs were grouped at the bottom in a kind of stepped-pyramid arrangement. Between them, silver-plated bars of crystal al-ternated with bars of gold-plated ivory.

There was no doubt in Evans' mind that the object of the game was to reach the "goal" at the top of the board before one's opponent; whoever got there first was the winner. The arrangement of the "moves" suggested that it must have been a game not only of skill but of chance. Played by dice-throwing? He thought it probable. When, nearby, the sifted earth yielded ivory "men," he could even conjecture the "rules." More, he could visualize the players: certainly of noble rank, relaxing after a day of ceremony, with their eggshell-thin pottery goblets filled with heady Cretan wine and a fluted bowl of fruit close at hand. Had they worn smoking jackets and stiff collars instead of embroidered loin-cloths, they might have been playing backgammon in a Victorian drawing room, on a truly elegant board. "It gives an extraordinary idea of magnificence," Evans wrote to his father.

Not long after the royal gaming board was discovered, the spade produced another fragment of wall decoration which, Evans reported in *The Times*, "supplies insignia of still more Royal purport. It displays the upper part of a head wearing a crown which terminates above in a row of five sloping lilies of varied metal-work, with a higher one rising in the centre. That the *fleur-de-lis* of our Edwards and Henrys should find a prototype in prehistoric Greece is a startling revelation; but it was perhaps fitting that, as last year's excavation in Knossos brought to light 'the oldest throne in Europe,' so the more recent researches should produce its most ancient crown." Evans promptly attributed the head, executed in plasterwork in low relief, to the priest-king himself.

When additional fragments were found and Gilliéron was able to piece out and restore the priest-king fresco, the regal youth that emerged was the embodiment of Minoan grace and elegance. He was smooth-shaven and wore his hair long and flowing. Clad only in a short kilt and wearing a narrow metal belt, he had the lithe but muscled body of a dancer, with a wasp waist that would have been the envy of a Victorian debutante. Evans marveled at how different these lissome Minoans were from all other ancients; how unlike the squat and dumpy Sumerians, the stiff hieratical figures of Egypt, the godlike statues of Classical Greece. There was spontaneity in their movements, refinement in their gestures. And always, in both sexes, there were those incredibly slender waists, invariably belted. Evans found only one statuette, of an older man, with a thickened waistline. He too was wearing a belt, but it had been let out to accommodate his years.

To Evans, drawing conclusions from frescoes, statuettes, and sealstones, it seemed clear that Minoan boys began wearing narrow metal rings around their waists from about the age of ten. Girls of the same age had their waists confined by tight girdles. "Considering the vital ducts and vessels involved by constriction below the ribs," he wrote with delicate concern, "this might have been thought an impossible interference wth Nature." However, after consulting "expert medical and physiological opinion," he concluded that the Minoans had achieved their enviable figures with no injury to health. ("Among other authorities who have kindly given me their opinion and who take this view: Lord Moynihan, President of the Royal College of Surgeons, and Sir Humphry Rolleston, Regius Professor of Medicine at Cambridge.") Once again the alluring Minoans had satisfied Evans, both scientific inquirer and aesthete.

The roster of one hundred men who had been working during Sir John's visit had nearly doubled. Mackenzie's red-thatched head towered over the dark-haired Cretans as he moved from one group to another, speaking softly and seldom but keeping a sharp eye on the work. Reticent, tireless, the Scotsman filled his Day Books with penciled sketches of pottery and diagrams of strata during the day. Each evening, when he returned to the house in Candia, he added more notes in his small, careful handwriting. It was no easy task to keep track of what was going on at Knossos.

On the western side of the Central Court, where the official and ceremonial rooms of the palace were located, attention was focused on the Throne Room. The temporary shelter erected the year before had already proved inadequate for the Cretan winter. Evans was determined not to let another season's rains fall on the room where the priest-king himself had once presided. But to support a roof it was necessary to replace the columns whose burnt remains and sockets were still visible. Moreover, the new columns must look as much like the originals as possible.

He found an exact model for their shape and coloring in the miniature Temple Fresco: downward-tapering columns painted a deep russet. The shape of these wooden columns, the exact opposite of the usual taper, was one of the most characteristic and distinctive features of Minoan architecture. The most likely explanation for the downward taper was that the tree trunks used in ancient times were unseasoned and the best way to keep unseasoned timber from sprouting was to plant it upside down. The Minoans had painted their graceful columns either red or black, with the capitals made wide enough to throw rainwater clear of the base, which might otherwise rot. Designed under Fyfe's supervision, the modern pillars substituted for the Minoan would have satisfied King Minos's own architect.

Meanwhile, the eastern side of the Central Court rang to the sounds of pick and shovel, of hammer and saw, as excavation preceded reconstruction. It was becoming very clear that in the Domestic Quarter people had lived and worked right up to the final day of the catastrophe. A stonecutter's workshop bore mute testimony: two alabaster amphorae were still waiting for his finishing touches. The heaps of lime cluttering the basement floors evoked an image of plasterers fleeing in the middle of their work. But the room that most stirred Evans' historical imagination was the one he called the "School Room."

Through the accumulated dirt and rubble, the chipped stones and the eloquent remains, he saw not only a classroom but the squirming schoolboys in it. Three of the walls had been lined with stone ledges, arranged in double gradation and sloping inward, like a modern lecture hall. Along the back wall ran a low stone bench, flanked at each end by a rounded stone pillar. What was curious about these pillars was their hollowed-out tops, shaped like bowls. One was the right height for a man, the other for a boy. They would be ideal for keeping lumps of clay moist, the clay from which scribes molded the tablets they wrote on. "May we perhaps imagine," Evans mused, "that the higher and lower stucco bowls were used by master and pupil respectively . . . and that the art of writing was here imparted to the Palace youth?"

It was a beguiling thought. One could picture him puzzling over the possibility, relishing the image; then scratching the far corner of his head the way he did when an idea titillated him.

The second season, like the first and all others to come, ended with a fine *glendi* at which the raki flowed freely. Another party was waiting for Evans back in England, where his homecoming was warmly toasted with champagne, both at Youlbury and Nash Mills. In June 1901 Arthur Evans was elected a Fellow of the Royal Society. It marked the first time in almost three hundred years that England's most distinguished scientific organization, founded in 1622, had included a father and son simultaneously. Sir John was equally pleased when the universities of Edinburgh and Dublin conferred honorary degrees on his son. Indeed, recognition of Arthur's discoveries was immediate and general, not only among scholars but among fascinated tourists who were already flocking in growing numbers to visit Knossos.

Only the Visitors of the Ashmolean Museum, it seemed, were still disinclined to take Evans' work in Crete seriously. Some of them were increasingly restive, even unfriendly; more annoyed with their absentee Keeper than impressed by the excavator of Knossos. To deal with them required a talent for compromise which Evans conspicuously lacked. If they tried his temper in Oxford, they thoroughly irritated him in Candia.

Chapter XIV
Fit for a Queen

Evans had hardly returned to Crete for the third season, in February 1902, when he received a disturbing letter from Charles Bell, his loyal assistant at the Ashmolean Museum. There had been trouble at the last meeting of the Visitors: the old story of pettiness and lack of vision, of grumbling and dissension. "No one can lament more bitterly than I," Bell wrote, "these things which look to you like inroads upon your prerogative—and are indeed such—because I *know*, as you are very well aware, that the great reforms of the future, necessary to place the study of Archaeology and Art upon any tolerable basis here, can only be carried through by you, and by you only with the use of autocratic power."

Evans reacted to Bell's letter with predictable asperity, but there was a disquieting undertone in his reply. He began firmly enough and became more mordant as he went on. "Board management," Evans fumed, "is at the root of a good deal of the difficulty and all modern tendencies at Oxford seem against simplicity in machinery." For his part, he wrote, he liked to keep things "trenchantly simple." All his instincts told him it was the best way and his methods certainly produced good results in Crete. Why not in Oxford?

Thus far the letter sounded like the familiar Evans, the man who knew only one way to work and who dealt summarily with his critics; the always-optimistic Evans, undaunted by obstacles. But what was Bell to make of the following sentence? "All this is rather pessimistic, but I am myself in a state of mental crisis, about which, however, I will not write now."

The weather was partly to blame. No one could remember when the spring rains had been so heavy and continuous. All of Knossos was an oozing sea of mud. In addition, Evans was suffering one of his periodic bouts of malaria, now feverishly hot, now chilled to the bone. Nor could he see any end to the work. He was overwhelmed at the amount still to be done. To cap matters, resurrecting the Minoans was proving to be not only a more extensive but a far more expensive undertaking than anyone could have foreseen.

Evans was deeply worried about finances. He had already spent a sobering amount of his own money. Less than half of his expenses had been met by the Cretan Exploration Fund (to which he, not to mention his father, contributed generously); and now, with who knew how many more years of excavation ahead, the fund itself was in trouble. It was hard to sustain popular interest in Crete indefinitely, especially with a war going on between the British Empire and some rebellious subjects.

England was bogged down in South Africa, fighting to maintain colonial rule over the Dutch Boer farmers who had originally settled there. Everyone had expected this struggle between the mighty British Empire and the simple but obstinate farmers to be quickly over. The Boer War had begun with the dispatch of twenty-five thousand English troops and assurance of quick victory. Contrary to all rational expectations, it took three years of bloody battles and three hundred thousand English soldiers to bring it to an end. It was surely not surprising that the war effort made prior demands on many potential subscribers to the Cretan Exploration Fund.

As Evans' expenses multiplied, contributions dwindled. The treasurer of the Cretan Exploration Fund, George A. Macmillan, was obliged to resort frequently to Letters to *The Times* in order to appeal for public support. Mr. Evans, he informed the readers, had already "drawn largely upon his own personal resources. . . . It is certainly not right that he should be allowed to bear so large a proportion of the cost of the undertaking, besides giving, year after year, so many months of personal supervision to the undertaking." He wrote fervently of Evans' "disinterested zeal which has carried him beyond the limits of prudence" in expending large personal outlays; of his strenuous labors and brilliant researches, and of the necessity "to complete one of the most fruitful excavations of modern times."

Macmillan was frequently seconded by ordinary citizens who invoked the good name of Britain to underscore their support. One such was a Mr. Charles Waldstein of King's College, Cambridge, who wrote that "work of this kind is national in character, and does more to maintain and increase the good fame of our country than most enterprises which advance our commerce, our industry and our wealth."

But despite all the publicity given to the Cretan Exploration Fund, contributions continued to fall off. David Hogarth had his own explanation for this public apathy, and it did not include the Boer War. Hogarth, as director of the British School of Archaeology at Athens, had helped to launch the fund. Moreover, because he had a living to make, he also drew on it for his own salary and expenses in digging, and perhaps that was what impelled him to begin an exchange of letters with Evans. Since both men were outspoken and crisply articulate, the exchange soon went from curt to caustic.

It was true, Hogarth wrote, that Evans took no salary and paid for much of the work at Knossos out of his own pocket. However, he could hardly complain about paying for expenses which were "avoidable had you so chosen. For example, the restorations and the very expensive building over the Throne Room after the frescoes had been moved."

Evans' reply crackled with indignation over what he took as an attack on his work. Hogarth hastened to assure him that he did not intend to imply "disapprobation" of his methods. Evans must have been reading between the lines. Nevertheless, Evans had to admit that such restorations were a luxury not everyone could afford, "and perhaps others can hardly be expected to pay for."

Clearly, the subject rankled. Hogarth may even have discussed it with Flinders Petrie, their mutual friend and colleague, who was excavating in Egypt. Or perhaps the comparison with Petrie in his letter was intended both to mollify and restrain Evans.

These expensive methods are yours in digging, as in collecting and in ordinary life. You are a rich man's son, and have probably never been at a loss for money. At the other pole to you stands Petrie—I see advantages in the methods of both. If you spend much more in proportion to Petrie, you produce far worthier results in published form, and one feels that nothing has been spared to obtain expert accuracy. One can't feel that with P.'s roughly drawn plans and illustrations; nor again does he leave a site so that it is a gain for the spectator. The drawback of your method is that it does not appeal to people's pockets.

Therein lay the crux of the matter. Public subscription could not be expected to support a rich man's way of work. He, Hogarth, was not imagining things. He had heard reports brought back by the big tourist parties about the "princely" way things were done in Crete. No wonder that even some of the old subscribers to the Cretan Exploration Fund had decided not to pay up again.

It was a long and explicit letter, and may have contributed to Evans' state of mental crisis. But whatever its effect on his spirits, it produced no change in his methods. With or without the Cretan Exploration Fund he intended to uncover and restore as much as possible of the civilization which had reached its pinnacle at Knossos. Fortunately the obliging Minoans cooperated. Early in the 1902 season they provided Evans with a vivid picture of what a Minoan city had looked like at the close of the eighteenth century B.C.

Bright bits of color caught the eyes of the men sifting earth in one of the basement rooms of the Domestic Quarter. Along with the pebbles and hardened lumps of clay remaining in their sieves, they had trapped scores of pieces of glazed porcelain. Washed clean of their 3500 years of dirt, the fragments glistened with colors as fresh as the day they were fired. Pieced together—or "reconstituted," as Evans preferred to describe the tedious process—they proved to be mosaic plaques averaging no more than four centimeters wide by four and a half centimeters high. And then came the revelation: each tiny plaque depicted the façade of a house.

The houses were two and three stories high; some even had fourth-story attics. Most of the roofs were flat, but there was one with a decided slope, probably to shed rainwater. Windows brightened the façades, windows with four and even six panes covered with some substitute for glass—oiled parchment, perhaps. The plaques themselves were made of exquisite faïence painted an overall pale gray, with timbering and other details brought out in brown, crimson, or green. They were works of art, and they told a story that amazed even Evans.

He was prepared for a sumptuous, multistoried palace. He would expect the mansions of the nobility to be more than one story high. But the tall houses shown in the Town Mosaic had been inhabited by ordinary Minoan citizens. It could mean only one thing: generations of civic living must have preceded such dwellings. Generations of well-settled urban life carried on by a highly gifted and advanced society. Placed side by side in rows, the mosaic plaques with their elegant proportions and their paned windows reminded Evans of the town houses of a modern street-front in London or Oxford. They wore an aura of permanency, poignantly affirmed by their almost miraculous rescue from the earth.

Evans' own living arrangements, meanwhile, continued to be temporary. He made only one improvement. This year, having long envied his friend Halbherr his swift Arabian mare, he too bought a horse. Evans loved going fast. Both he and the horse seemed to take pleasure in shortening the distance each day between Candia and Knossos. But though he might outride Mackenzie and Fyfe to the site, he invariably found Gregorios Antoniou, the new foreman, waiting for him when he got there.

Gregori, as everyone called him, was a valuable addition to the team. Born in Cyprus, he had spent his youth robbing tombs on his native island. To this felicitous background he had added the experience of working on a succession of British digs in Cyprus, as well as for Hogarth in the Dictaean Cave and at Zakro. He had thus joined training to instinct. "The most expert tomb-hunter in the Levant," Evans called him. Gregori could ferret out the most likely places where *antikas* lay merely by noting the presence of certain wild plants—the wild licorice plant, for example. Wherever it sank its roots, sometimes to a depth of over twenty feet, there would be evidence of undisturbed human habitation nearby. Moreover, though his muscles bulged and he had a neck like a bull, he could remove the most fragile objects from the earth without breaking them.

Most important of all, however, Gregori knew how to keep his men at work. With as many as 250 diggers, sifters, pottery washers, carpenters, and masons on the site during most of the season, this alone was no small task. But he was often called upon to perform even more heroic labors, including one which saved the "recompacted" Grand Staircase from possible reburial.

The wall at the top of the main staircase, made of masonry a solid meter thick, was found to be sloping forward at a seventy-five-degree angle. If it crashed down, its tremendous weight would pulverize everything that lay below it. The question was how to restore such a mighty mass to an upright position. Evans answered the question with brisk understatement: "In this emergency I had recourse to a novel expedient."

Under the eye of the trusty Gregori, a hand-picked group of men began by trussing up the wall, which was leaning like the Tower of Pisa, with ropes and planks. Then they cut a deep slit in the ground along both sides of its whole length. They pounded a solid wooden baseboard along the inner slit. For the outer slit they prepared wedge-shaped stones and cement, ready for use when the time came. Now came the moment when everybody on the spot held his breath.

Sixty men stood on the terrace above, holding on to the ropes fastened around the wall. A "heave-ho" from Gregori; a collective bellow from the men, ending in loud grunts. The process repeated and repeated. Slowly the enormous mass of masonry began to move. Inch by inch it was pulled backward. At last it settled itself into the inner slit, came to rest against the baseboard, and stood upright. Quickly the men below inserted the stone wedges and poured cement into the outer slit. This done, they removed the baseboard from the inner slit and the original Minoan wall once again handsomely guarded the top of the Grand Staircase.

Work could now continue in the Domestic Quarter. In the previous years the spade had uncovered the throne and ceremonial rooms of the priest-king. This year it focused attention on the private apartments of his queen.

Shovelful by shovelful, the diggers turned over the earth and followed the clues left by residual walls and pillars, by carbonized remains of benches, by fragments of broken plaster. These led to a short, twisting corridor with a sharp double bend, guarded by doors at both ends. Evans descriptively named it the "Dog's Leg Corridor." It had obviously been designed to give privacy, not easy access, to the room beyond—the room he called the "Queen's Megaron" (Megaron means hall or principal room). He so designated it from the archaeological evidence, which he read as though it were a photograph in full color.

To begin with, there were the benches. So much remained of their structure, including a good deal of the carbonized wood itself, that it was possible to restore them in their original form. The benches turned out to be only thirty-eight centimeters above floor level, which seemed, Evans tactfully suggested, "to be best in keeping with female occupants." Already, from the accumulating fragments of painted plaster, it was obvious that the walls of the room had been decorated with feminine lightness and grace. As the rubble was carted away and the digging proceeded, what slowly emerged were chambers fit not just for a lady but for a queen.

During the 1902 season Evans managed to clear out the whole area and to salvage whatever relics were found. Digging continued, with interruptions, for twenty-seven more years. New finds often necessitated changing old plans. Successive layers of the palace's history were laid bare. Architects reconstructed walls. Monsieur Gilliéron covered them with frescoes, copies of the originals pieced together from fragments. Not until 1929 would the final excavation be completed and the Queen's Megaron restored to the comfort and opulence it had attained in the Golden Age of Minoan Crete, somewhere around 1500 B.C.

Pillars set on a wide balustrade separated the queen's salon from its own private portico and light well. Vertical shafts, or light wells—really small interior courtyards—were a special feature of Minoan architecture. Often used in modern office buildings, they were particularly suited to the Cretan climate. The light well shut out the winds of winter and the intolerable summer heat, while at the same time letting sunshine into the room it illuminated. The queen's salon, thus bathed in a soft, diffused light, glowed with color. Its walls were covered with frescoes, painted in the first truly naturalistic style to be found in ancient art. On one wall swam blue dolphins with orange-yellow sides and creamy-white bellies, surrounded by smaller marine life. On another wall was the fresco of a dancer wearing an embroidered jacket and flounced skirt, her braids flying out to indicate the motion of her twirling. Painted stucco reliefs of spirals, rosettes, and papyrus plants framed the doorways.

A second light well at one side of the room filtered the sun's rays and provided a cross-draft of fresh air. Beyond it, at the far end of the salon, there was a private inner staircase leading to the rooms on the floor above. The pavement was made of gypsum. The ceiling was decorated in an intricate spiral pattern. All was lightness, beauty, and color.

Evans pictured the benches covered with pillows, their colors sparkling by day. He visualized the room lighted at night by one or more of the tall pedestaled lamps made in the palace workshop. He could almost overhear the court ladies, in their flounced costumes, gossiping as they sat along the walls or on the balustrade. "For conversation the room was ideal," he slyly noted, "with its seats both back to back and at right angles to one another." But the main surprise was yet to come.

At the far end of the salon stood a second row of downward-tapering pillars, set on a broad balustrade whose L-shaped extension formed an enclosure. When the painted clay fragments found within the enclosure were reconstructed, they revealed the function of the small chamber. It was the queen's bathroom. The restored tub, a small hip bath, anticipated its successors in shape but outdid them in elegance. It was painted inside and out with a motif of reeds and papyrus. Since there was neither sink nor drain in the room, it must have been filled by hand; but then, it was unlikely the queen had lacked for handmaidens. Nor for other, more "modern" conveniences.

Behind the bathroom, in a small room which Evans with Victorian nicety named the "Toilette Room," he found the remains not only of a sink but of a toilet—a toilet flushed by water, as evidenced by a small duct leading from it to the main drain. The plumbing in the queen's apartment was as plush as the appointments.

Minoan engineers, 3500 years ago, had foreshadowed the future when they designed the sanitary arrangements of the palace. Each individual quarter had a drainage system of its own, connected with the main channels. These were made of stone, ventilated by air shafts, and made accessible by manholes. The Minoan plumber could clean the drains with ease. "They were so roomy," Evans reported, "that, in the course of their excavation, my Cretan workmen spent whole days in them without inconvenience."

As for the pipes, they were made of terra-cotta and designed for maximum efficiency. Each was about seventy-five centimeters long, narrow at one end—with a stop-ridge to prevent it from jamming into the next pipe—and wide at the other end, with a raised collar to absorb the pressure of the stop-ridge joined to it. Once snugly fitted together, the pipes were bound with cement. Their tapering form gave a shooting motion to the flow of water and prevented the accumulation of dirt. But Minoan hydraulic engineers had had to face more serious problems than sediment.

When it rained in Crete, as Evans could testify, the water came in savage torrents, turning wadis into streams, streams into rivers. Moreover, the Palace of Knossos was built on a hill. To prevent flooding, the Minoans had cut a channel at each side of the majestic staircase leading from the Central Court down to the basement level of the palace. Each flight of stairs, however—there were once five flights—was at right angles to the next. The question confronting the engineers was how to slow down the water in its downward rush so that it would not overflow onto the landings.

They solved the problem by constructing the steep water channels in a series of natural curves, the curve being the parabola. The rate of flow was cut in half. "Nothing in the whole building," Evans wrote in admiration, "gives such an impression of the result of long generations of intelligent experience on the part of Minoan engineers as the parabolic curve of the channels." Furthermore, thanks to a series of catchments that collected the sediment along the way, the water was pure and clean when it reached the bottom. Trapped there in a large basin, it could serve for the palace laundry, Evans attractively suggested. "The special fitness of rain-water for washing linen warrants the conjecture that the tank was used for this purpose."

So this ancient people had known how to harness water for sanitation and cleanliness. They had also learned how to use it to cool and beautify, by means of fountains. On a fresco Evans found a painted design showing a central column of water and falling drops. It pleased him, whose own aesthetic bent was so strong, to imagine the gardens in which those fountains had played and to picture the houses aglow with each season's flowers. The image he conjured up of fountain spray, of scented gardens, of tall vases filled with flowers threw "an agreeable light on the population."

Chapter XV
The Earth-Shaker

A *glendi* like the one taking place in the spring of 1903—
in the newly excavated "Theatral Area"—had not been seen
in Knossos since the days of the Minoans. Evans was giving
a party. The occasion was the visit of Dr. Wilhelm Dörpfeld,
former assistant to Schliemann, and the group of tourists
participating in his annual island cruise.

The enthralled spectators could hardly believe that the area
they were now gathered in had been filled with rubble only
a few weeks before. The bright Cretan sun shone on a large
paved rectangle about twelve meters by nine. Tiers of low
steps, at right angles to each other, enclosed two adjoining
sides of the rectangle. Between these tiers, one of which
was still eighteen steps high, was an oblong block of limestone
forming a tribune, or dais. This, Evans explained to his guests,
had probably served as a kind of royal box. Judging from
the fragments of painted stucco found there, it may even
have been covered with a decorated canopy to protect the
priest-king and his retinue from the sun.

The uppermost step widened into a platform broad enough
to seat other distinguished spectators. However, since the
rest of the steps were so shallow, most of the ancient audience
in their long skirts or kilts—like the present one in their
traveling outfits—must have stood to watch the performance.
Evans estimated, by allowing forty-six centimeters per person,

that there could have been room for some five hundred people.

What happened on the "stage"? Principally, religious rites and ceremonial receptions. The space was too small for bull-leaping, but Evans could imagine spectacles such as boxing and wrestling matches. And, undoubtedly, dancing. The evidence painted on frescoes and pottery, engraved on seals and gemstones, all showed the importance of dancing in Minoan life and religion. Homer, referring to Crete, sang of "the twinkling of the dancers' feet." An old legend told how Theseus composed a twisting, snakelike dance to symbolize the Labyrinth from which he and his companions had escaped. To this day the Cretans were splendid dancers, as Evans' guests would now see for themselves.

The "Theatral Area" resounded to the rhythmic beat of music. A group of workmen and their womenfolk, dressed in their holiday costumes, formed a colorful circle, sometimes holding hands, sometimes linked only by kerchiefs. Their movements followed the haunting melodies of the musician seated within the circle. He was playing the *lyra*, the special instrument of Crete, a descendant of the ancient seven-stringed *cithara*, or lyre, of the Minoans. The dancers swayed and bent, wound in and out, performing "chain-dances" as old and traditional as the legends themselves. Their steps were now rapid, now sinuous, but always graceful and dignified.

For the tourists watching the dancers, it was a scene they would describe in their diaries as "unforgettable." For Evans, it was a pure evocation of the past. Inanimate ruins spoke. The Theatral Area was once more a stage on which the drama of Knossos, with its cast of characters and its plots within plots, continued to unfold. Like a latter-day Theseus following Ariadne's thread, he had no choice but to follow the archaeological clues that led out of the Labyrinth.

"There seems to be no finishing this year," he wrote his father in 1903. Heavy rains had produced another dramatic clue outside the palace limits. At the foot of a steep bank overlooking the Kairatos stream the sodden earth showed the clear marks of protruding doorjambs. But to unearth whatever building they gave entrance to was miners' work, and Evans again called on his Laurion miners.

They began by digging an exploratory tunnel into the hill-

side. Luck was with them. Almost immediately they came
on a bulwark of solid masonry which kept the hill from
caving in. A short distance brought them to a double doorway.
Farther on was a wall. Evans, Mackenzie, and Fyfe, making
their way through the tunnel with candles, could see by the
flickering light that the wall was made of fine gypsum blocks.
When the workmen had mined their way up a flight of gypsum
stairs to a landing ten steps above, Evans decided on a full-
scale excavation.

Nothing less than a royal villa was eventually uncovered.
It must have housed an important functionary. It may even
have served, Evans speculated, as a summer residence for
the priest-king himself. Built into a cutting in the hillside,
it profited from cool breezes yet was shielded from the sun.
A wide central flight of stairs with a narrower flight on each
side rose from ground level to the third floor. It was a stately
mansion—not as sumptuous as the "Little Palace" still awaiting discovery, but without question one of the many dependencies of the palace complex.

Meanwhile, as digging continued at the Royal Villa, there
was commotion elsewhere in the palace. A slight depression
in the floor of a room already excavated led Evans to discover
treasures that only the most privileged Minoans had ever
seen. Exposure to the elements had caused a small chamber,
located on the ceremonial west side of the Central Court,
to "settle." Its sagging pavement caught his eye. He had
some of the slabs removed. Underneath them he found not
the usual Neolithic stratum that underlay the palace but loose
earth. It was most curious.

Downward probing revealed first reddish clay, then darker
earth mixed with charred wood and fragments of gold foil.
Still lower, a layer of terra-cotta vases; beneath that, a thick
seam of "fatter and more compact" earth; and at the bottom,
two stone cists, or vaults, whose contents inspired and merited
the name he gave them: the "Temple Repositories." The
keepers of the palace had done well to hide such treasures
until Evans, and not some tomb-robber, had come along.

There were masses of petal-shaped gold foil. There were
molded glass beads, thin-walled painted cups and vases, exquisite plaques made of faïence, objects carved out of bone

and ivory. But the masterpiece was the elegant faïence Snake Goddess, perhaps the finest example of Minoan glazed ware.

Reconstituted, the Snake Goddess stood 34.29 centimeters high. She was dressed in the latest fashion, but what struck the eye were the three snakes coiled so intricately around her body that they seemed part of her costume. One snake, whose head she held in her right hand, wound its way up her arm, over her shoulders and down the other arm, its tail ending in her left hand. The other two were twisted like a girdle over her hips and tiny waist. One of them coiled upward and around the tall hat she wore, its head rising above the crown. The other coiled downward, looping itself almost parallel to the embroidered circular band of her apron. Under the apron her skirt fell to the floor in flounces. A richly embroidered bodice, tightly laced at her waist, bared her breasts. She wore a necklace around her neck, a bracelet on her wrist. Her black eyes blazed under black eyebrows, shown in relief. Her milky-white skin dramatically contrasted with the purple and brown of her costume and the green snakes with purplish-brown spots.

The Snake Goddess was the chthonic, or underworld, form of the Mother Goddess herself. She played a prominent role in everyday Minoan life. Far from arousing horror, the snake was looked upon as a symbol of rebirth and immortality. It was revered as a reincarnation of the dead. To harm it would be like desecrating a dead ancestor. The Minoans had shared these beliefs and the practice of the snake cult with most of the ancient world and indeed some modern societies. Evans remembered the peasant huts he had visited around Ragusa: the dish of milk set out by the hearth for the family snake and the peasants' regard for the reptile as a kinsman, a friendly spirit bringing luck to the household. He had been a guest in Greek and Albanian homes where the snake was called "master of the house." To him, the relics of the age-old cult buried in Knossos were not a throwback to primitive beliefs but a reminder that the beliefs still persisted.

The clay cylinders, or "snake-tubes," which the Minoans had provided for their reptilian tutelaries were ingeniously multipurposed. Cups were attached to their sides, from which the snake could partake of the drink offerings. Having drunk, it could then crawl inside the tube for rest or shelter. Some of the cylinders themselves were shaped like snakes, as though to make their purpose more explicit. In addition to the snake-tubes there was the snake-table. This was divided into four separate compartments, to accommodate two pairs of reptiles at a time, with a raised bowl in the center for food. The addition of a clay "hearth" at which the snake could warm itself completed the reptilian sanctuary.

Such elaborate fittings had little in common with the humble dish of milk at peasant firesides. Remembering his Bosnian wanderings, Evans pondered the ancestral cult which, stripped of its refinements, was still so tenaciously observed in remote mountain villages where no one had ever heard of the Minoans. Still, it was purely by coincidence that the year 1903 began with the discovery of the Snake Goddess and her reminder of Slav villages and ended with another echo from the Balkans.

No matter how jealously the Minoans claimed Evans' attention, they never succeeded—any more than Margaret had, or the Ashmolean Museum, or Nash Mills—in blotting out the Balkans. Evans' removal from his adopted Slavs was purely geographical. He had never abandoned their fight for freedom. His continuing devotion to their cause produced periodic interludes in his life when the archaeologist he was reverted to the polemicist he had been—even when it was inopportune or even risky to voice his opinions. No one who knew him was surprised to read his Letter to *The Times* in October 1903 and Evans, for one, was not unhappy when the Balkan Committee reprinted and widely distributed it under the inflammatory title, "Extermination in Macedonia." He followed up his first letter with a second one in November, vehemently criticizing political meddling in the Balkans. This time his anger was directed not against the sultan but against Greece, which was laying claim to Macedonia, still under Turkish rule.

Margaret would have recognized her husband's unswerving principles in the indignant prose. Edward Freeman, too, would have relished every word. Sir John, who had just celebrated his eightieth birthday, thought it entirely characteristic of his son to write such imprudent letters at such a time. Anyone

else excavating Knossos would have thought twice before publicly attacking Greek politics. Prince George of Greece was
the royal patron of the Cretan Exploration Fund. Crete was
a Greek protectorate. The authorities in Candia were heavily
dependent on the Greek mainland for conducting affairs on
their island and so, in the final analysis, was Arthur Evans.

Taking none of these facts into consideration, Evans sternly
informed the readers of *The Times* that Greece had no rights—
either ethnological or linguistic and certainly not humani-
tarian—to the territory of Macedonia. That unhappy land's
answer to Ottoman oppression lay in reforms, not annexation.
Until those reforms had been achieved and had paved the
way to freedom, he would continue cooperating with Balkan
patriots in their life-and-death struggle for independence. His
friends knew, and his critics soon learned, that Evans never
abandoned a principle or a goal.

Ironically, in a lifetime of pursuing his own ends, only
one achievement eluded him: the decipherment of Minoan
script. He had discovered Linear A and Linear B tablets
in the first week of excavation. He spent the rest of his
life trying to read them, without success. It was not for want
of trying. He pored so long over the ancient hieroglyphs
and symbols, that they became as familiar to him as the
English alphabet. Laboriously he copied them out. His own
handwriting, never very legible, began to take on a Minoan
look. No incision of the scribe's stylus escaped his notice,
no stroke, curve, broken line, or pothook.

What made his task so difficult was the absence of any
bilingual inscription which could offer clues in a known language to the decoding of the unknown. The Knossian earth,
so generous in other respects, yielded nothing comparable
to the Rosetta Stone, which had made it possible to decipher
Egyptian hieroglyphs; or to the trilingual Behistun Rock,
which provided the key to Babylonian cuneiform. By the
time Evans finished excavating in Knossos he had accumulated
some three thousand tablets inscribed in Linear B script.
Had even one of them been written in two languages—a
bill of lading to an Egyptian merchant, for instance, or a
receipt—he might have realized his dream: to read about
the Minoans in their own tongue. For he naturally assumed

by now that their script, long dead, was of Cretan invention and not, as he had speculated in his article in *The Monthly Review*, a form of archaic Greek.

Nevertheless, through observation, intuition, and long study, Evans was able to arrive at a surprising number of conclusions. The earliest form of Cretan writing had, of course, been hieroglyphic. The Linear A script which succeeded it—called "linear" not because it was written in a straight line, but because a few stylized strokes took the place of a picture—made the scribe's task much easier. Then, somewhere around 1450 B.C., during the Golden Age of Knossos, came the invention of a new script through modification of Linear A. This was the Linear B, which kept Evans at his desk into the candle-lit hours. It taught him a great deal about Minoan efficiency and organization.

The tablets were roughly similar to the contents of a filing cabinet in a modern business office: lists of supplies, accounts, inventories, work records. Each tablet had been neatly marked with crosslines before it was handed over to the scribe, much like the ruled pages of a stenographer's notebook. The rapid flow of the writing showed great practice. Sometimes, for extra clarity, the clerk drew a pictographic design in the margin: a horse, a chariot, a weapon. The numbering system was based on the decimal and included fractions, making it easy to add or subtract and keep accurate accounts.

Important documents or packages were secured by clay sealings onto which an official pressed his signet. On very important documents his signature was countersigned and endorsed by that of his superior. However, the majority of the tablets were stored in wooden boxes, labeled with ink-written inscriptions. Early in the excavations Evans had found two cups with linear writing on the inside. Noting that "the lines of the letters show occasionally a tendency to divide," he concluded that this pointed to the use of a reed pen with a split point. Unlike a stylus, an instrument intended for clay tablets, a pen was something one dipped in ink and used—on parchment? On palm leaves? Perhaps on wood, leather, or papyrus, none of which would have survived the Cretan dampness.

Tirelessly examining the evidence, Evans drew conclusions.

Archives so meticulously kept were the work of a well-ordered bureaucracy. They reflected "a legalized administration and Treasury devices of a highly modern kind, such as never before were seen on any fraction of European soil." They helped to explain the traditional image of King Minos as a great lawgiver and enlightened ruler, whose influence spread far beyond his island. When traces of Linear B writing were found painted on vases in Thebes on the Greek mainland, it only confirmed Evans' theory of Cretan preeminence in the ancient Aegean world.

In 1909 Evans published his *Scripta Minoa*, Volume I, containing the earlier hieroglyphic tablets and a few inscribed in the Linear A script. Two more volumes would be forthcoming, he announced, "devoted to the advanced Linear Scripts of Crete of both Classes (A and B)," in accordance with his promise to the learned world that he would share his findings for mutual study. Unfortunately, it was a promise he never kept and for which many scholars have never ceased to reproach him. He did publish a handful of Linear B tablets, and a Finnish scholar named Professor Johannes Sundwall managed to get hold of a few others, much to Evans' rage, but the vast bulk of the precious documents remained locked up at Youlbury for half a century. It was not in Evans' nature to admit defeat. Did he keep Linear B for his very own so that he and he alone would decipher it? Was he determined to be the first to read that "Mycenaean" type set up for him by the Oxford University Press? Or was it because, as some critics have implied, he became overpossessive of his finds? "His" Minoans?

Whatever the case, the Minoans, who had revealed so much to him, withheld this one final secret. The Linear B tablets were not published until 1952, eleven years after Evans' death, when his good friend John Myres, himself an octogenarian by then, undertook the monumental task. It was the same year in which a young, hitherto-unknown scholar named Michael Ventris broke the communications barrier, working from tablets found not by Evans but by Carl Blegen, an American archaeologist, and deciphered Linear B with totally unexpected and far-reaching results. But all this was still far in the future.

During the first six years of the twentieth century Evans
continued to explore Knossos and its environs and to publish
his findings in the Annual of the British School at Athens
and other learned journals. Mackenzie did his share, too,
to keep the scholarly world informed. The article the Scotsman
wrote in 1902 for the *Journal of Hellenic Studies*, entitled
"The Pottery of Knossos," gave a thorough review of the
evidence accumulated during the first three seasons' digs and
formulated several basic theories which Evans held to all
his life. One was that the clay tablets inscribed in Linear
B were contemporary with the spectacular "Palace Style"
of pottery which Mackenzie ascribed to approximately 1450
B.C. Another was that the pottery produced after the destruction
of the palace was inferior and "decadent," thus indicating
a partial and later habitation of the ruins. And in the same
article Mackenzie proposed a tripartite chronological scheme,
which Evans later elaborated on when it came to final dating.
One of the questions archaeologists have been asking ever
since is how much Mackenzie drew from Evans for his theories
and how much Evans from Mackenzie.

Two years later the full account of the British excavations
at Phylakopi on the island of Melos finally appeared and
contained a chapter by Mackenzie entitled "The Successive
Settlements at Phylakopi and their Aegeo-Cretan Relations."
In it he postulated that the "latest rulers at Phylakopi were
a mainland people," and went on to say, in speaking of
the incursions from Greece, that "One of the causes which
contributed toward the break-up of the Minoan civilization
in Crete was undoubtedly invasion from the mainland." This
statement, too, would have repercussions—but much later.
In 1904 Evans was too busy adding new discoveries to engage
in present arguments with Mackenzie or worry about future
ones.

He found a large cemetery and opened up some one hundred
tombs; excavated a princely royal tomb overlooking the sea;
and came upon the "Royal Armoury" with its store of some
eight thousand arrows. He also continued with his test probes
into the mound of Knossos, reaching in some places an impressive depth of over twelve meters of habitation debris.

In 1905 he uncovered "the oldest paved road in Europe,"

leading from the Theatral Area to the remains of a large building which he called the "Little Palace," the largest of the palace dependencies. Thus added to the vast complex, it resumed its position opposite the palace itself and the Royal Villa beyond. Behind the Little Palace he noted the remains of still another building which he left unexcavated, appropriately naming it the "Unexplored Mansion." It ran deep into the hillside beneath an olive plantation, but its Eastern façade wall was visible for a length of twenty-six meters. Evans described and illustrated the fine limestone construction, and the ashlar blocks which formed a wall, in regular parallel horizontal courses, with the vertical joints at approximately right angles. He noted that "about a meter higher than the Minoan floor level are well-preserved remains of a room of a Greco-Roman house with traces of decorative wall paintings showing upright marbled bands of green and red." He would have been pleased to know that almost three-quarters of a century later other archaeologists would excavate the Unexplored Mansion and prove him right.

And all the while he was studying the palace stratigraphy and trying to arrive at a chronology. By April 1905 Evans was ready to attend an archaeological congress in Athens and propose a historical framework for the Cretan Bronze Age. He had two advantages: his geological upbringing and the fact that the stratigraphical evidence at Knossos, although enormously complex, had lain relatively untouched over the millennia and was almost entirely complete and conformable.

It was fairly easy to distinguish one layer of habitation at Knossos from another. Dating them was more complicated. Sometimes Clio the Muse of History cooperated by "planting," as it were, an object of known date—like the figure of the Egyptian called User who, discovered during the first season, had stamped approximately 2000 B.C. on his stratum; or the lid of an Egyptian alabastron, found the year after, and obligingly engraved with the name and titles of Khyan, the Hyksos king who had reigned around 1200 B.C. But more often Evans had to rely on "the archaeological law that the small relics found on floors belong to the last moment of occupation," and on the "pottery sequences": the dating of pottery types based on stratigraphic evidence. This was one of the most valuable tools in the archaeologist's kit.

Clay, once fired, is practically indestructible. Clay pots may be broken, but their sherds, or fragments, remain to tell a story of advancing techniques, of changing fashions, even of life-styles. Handles evolve from rudimentary to fully developed. Shapes and painted designs become more sophisticated. New forms are created to satisfy new needs. In the correlation of the architectural strata with the pottery embedded within them, Duncan Mackenzie, who had perfected methods of his own during his excavations at Phylakopi, was of great help.

Speaking at the archaeological congress held in Athens in April 1905, Evans proposed a timetable for the Cretan Bronze Age which rendered out-of-date all books published before 1902 on the general subject of ancient Greece. He classified the Minoan civilization into three periods—Early, Middle, and Late Minoan—and further divided each into three subdivisions, making nine periods in all. They corresponded roughly, as determined by the synchronization and correlation of archaeological evidence, with the Old, the Middle, and the New Kingdoms of Egypt. (For quick mnemonic purposes, the dates were approximately 2500 B.C., 2000 B.C., and 1500 B.C. For more precise and detailed dating, see Chronology on page 265.) Thus Evans brought a long-forgotten civilization into step with the march of history. On the calendar of the palace itself the vagaries and chemistry of survival had red-lettered certain epochal dates.

The first, or Old Palace of Knossos, was built around 2000 B.C., on top of the relics left behind by the Neolithic and Early Minoan inhabitants of the site. The finest artistic legacy bequeathed by the builders of the Old Palace to their descendants was the splendid painted pottery called Kamáres ware. Even more important, however, was the *joie de vivre* they must have demonstrated at the beginning of the twentieth century B.C., alone among their contemporaries, in order to build so splendid a palace. It was not only a center of government and religious life but also of arts and crafts and industries so flourishing that Cretan products were in demand abroad. This joyous outburst of creative energy was not confined to Knossos. The Minoan genius also created palaces at Phaistos, Mallia, and elsewhere; but Evans' audience would understand if he concentrated his remarks on the excavations he himself had conducted.

In approximately 1700 B.C. a devastating earthquake reduced the Old Palace of Knossos to ruins, together with villas, workshops, and the dwellings of the humble. Evans knew that Crete, an earthly paradise in so many respects, was especially prey to violent tremors. The medieval and modern history of the island recorded six destructive earthquakes in six and a half centuries. However, the resilient Minoans were no different from modern victims of a natural disaster. Far from abandoning their homeland, they went to work, rebuilding their palace more sumptuously than before.

This time, with their greater technical skill and improved materials, they built a framework of vertical and horizontal beams into the walls as a precaution against earthquakes. Then they splashed those walls with the brilliant mural paintings Gilliéron was later to attempt to restore. They also created the stone and ivory carvings, the glorious faïence figures, and the elegant ceramics that made the Minoan civilization the most purely delightful of the Bronze Age world. They added on to the east side of the Central Court a large new residential wing, Evans' Domestic Quarter. Ruins became homes again. Fields and vineyards flourished. Trading vessels put out to sea. The Minoan equivalent of the god Poseidon was appeased. Homer's epithet for Poseidon was the "Earth-Shaker," whose symbol was the bull. He was the ruler of the sea and of the stormy flood, the god who both supported the earth and could shake it with the blows of his trident. For well over a century Poseidon was quiescent and Crete prospered.

And then, around 1580 B.C., another mighty earthquake struck the Knossos area. So violent were the tremors that a massive wall of the palace fell outward, hurling huge blocks of stone—some weighing more than a ton—for distances of over six meters, and crushing the simple houses of artisans and townsfolk clustered below. The home of the craftsman who made stone lamps was so badly damaged that he never rebuilt it. Had he perished in the ruins? If so, he had been given a decent burial; the only remains left behind for Evans' workmen to find were eight unfinished lamps, mute testimony to diligence. Nor was the house next door ever reoccupied. Evans called it "The House of the Sacrificed Oxen." Sealed in with the debris were the heads of two wild oxen of a breed now extinct, with horns measuring thirty centimeters at the base. In front of them lay the fragments of portable terra-cotta altars. This sacrificial offering to the Powers below told a poignant story of human suffering and indomitable will.

For what the Unseen had destroyed, the people once again restored. Minoan Crete now entered into the full flowering of its Golden Age. The priest-king of the House of Minos was the most powerful ruler on the island. "Broad Knossos" was its imperial city. It covered a considerable area, from the palace at its summit and the humbler residential district below to the outlying Harbor Town beyond. Evans estimated that the city could have sheltered up to one hundred thousand souls (a figure now considered exaggerated).

Unlike other cities of antiquity, no walls ringed Knossos. No citadel betrayed the fear of invasion, no fenced-in areas sacrificed expansion in return for safety. Surrounded by waters they controlled, the islanders lived in peace and security, expressing a zest for life in the very exuberance of their pottery, the refinement of their arts. The goldsmith, using a crystal lens as a magnifier while he executed his miniature figure of a lion—only fifteen millimeters long, yet so beautifully modeled that every muscle rippled—how could he foresee disaster? What merchant, fisherman, or potter, going about his busy day, dreamed of tragedy?

The disaster that befell Crete in about 1450 B.C. was the most catastrophic of them all. Knossos recovered sufficiently— very likely under a change of dynasty, Evans thought—to enjoy another half-century of high prosperity, during which it created its incomparable "Palace Style" pottery, but it was no longer strong enough to avert the final, tragic end. Though "squatters" had partially occupied its ruins for perhaps another two hundred years, the magnificent palace as it was in its days of glory was forever destroyed, Evans estimated, in approximately 1400 B.C. Again by the Earth-Shaker? Or was it foreign invasion that brought so brilliant a civilization to a close? Local insurrection, civil war?

At the archaeological congress in Athens in 1905 Evans was not yet ready to arrive at conclusions, nor would the scholarly community have been prepared to discuss them. His colleagues, listening raptly as he reconstructed a buried culture and framed its weathered layers within a time span, had quite enough to ponder—and so had he. With five seasons of extensive excavations behind him, he still had years of work ahead. Years not only of more digging but of study and research. The twice-daily horseback rides from Candia to Knossos were tiring and time-consuming. Evans decided that the time had come to build his Cretan home within walking distance of the Minoans.

Sir John, meanwhile, had been planning a home of his own. Nash Mills was no longer the stately, white-stuccoed family homestead it had once been. Over the years the expanding paper mills had grown closer and closer to the house, filling the air with steady noise and smudging the starched curtains at the windows. The garden with its chestnut trees and raspberry patches was hedged in by whirring machinery. England's demand for paper seemed to be insatiable and in order to keep up with it, Sir John came to a decision that would have daunted most men of his age. At eighty-two, he made up his mind to convert Nash Mills into an office and live elsewhere.

For months he had been poring over architects' plans. The handsome new red-brick house he was building for his wife, Maria, and their thirteen-year-old daughter, Joan, would soon be ready.

Chapter XVI
The Villa Ariadne

John Evans had lived at Nash Mills for more than half a century. Within its walls he had heard the quarrels and laughter of five children and suffered the loss of two wives. From it he had traveled all over England and abroad to explore in likely places for relics of man's prehistoric ancestors. There was hardly a learned society, an antiquary, or a dealer in all the British Isles who didn't know his address. When Sir John left Nash Mills, he had more than memories to take away with him.

His collections, reflecting a lifetime of scholarly pursuits, filled his library and overflowed into the rest of the house. Walls were lined with cabinets containing stone and bronze implements, ancient pottery, and early Teutonic metalwork. Glass cases and countless drawers were filled with coins and medallions, with Anglo-Saxon jewelry and Roman glass. Nash Mills had had the time and capacity to absorb them all. The new house would not, and Sir John decided to hand over most of his collections to his son Arthur. Nothing Arthur could say would dissuade him.

On a wintry day in January 1906 the paper mill's biggest van was backed into the Nash Mills drive and loaded with boxes of stone implements for delivery to Youlbury. No sooner had the driver started moving toward the gate, however, than the bottom of the van dropped out. The stone implements alone weighed four tons, and were only part of the thousands of objects destined for shelf-room at Youlbury. No wonder that Arthur, writing to tell his father that the vans had finally arrived safely, found it difficult to sound enthusiastic. "As I said before, I would rather you had kept the collections."

The cabinets, he wrote, fit in very well, but he was hard put to find enough drawer space. Much of the pottery, he suggested, should go to the Ashmolean Museum. He hadn't realized how immense the collections were. "Anyway I hope I may learn something from them and I do realize your kind intentions." He didn't add that most of the boxes were taken down to the cellar without being unpacked at all.

Arthur Evans preferred to fill Youlbury with his own treasures. He found exquisitely engraved Cretan sealstones more aesthetic than stone hand-axes. He liked fine paintings on his walls: a portrait of a lady by Bronzino, a splendid Caravaggio, beautiful canvases of the Venetian and Veronese schools. His house was filled with colorful Mediterranean embroideries that reminded him, as dark wood cabinets could not, of Ragusa and his life with Margaret.

To his great sorrow they had never had children. He came as close as possible to having a son of his own when Margaret's nephew Lancelot Freeman, whose parents were settling in Virginia, came to live with him in Youlbury. Lance was not very strong physically or overly intellectual, but he was warm and affectionate—and he was a child. He became the object of every attention Evans could bestow. Whenever Lance was home from school, the house rang with the voices of young people. Soon the grounds, too, resounded to the shouts of youngsters in scout uniform when Evans added still another cause to his wide-ranging interests.

The Boy Scout movement was founded in 1908 by Lieutenant General Sir Robert Baden-Powell. Evans became one of its first and staunchest supporters from the day when some ten or twelve village boys rang his doorbell at Youlbury. They had formed themselves voluntarily, their scoutmaster Arthur Shepperd explained, into a troop. For weeks they had been busily making bonfires, practicing knots, and earning their badges on the slopes of Boars Hill, where Evans' neighbor Lord Berkeley owned a big field ideal for their purposes.

Unfortunately, Berkeley's gamekeeper had complained that they disturbed the pheasants. Now they were homeless; and they wondered whether—

It was the beginning of a long association between a famous archaeologist, who spent much of his time in Crete, and the Boy Scout movement which started in England and became a worldwide organization. Evans invited the scraggly troop into his home, where they stared speechless at the maze and the Minotaur on the floor of the vast entrance hall and where a not-altogether-approving housemaid served them cocoa and biscuits. While the boys fell to, Evans discussed future plans with their scoutmaster. The Boy Scouts could have free run of the Youlbury woods, he told Shepperd, and use of the lake, provided that every boy be taught to swim before receiving his badge. More, he would turn over to them as a temporary headquarters the tree house he had built for Margaret on the edge of the lake. He heartily endorsed the scouts' aims to teach nature lore and outdoor skills to the young and to instill in them good citizenship, and would do everything he could to further their goals.

One small lad among the group devouring the biscuits attracted his attention: he looked so pale and sickly. When Shepperd told him it was one of the Candy children, Evans remembered the little fellow he had lifted onto his shoulders so that he could see the tug-of-war that had topped off the flower show. James Candy, or Jimmie, as Evans always called him, was then about ten. He had had an operation for mastoids at the age of six months which had left him with impaired hearing and a constantly discharging ear, with serious effects on his health, his schoolwork, and his self-confidence in general. His parents, poor tenant farmers living on Boars Hill with five children besides Jimmie to raise, had done everything they could for the child. Evans determined to do more.

He visited Mr. and Mrs. Candy several times to talk about Jimmie's future. Finally he persuaded them to allow him to become the child's guardian. He had no thought of supplanting their role as parents, he assured them. He wanted only to provide the medical care and education the boy needed. He would see to it that he got the best treatment London's Harley Street specialists could offer, and would arrange proper schooling for him. Reluctantly, the Candys had to agree that Evans' means of insuring their son's future far exceeded their own. With the understanding that Jimmie would spend the first fortnight of his holidays with his parents and siblings—and every Sunday after church, until dinnertime—Evans took the boy to live with him at Youlbury.

For Jimmie it was the beginning of a new life; for Evans a surrogate family, completing the transformation of Youlbury from a bachelor's fief into a home. With both Lance and Jimmie at Youlbury, he engaged a governess to look after them. Miss Mary Wiggins became a full-fledged member of the household, and her nephew Denis often augmented the resident young. Denis's sister Nancy also spent occasional weekends with them, although Evans never felt quite as relaxed with young ladies as with their opposite numbers.

Youlbury settled into a surprising domesticity when the boys were home from school. Gongs regulated the day, from the breakfast gong at nine in the morning to the dinner gong at seven on the dot. Breakfast was a hearty meal: porridge or cornflakes, cold ham, eggs and bacon, kidneys or fish, toast, marmalade, and coffee. Evans sat at the round table in the morning room reading his mail while he ate, regally tossing the letters over his head onto the floor when he had finished with them. Immediately after breakfast the boys would go off to their lessons. Evans retired to his library. After-lunch activities varied with the weather until teatime. At six o'clock Evans would return to his library to write letters. Promptly at seven whoever was in the house was expected to appear for dinner, the boys in their Eton jackets, and everyone else in formal attire. Mackenzie, who spent most of his time at Youlbury when he wasn't in Crete (or off in his "lair," as Evans called it, in Scotland), wore his plaid kilt. The dining-room table, like the one Evans grew up with in Nash Mills, was enormous and was seldom laid for fewer than ten or twelve people and often more, especially in summer. Among the frequent guests was Evans' friend John Myres and his family.

Many years later, the younger Myres reminisced about those holidays with nostalgia. "Youlbury was a marvelous place for children: the mysterious rambling house, miles of wild

woodland gardens, a lake with boats and bathing, peaches
and grapes in one's bedroom before breakfast, everything
a child could want. His garden and lake were always full
of the neighbours' children."

After the Youlbury Scout Troop was formed, the thickets
swarmed with boys of all sizes and ages in scout uniform
as well. "There were Boy Scout camps all over the place,"
Myres recalled. "Too many really for my liking, but it did
not seem to worry Evans. He never tried to organize our
activities, but was always kindly and unbothered by what
we did. He seemed to radiate an air of spaciousness and
unfussy sympathy which gave one confidence. I look back
on those times at Youlbury with immense pleasure. Evans
may have been a difficult man for grown-ups to know, but
he was fascinating with children, and very generous."

James Candy, too, long after he was a successful businessman, married, the father of four children, and a grandfather, retained his own glowing memories of the many years
he spent at Youlbury. During his first lonely weeks there,
a frightened and homesick ten-year-old, he would sometimes
have nightmares at night and awake screaming. His new guardian would come running to comfort him, looking like a benevolent gnome in his nightcap and a nightshirt that came
down to his ankles. Evans' bedroom was next door to Jimmie's,
who would never forget his surprise the first time he saw
it. In addition to an old-fashioned horsehair sofa piled high
with English mystery stories and French novels, it contained,
underneath the bed, a tin bathtub. The boy marveled that
the master of a house with a tiled Roman bath still took
his ablutions in the Victorian Nash Mills manner.

Candy treasured the weekly letters Evans wrote to him
when he was away at school, often beginning "My dear kid":
"I am not very good at finding ties—the colours are generally
not what I like! But I am sending you three which I hope
you will like." Or, "The GARDEN RABBIT is growing fatter
every day. (That sounds like a sentence to turn into French.
'Le lapin du jardin s'ongraisse [sic] tous les jours.')" He
especially liked the letter to his mother: "You know that
I have really given Jimmie a little bit of my heart. . . ."

The schoolboy and the archaeologist used to take long

walks together through the woods. Suddenly Evans would grow quiet, lost in thought, and then become as though jet-propelled. He would dash off like an Olympic sprinter, stopping himself yards ahead when he remembered the boy struggling to catch up. What idea, what vision, what new theory had taken hold of his fertile brain and given flight to his legs?

They often played croquet on the lawn, a game Evans loved (he had to put on his pince-nez to see the ball) and billiards in the dining room—the room was so large that the billiard table was lost in a corner. Sometimes Mackenzie would join in the fun: chasing rabbits through the Youlbury woods, hunting for badgers, catching butterflies. The boys were all fond of Mackenzie with his soft voice and great height, his mustache that got entangled in the breakfast porridge, and the ghost stories and fairy tales he would tell them at twilight. It was the best time, the Highlander explained, to hobnob with ghosts and the "wee ones." But most of Candy's memories revolved around Evans. The evenings in the drawing room, with Miss Wiggins playing the lovely grand piano. The trips to Oxford to have the boys' clothing and shoes custom-made. The cricket match Sir Arthur organized on his own grounds between the "Youlbury Eleven" and the scouts. The pogo sticks Jimmie, Lance, and Denis bounced around on—they were the first boys on Boars Hill to have pogo sticks. To his fellow archaeologists Evans may sometimes have seemed a tyrant, but to the boy transported from farmhouse to luxury he was "the most lovable man I ever knew and the kindest."

It would certainly have come as a shock to Evans' colleagues to see the discoverer of the Minoans crawling on his hands and knees through the bracken with the Boy Scouts, "like one of us." Or rolling up the legs of his trousers to go paddling, and inviting twenty or thirty scouts every week to his home. The troop would go up to the "solar" room through the servants' quarters—Evans' concession to the housekeeper Mrs. Judd—to gather around the piano and sing songs, play games, and devour the "eats." There was none of the autocrat in the man who played bridge of an evening with Jimmie, Miss Wiggins, and Denis (being no mathematician, Evans was a poor player; he did much better at Whist or Patience) or chose esoteric words to act out in charades. Years later Jimmie could still see Evans acting out the word Popocatepetl.

He kept a huge box in his library filled with Balkan trappings: guns, swords, beautiful tapestries, lengths of embroidered cloth. What games they inspired! There were the summer holidays to Barmouth, with historical side trips for the boys' edification: visits to Caernarvon Castle, Harlech Castle, old Saxon and Norman churches. Evans would have peaches and nectarines sent from Youlbury twice a week by train from Oxford in a specially cushioned wicker basket. There were also archaeological expeditions to Cornwall to look for beehive huts, with all of them tramping over the moors and Evans finding his quarry like a dog sniffing for rabbits. He would take out his tape measure to start measuring and use his "pocket excavator's tool" to scrape at bits of mud or rock. This latter was his own invention: he kept the nail of his small finger on the right hand a quarter of an inch longer than the other nails. It, together with the tape measure, the stub of a pencil in his vest pocket, and the magnifying glass made up his portable archaeological equipment.

Evans' Christmas parties at Youlbury, like the ones he and Margaret used to give at Ragusa, were the social event of the year at Boars Hill. He invited all the children from the village, together with the offspring of Oxford dons and other friends, to a celebration none of them ever forgot, either the small girls in their fancy dresses or the boys in their Eton jackets and ties. Their host, with his instinctive understanding of the very young, contrived to make the party both a grown-up affair and a rollicking event, and to inject a bit of Minoan history into the festivities as well.

The party started off like a Victorian ball. Seated on the wide gallery overlooking the first floor was an orchestra for dancing. Each boy or girl was given a different-color ribbon and danced the first cotillion, led by Evans himself, with the partner whose ribbon matched. But the man who could keep an audience of archaeologists spellbound could also invent games. The one that elicited the most shrieks of delight was the bull-game. One by one the children would thread their way through the black maze on the floor of the entrance hall until they reached the Minotaur, where Evans was waiting to catch them with a roar and toss them up into the air.

With the refreshments came the high point of the evening. In each of two enormous cakes, one for the boys and one for the girls, the cook had hidden a black bean. As the children ate their way through the cake to see if their slice contained the surprise, their suspense and excitement mounted (and was compounded one year when none of the boys claimed the black bean until the smallest among them confessed to having swallowed it). The lucky pair who retrieved the bean were crowned King Minos and his Queen and were seated with solemn ceremony on the two mahogany replicas of the Minoan throne.

This was a side of Evans few people saw. The man was as complex as the *tell* of Knossos. Only those who knew him best were aware of his delight in simple pleasures and his capacity for anonymous giving. His family and close friends could let his imperious moods pass, knowing that warm interest and concern would succeed them. They accepted his high-handedness, they lived with his intimidating energy. They endured his asperity. Let any one of them be in trouble, he could count on Evans' help and support. Moreover, besides being a loyal friend and a fine host, Evans made lively, if strenuous, company.

Long before it was "done," he bought himself a car. His elegant Wolseley with its luxurious upholstery and gleaming black, hand-painted body was the first car on Boars Hill. While others still eyed the combustion engine with distrust, Evans loved to sit beside his chauffeur and be driven about the countryside at what was then considered outrageous speed. He would drop in to visit his brother Lewis and his sister Harriet Longman, who lived nearby with their families. He would take Lance, Jimmie, Denis, and their friends for a thrilling ride. Older guests remembered the botany that accompanied the tours, as their host pointed out the local flora. Evans relaxed in company as intensely as he worked in private.

When he was in his library, no one entered uninvited. This was the inner sanctum of his Oxford labyrinth. It was a room that met his requirements as fully as the library at Nash Mills had suited his father. The carpet behind his desk was strewn with the opened and unopened letters he tossed over his head onto the floor. There was no Margaret to sort them out and no maid who dared to.

The piles of black-edged paper on which he wrote with a white goose-feather quill pen were stacked high. When he wasn't working on his *Scripta Minoa,* he was preparing public lectures, writing for professional journals, or carrying on a learned correspondence with colleagues. The letters he dashed off in free moments to his family and the boys away at school were witty, observant, ironic, always warm and affectionate. They sometimes took longer to read than to write. In his tiny, angular scrawl he crowded every page, even the margins. Like most Victorians, Evans hated to waste paper.

Even more, he hated to waste time. Having made up his mind to move nearer to Knossos, he instructed Christian Doll, then architect at the British School of Archaeology at Athens, to build him a house and told him precisely where. When it was completed, in October 1906, it stood on the same slope overlooking the palace site where, picnicking with John Myres eleven years before, he had said, "This is where I shall live when I come to dig Knossos." He called his Cretan home the Villa Ariadne.

Christian Doll was the architect, but it would be an exaggeration to say that he planned the Villa Ariadne. As usual, Evans knew exactly what he wanted. The house (which would eventually serve as headquarters for the students from the British School of Archaeology at Athens) had to be a comfortable place in which to work as well as to live, adapted to the Mediterranean sun and rains, the searing winds from the south, and the winter dampness. And who had better understood the island's climate than King Minos himself?

The villa, like the palace, had basement rooms for coolness. It too had a flat roof, and was built of sturdy stone with an imposing flight of stairs leading to the main entrance. But with the hindsight of thirty-five centuries and the technology of his day, Evans was better able than the Minoans to protect his home from the Earth-Shaker. He made sure that the framework of the Villa Ariadne was constructed of solid steel and cement and that the walls were almost a meter thick.

No house of Evans' could be without its garden. Exotic shrubs fattened in the prodigal Cretan sunshine. Hibiscus bushes with their showy flowers grew as large as trees. The flaming-scarlet blossoms of pomegranate trees subsided into the yellowish-to-purple reds of their fruit with the seasons. Olive trees and palms proclaimed their perennial rights to Cretan soil. There were masses and masses of roses. Honeysuckle and jasmine perfumed the terrace where Evans and his guests took their evening meals.

Indoors, the long dining room was cool, even at midday. The faithful maid Maria, muffled in black like all the island's women, shuttered the windows at the sun's first rising. Reared in village ways, she was accustomed to do her daily cleaning by splashing pails of water over tiled floors in rooms sparsely furnished. The carpets and sofas, the curtains and bookshelves that graced the villa would have been more familiar to a Victorian housekeeper. While Evans enjoyed the easygoing Mediterranean informality, he liked decorum and comfort as well.

The Villa Ariadne geared itself for its owner's yearly comings. When the master bedroom was occupied, life took on style. Visiting scholars went home with memories of splendid parties in the garden, of tinned meat from Fortnum & Mason served at luncheon with French wines or champagne, of animated talk with other archaeologists—French, Italian, Greek, American, German. Tourist notables sat under the olive trees to listen to the peasants' mandolins and lyres and watch the new-old Cretan ring dances. But above all, the master's presence in the Villa Ariadne meant a season's wages to scores of Candia's breadwinners. Digging at Knossos continued on a grand scale.

There were over one hundred men at work in the spring of 1908 when the news came from England that Sir John was seriously ill. Evans wrote his stepmother immediately—"My thoughts are very much with the Padre"—but added that he had his hands full in Crete. It would be difficult to leave with excavations in full swing. He was much relieved to get his father's message insisting that he should not interrupt his work. Evans, Mackenzie, and the foreman Gregori had instituted the "wager system" to speed operations wherever feasible. The dirt was fairly flying.

When a particular area being cleared was found to have no important deposits above a certain level, the "wager system" went into action, with a prize of money awarded to the fastest workers. The area was marked off into squares of four or five meters and from three to five men were assigned to each section. As they dug, groups of villagers stood by with sacks, ready to be filled with the earth thrown up by the diggers and then carried off by donkeys to the nearest dumping ground. The group of workers who first reached the predetermined level where important finds might be expected carried off the prize, to general applause. Meanwhile, two or three times the usual amount of earth had been excavated and removed in a given time.

Yet there was no hurrying a site like Knossos and no finishing it either, it seemed. Evans continued to widen his explorations from the palace itself to the surrounding area. A peasant working his fields would accidentally turn up fragments of pottery and the call would be sounded. A preliminary probe, a promising find, another crew of men assigned— so it went. Sir John, mortally ill yet urging his son to go on with his work, had understood this; and thus it happened that there was no final farewell between these two strong and gifted men, so alike, so different, so bound up one with the other.

John Evans died on May 31, 1908. Arthur returned to England in July, after having finished the season's dig. The Padre, he knew, would have conceded priority to the Minoans, but Arthur sorely missed the penetrating questions he would have asked about the new finds. Their personalities had often clashed, their intellectual interest never. For all the latent rivalry between them, each had respected and been proud of the other. Now the son would no longer need to assert his own tastes and views. All that remained was filial love and a deep sense of loss.

With his father's death Arthur Evans became a rich man in his own right. Five months later he inherited an even greater fortune. His maternal grandfather, John Dickinson, founder of the paper mills, had left his vast estate first to his son and then to his grandsons. When the last of these heirs died prematurely, Evans found himself a wealthier man than Sir John had ever been. At last he could afford his Knossos: not only to uncover it in all its immensity but to restore as much as possible of its ancient splendor. The prospects were exhilarating. The circumstances were unique. The annals of archaeology record no other site owned outright by one man and excavated and reconstructed largely out of his own personal fortune.

Evans had long wanted to resign from the Keepership of the Ashmolean Museum in order to devote himself entirely to Crete. Now he did, and marked the occasion by giving some of his father's collections to the museum. More treasures would follow. Indeed, were there competition today between the distinguished father and his famous son, it would be in the number of visitors attracted to the two rooms in the Ashmolean which bear their names: the John Evans Room and the Arthur Evans Room. Both men would be content to have handed over their life's work to new generations of scholars and students who come from all the world, pad and pencil in hand, to study man's past.

In January 1909 David Hogarth succeeded Evans as Keeper. The thorny budget problems, the administrative details, the lengthy meetings with the Visitors—all these were now Hogarth's concern. But Evans, appointed Honorary Keeper with a permanent seat on the Governing Body, had no intention of retiring to passivity. Twenty-five years before, in his inaugural address, he had projected the image of the Ashmolean "as a future home for archaeological research and teaching." Thirty-two years later he would still be pursuing his objectives. His last visit to the museum took place only a few days before his death. Anyone studying his portrait in the Ashmolean might have predicted as much. The portrait was painted by Sir William Richmond and presented to the museum by subscribers in December 1907, only five months before Sir John's death. The ceremony at which it was unveiled was the last public occasion on which a proud father was present to see his son honored. Richmond, a frequent visitor at Youlbury, knew his subject well. Though the Arthur Evans who looked out from the canvas was surrounded by artifacts from the past, he seemed to be peering far into the future as well.

Honors continued to pour in on the Honorary Keeper. In March the Royal Institute of British Architects presented him with its Royal Gold Medal. Only Schliemann, discoverer of Troy and Mycenae, and Layard, excavator of Nimrud and Nineveh, had preceded him as archaeologists so honored. In June the University of Oxford appointed him Extraordinary Professor of Prehistoric Archaeology. Two years later, in 1911, he was knighted and elected president of the Hellenic Society. Though it might have seemed that the son was following more and more in his father's footsteps, Sir Arthur in fact became increasingly his own incisive self. No gathering of his colleagues could ignore his well-modulated voice or the growing authority with which he spoke. His presidential address to the Hellenic Society provoked consternation among the orthodox classicists present.

The address, entitled "The Minoan and Mycenaean Element in Hellenic Life," foreshadowed the major fixation which would dominate Evans' thinking for the next thirty years. The Mycenaean inhabitants of the Greek mainland in the Late Bronze Age, he claimed, were completely lacking in originality. Their culture was "only a provincial variant" of the Minoan. Indeed, the whole Classical Greek civilization owed much of its inspiration, particularly in the areas of art and religion, to sources rooted in a far earlier, non-Greek past. Those sources, he hardly needed to add, were Minoan. With this pronouncement Evans completed his progression from the student at Oxford who had criticized the narrowly classical curriculum to the eminent archaeologist prepared to defend his theories against all challengers. Scholars who dared to lock horns with him would find him a relentless opponent, hardly capable of friendship or even tolerance. Only privileged friends were mindful of the kindness beneath the Olympian exterior and even among them few knew the extent of his generosity.

One beneficiary of that generosity expressed his gratitude long after Evans' death. In 1913 Sir Mortimer Wheeler was a young man at the beginning of his career. He had applied for an archaeological studentship newly established by the University of London and the Society of Antiquaries. Sir Arthur, he wrote in his book *Still Digging*, was a member of the prestigious committee set up to choose the successful candidate. Wheeler was delighted when he was granted the studentship, but deeply concerned about finances. Engaged to be married, he faced new responsibilities with a sense of anxiety. How would he manage on £50 a year for two years?

"As I walked away slowly and thoughtfully down the long corridor, I became aware of light footsteps hurrying after me. I turned and found myself looking upon the small, slight form of Arthur Evans, a little breathless with his running. 'That £50,' he said in his quiet voice, 'it isn't much. I should like to double it for you.' And he was away again, almost before I could thank him. That characteristically generous act of Evans's changed the whole climate of the situation. For the moment I was saved, and I have never ceased to recall with gratitude the kindly impulse that saved me."

In all probability, Sir Arthur would have been more embarrassed than pleased with this tribute. He drew a sharp curtain between the private and the public Evans. He followed the young Wheeler's career from afar, as he followed the careers of so many others. But his own concentration was focused always on his own work. He remained obsessed with the same two goals: the one was to resurrect the Minoans; the other was to celebrate the end of Turkish dominion over the Slavic nations.

Sometimes the rumblings in the Balkans were underground and muffled, sometimes they surfaced. In the fall of 1912 they erupted like a volcano. On the fifteenth of October Turkey declared war on Bulgaria, Serbia, and Montenegro. Three days later Greece joined her neighbors against the Ottoman sultan and the First Balkan War broke out. The campaign was as decisive and short as a burst of machine-gun fire, and it ended in Turkish defeat. Evans exulted that "in little more than a month, the whole political figuration of the Balkan Peninsula has been changed." Even more than the victory, what astonished him was that quarreling neighbors had for once set aside perpetual rivalries in order to unite against their common enemy.

Evans closely followed the proceedings at the Peace Conference that was arranged in London by the Great Powers. He knew many of the Slav delegates, come from those parts of Europe with which so much of his life was bound up. In January 1913 he entertained them at Youlbury. Together they raised their champagne glasses to toast a future in which the Balkan Peninsula and the Aegean Sea would be purged of Turkish domination. But the dreams of freedom turned out to be premature.

Within three weeks the peace negotiations broke down. Six months later the Second Balkan War was taking its toll of bullet-ridden villages and ravaged fields. It was only the prelude to far worse: to catapulting events that would eventually engulf the whole world in war. The final, fatal spark was ignited at Sarajevo, the capital of Bosnia.

Evans had vivid memories of Sarajevo. His first visit, with his brother Lewis, went back almost forty years, but the city's original impact had not dimmed. He could still evoke that sense of impending collision between Turk and Slav, between Muslim and Christian. He remembered the mysterious alleys with shopwindows shuttered against violence, the crowded bazaar echoing to rumors. Even the smells of the spice stalls came back to him as he picked up *The Times* on June 28, 1914, and read the headline: ARCHDUKE FRANCIS FERDINAND ASSASSINATED AT SARAJEVO.

The archduke was the heir to the Austro-Hungarian throne. The assassin was Gavrilo Princip, a young Bosnian revolutionary acting as an agent for the Black Hand, a terrorist organization sworn to agitate on behalf of Serbian aspirations. From that act, from that bullet, historians would date the beginning of the First World War ever recorded in the age-long and often violent human epic. A Europe held together by uneasy alliances, by mutual distrusts masked by paper assurances, by secret treaties arrived at in corridors, slowly came apart. On July 28, one month after Princip shot the archduke, Austria declared war on Serbia. The next day the

Russian tsar ordered general mobilization against Austria. Germany reacted at once by declaring war first on Russia, then on France and Belgium. On August 4, 1914, Great Britain declared war on Germany.

Characteristically, Evans' thoughts went immediately to the Boy Scouts in tents all over the Youlbury grounds. Among them were about a dozen seventeen- and eighteen-year-olds who would inevitably become soldiers. The number of troops had grown to four by now, their ranks swelled by youngsters who lived six and eight kilometers away. Evans had bought them all bicycles so they could ride back and forth from their homes: he wanted the scouting movement to spread as widely as possible and to encompass boys of all types and classes. On that fateful day of August 4, 1914, he asked the then scoutmaster Frank Gilliams to blow his whistle and call all the scouts together. Their reaction to his announcement that England was at war brought shouts of "Hooray! Hooray!" from youngsters for whom the word had no meaning beyond the bang-bang of toy pistols and the capture of "prisoners" in mock games. It wouldn't be long, however, before the same youngsters, Jimmie among them, would be saying a tearful good-bye to brothers older than they.

Before the end of 1914 an assassin's bullet had ricocheted into an ever-widening conflict between Germany, Austria, and Turkey on the one hand and the rest of the world, almost literally, on the other. Even faraway Siam would be drawn into the struggle before the last shot was fired. No one could possibly have foreseen that World War I would last four years; that over thirty countries would be involved in one way or another; that an estimated 10 million men would be killed and another 20 million wounded. By finally exploding, the Balkan volcano had set in motion a tidal wave of events that unalterably changed the face of Europe and, with it, the map and configuration of world politics.

The war brought almost immediate personal tragedy to Evans. His nephew Frederick Longman, Harriet's son, was killed in battle barely ten weeks after British troops went into action against the Germans. How many more of the boyish voices he occasionally overheard in his library would be silenced?

One by one, the scouts who roamed the woods reached military age and exchanged playing at soldiers for the real thing. Before long it was Lance Freeman's turn to put on a uniform.

There was no question of continuing the excavations at Knossos or even of maintaining close communications with Crete. The only way Evans could safeguard his find of a lifetime was on paper. He plunged into the monumental task of writing *The Palace of Minos*.

Sir Arthur defying the elements at Knossos. *Courtesy of the Ashmolean Museum.*

(CLOCKWISE FROM ABOVE) A "massed attack" on a large stone block at Knossos. Evans supervising a group of workers. Excavating the Temple Tomb. Storage jars, some of them as tall as a man. *Courtesy of the Ashmolean Museum.*

(ABOVE) Mackenzie and Evans at Knossos. *Courtesy of the Ashmolean Museum.* (OPPOSITE ABOVE) The Theatral Area at Knossos today. *Courtesy of Vincent Czarnowski.* (OPPOSITE BELOW) Work in progress on the Little Palace. *Courtesy of the Ashmolean Museum.*

(TOP TO BOTTOM) Youlbury in 1919, the south side of the house facing the Berkshire Hills. The drawing room at Youlbury. The entrance hall at Youlbury. *Courtesy of P. Denison Haskins.*

(LEFT) Evans with Denis (foreground), his nephew Jack, and Jimmie (standing). *Courtesy of P. Denison Haskins.* (BELOW) Excerpts from Evans' letters to Jimmie and Mrs. Candy on his distinctive black-bordered stationery. *Courtesy of James S. Candy.*

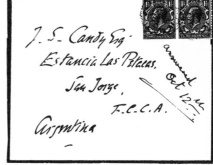

Envelope addressed:

J. S. Candy Esq.
Estancia Las Petacas,
San Jorge,
F.C.C.A.
Argentina

Two letters on black-bordered stationery headed "YOULBURY, BERKS, Nr. OXFORD."

Oct. 12.
1914

My dear Jimmie,

I am not very good at finding ties — the colours are generally not what I like! But I am sending you three which I hope you will like —

I saw your Mother yesterday & was very sorry to hear that owing to the war Monsieur Barguin has had to throw over poor Dick as he can't carry on with his Motor works. It is

Second letter:

June 21. 1914
(Sunday)

Dear Mrs. Candy,

I am rejoiced to hear such a good account of Jimmie's ear. I only hope that Dr. Hayward's hopes are justified. But, indeed, I have had too sad experiences to be ever over sanguine in such matters. & I greatly realize the need of taking every possible precaution for some time to come — even though it meant to be irksome to the

(ABOVE) Evans on the occasion of the unveiling of his bronze bust
at Knossos, 1935. (BELOW) Evans surrounded by notables at the
ceremony at Knossos, 1935. *Courtesy of the Herakleion Museum.*

Chapter XVII
The Great War

Unlike the other rooms at Youlbury with their curtained arches, Evans' library was the only room on the ground floor with a door. Mrs. Judd was permitted entrance when she came to confirm the day's menus, written in chalk on a large slate. A housemaid might knock to announce that the car was outside. Otherwise the library, where confusion reigned unchallenged, belonged to Sir Arthur alone when he was working. Mackenzie was one of the few trespassers, the painter E. J. Lambert another. Lambert, who lived in London, spent part of his summers at Youlbury, where he worked on the illustrations for Evans' book during the morning and painted beautiful landscapes after lunch. Under five feet tall, with bandied legs, Lambert had to scurry to keep up with Mackenzie. Jimmie and the other lads were as diverted by the sight of the dwarf arriving with the giant for afternoon tea as they were awed by their glimpses into the library when Sir Arthur emerged to join them.

How he managed to find the precise notebook or exact reference he was looking for was a mystery to everyone but Evans. The room was filled with bookshelves, piled high with papers in several languages, and studded with trestle tables, on one of which stood Gilliéron's facsimiles of the gold Vapheio cups. The stacks of letters went back several years. Fortunately, the floor space was immense—vast enough to accommodate a new trestle table about two and a half meters long for each new section of *The Palace of Minos*. It was a splendid way, actually, of organizing the almost overwhelming masses of material he was working on.

Evans had conceived his great work not merely as a technical report for specialists but as the saga of a unique civilization, and he wrote with a literary eloquence not all archaeologists command. The task he had set himself was formidable: to give a sweeping chronological account of the Minoan civilization with the Palace of Knossos as its focus, but incorporating all the additional evidence found by other archaeologists working in Crete. Since every dig at each site turned up fresh evidence, there was constant need to revise and to amplify. The book changed as it grew. Writing *The Palace of Minos* was like trying to compose a mystery story with no preconceived plot.

Nor did he employ a collaborator to make the work easier, or an assistant, a secretary, or even, for that matter, a typewriter. It could be said that the functionaries at Knossos, dictating to scribes, used more "modern" methods than Evans. He wrote each word by hand with a white goose-feather quill pen, in a handwriting that grew more and more stylized and became the despair of the printers. Fortunately, his friend George Macmillan, who had offered to publish the great work and share profits (if expenses were met), had also agreed to have it printed at the Oxford University Press.

There was only one typesetter at the plant who could decipher Evans' calligraphy. When a word or a sentence proved too baffling even for him, Evans would order the car and go down to Oxford to help out. This happened at least three times a week. Too often, while unraveling his own handwriting, he decided to change or add other sentences. Even when faced with page proofs he could not forgo the desire for improvement. His need to refine and revise led him not only to correct errors but to rewrite whole passages. The history of publishing must include few other books where the cost of corrections exceeded the cost of composition.

"Each step forward was a step in the dark." So Evans, in his preface to Volume I, described the early days of the dig at Knossos. The words were almost equally descriptive

of those early days in his library. To the accompaniment
of fresh outbreaks of war he set up one trestle table after
another and moved among them like a navigator charting
a course. There would be at least two volumes, he knew,
and possibly a "third and supplementary volume on a smaller
scale." He underestimated by more than half. When completed, *The Palace of Minos* filled six enormous volumes with
the index making a seventh. There were three thousand pages
of prose, ranging from the highly technical and scholarly
to flights of Homeric fancy. More than twenty-four hundred
maps, plans, drawings, and photographs, many of them in
color, illuminated the text.

For the reader lost in the labyrinth, Evans' felicitous names
served as signposts. Who, locating the Court of the Distaffs
on a map, could fail to find his way to the Hall of the
Colonnades? Who could forget the Room of the Lotus Lamp?
The Hall of the Jewelled Fresco, the Megaron of the Spotted
Bull? Through names that evoked function he brought the
palace alive: the School Room, the Sculptor's Workshop, the
Room of the Archives. The Corridor of the Procession. The
Magazine of the Knobbed Pithoi.

His historical imagination was ceaselessly at work. The
past was a natural dimension for Evans in which he moved
about freely, adjusting his perspective to the centuries like
a camera lens focused now on the foreground, now on the
distant backdrop. What, he mused in *The Palace of Minos*,
did the ancient world see of Knossos in, say, 1300 B.C.?
The fabled Labyrinth built by Daedalus would have been
standing aboveground, damaged but not buried. The Grand
Staircase probably still rose to its full majestic five flights.
But most important of all, the frescoes on the palace walls
would have been intact, or nearly. What a difference! He
could imagine himself joining the Greek newcomers to the
island and gazing with awe upon the fresco of the great
bull—not only the head, which had survived time and been
restored, but the whole body as well, in all of its brilliant
coloring. Who seeing it could have forgotten the legendary
Minotaur? What other wondrous frescoes, now disappeared,
had the ancients seen? What unknown works of art?

"So much," he concluded, "may be safely said. In all

future speculations regarding the fabulous lore that grew up around the site of Knossos strict account must be taken, not only of the considerable remains of the 'House of Minos' as they existed in early Greek days, but of the artistic creations on its walls."

Tantalizing evidence of those artistic creations had been trapped by the sieve, in literally thousands of fragments. In his preface to Volume I, Evans paid tribute to the men who had salvaged them from the scrap heap. Monsieur Gilliéron with his "fine artistic sense and archaeological intuition" had painstakingly pieced them together. Noel Heaton, consulted for his "expert chemical and technical knowledge," had examined them and found them to be true frescoes painted on pure lime plaster. With equal generosity Evans thanked his many colleagues who had helped fill the "gaps in the Knossian evidence": Federico Halbherr, Harriet Boyd, David Hogarth, John Myres, Flinders Petrie, and others.

There was one friend and scholar, however, to whom he could not express his gratitude until long after the war was over. Professor Georg Karo, author of a magnificent work, *The Shaft-Graves of Mycenae*, was a German. Evans never forgot, he would write of Karo in his preface to Volume IV, that "at a time when the Great War had already broken out, and national animosities were at their height, as a friend and fellow worker in the same field of research, he had found means to send me the first proofs of the text." Unfortunately, Karo was an exception among German intellectuals. Even from famed seats of higher learning came voices of hatred and rabid nationalism. It was particularly distressing to Evans, who had had German friends since his university days at Göttingen and for whom knowledge transcended borders. With growing horror he watched the world around him disintegrate into chaos.

By the end of 1914 the armies of ten countries had been mobilized and even the small world of Oxford and Boars Hill had changed. Gas and food rationing brought the battlefield nearer home. Men disappeared from farms, factories, and classrooms. The families they left behind, in those days before radio and television, waited anxiously from one day to the next for the newspaper or the news bulletins posted on the town hall. It was typical of Evans that he thought to speed up their tidings by sharing with them his own source of advance information. His friend Seaton Watson, the editor of *The Manchester Guardian*, telephoned him every morning at eleven to read out the headlines that would appear in the next day's edition. Evans then spread the news to the people around him in his own dramatic way.

Just before the outbreak of war he had built a watchtower at Youlbury for people to see the view. A steep flight of stairs led to a veranda where the less hardy could terminate their ascent. For the bolder there were more steps ending in a railed-in platform and for the really daring still another flight to the summit, well over 180 meters high. When the war began Evans installed a flagpole at each corner of the crest. If the news telephoned by Watson announced a battle won against the Germans, the flag of the victorious army was raised: English, French, Russian, or one of the other Allies. If there was no flag at all, it meant that the Germans were advancing. The people living on or near Boars Hill were among the first in England to know what was happening in the trenches.

The war brought visible changes to Youlbury, too. With the need to conserve electricity, the great house was no longer ablaze after dark. Evans had special round candlesticks made, glass-encased so that candle wax would not drip onto the carpets. Candles were no hardship for the man brought up at Nash Mills—he actually preferred their soft light to the glare of electric bulbs—but it came as a surprise to his overnight guests when they were each handed a candlestick and told to go upstairs to their bedrooms without turning on the lights.

To save gas Evans bought himself a small French car with a "dicky" seat that opened out at the back, the delight of young passengers invited to accompany him to the Ashmolean Museum or the Oxford University Press. On one memorable holiday with Jimmie, Miss Wiggins, and her nephew Denis he dispensed with a car altogether and hired a brougham drawn by two horses. The travelers got as far as Marlborough the first night and put up at a hotel. But when Sir Arthur, having given the best room to Miss Wiggins, was shown up to a small inner room, dark and airless, the man who preferred candles and who still used a tin bathtub became so infuriated that he threw all the bed linen and blankets down the well onto a back court. Victorian austerity and wartime restrictions were one thing; affront to rank quite another.

Youlbury lost none of its discipline and conventions during the war. Mrs. Judd, assisted in the kitchen by an under-maid and a scullery-maid, was as exacting as her employer. The head parlormaid, Emma, a severe and elderly woman, still cleaned the silver every day in a room set aside for the purpose and supervised the two under-parlormaids who took care of the downstairs rooms. The head housemaid, Ada, still kept a sharp eye on the two under-maids who were assigned to the upstairs rooms. All of them wore striped uniforms during the morning to do the housework. At midday they changed into black dresses with white caps and white pinafores tied at the back, black stockings and black shoes. The occasional under-parlormaid who was flighty enough to wear makeup or silk stockings didn't last very long. Sir Arthur maintained the staff and the standards at Youlbury as though Queen Victoria were still on the throne, and added a few stringent rules of his own.

One of them was no smoking: he couldn't abide cigarettes. Another was no telephones, at least not in his part of the house. Any guest wishing to use that modern means of communication, with which Evans never felt quite at ease, was obliged to go to the servants' quarters as he did every morning at eleven. Standing on a box to reach the wall telephone, he would take down the headlines relayed to him by the editor of *The Manchester Guardian* with no unnecessary exchange of words; no waste of time.

Evans begrudged even the time it took to dress. Although his clothes were made for him by the best tailor in Oxford, they were designed to his own specifications for quick donning and never seemed to change in style. He wore trousers without turned up cuffs when nobody else did, because cuffs were mere dirt-catchers and a nuisance. His dress shirts were made with stiff collars and cuffs, but in such a way that they required no studs. He ordered special ties that he could slip over his head without knotting them. He never wore shoelaces; his bootmaker put tabs on his shoes so that they could be pulled on or off with one motion and exchanged for the black or brown slippers Sir Arthur wore in the house. In summer he sported a Panama hat and a black alpaca jacket; the rest of the year a homburg and an ordinary jacket and waistcoat, with a watch chain.

Tirelessly, Evans continued to work on *The Palace of Minos*, reconstructing an ancient and peaceful past, but his overriding concern was for the war-torn present. His library at Youlbury became both a scholar's workshop and a pulpit.

The German Army brought the year 1914 to a close with an appalling atrocity by setting fire to Louvain in Belgium. This lovely city had long been one of the world's leading centers of Catholic learning. Its university, founded in 1426, was among the oldest in Europe. The rare books and precious manuscripts that German soldiers burned to ashes in the university library were irreplaceable. Evans, as president of the Society of Antiquaries, excoriated this "sin against history" and demanded retribution from Germany and the restoration of Louvain. Yet he never allowed his indignation at such acts of barbarism to degenerate into blind hatred or bigotry.

As a member of many learned societies, Evans refused to countenance the expelling of foreign members simply because they happened to be citizens of an enemy country. On the contrary, he fervently pleaded, "We have not ceased to share a common task with those who today are our enemies. We cannot shirk the fact that tomorrow we shall be once more labourers together in the same historic field. It is incumbent upon us to do nothing which should shut the door to mutual intercourse in subjects like our own, which lie apart from the domain of human passions, in the silent avenues of the past."

He fought the vagaries and outrages of war with pen, eloquence, and action. When some refugees from Ragusa were interned as enemy Austrians, Evans protested so vigorously that the port officials handed over their prisoners to his personal custody. He sheltered them at Youlbury until he could obtain their release. The house and grounds were already filled with a group of Serbian students stranded by the war at Oxford, and Evans found himself once again speaking the tongue of his adopted motherland and recalling other times. He also provided refuge for four Belgian families and turned the "solar" room at the top of the house, where the scouts used to gather to sing, into a nursery for their small children. "They found lots of toys up there," he wrote to Jimmie. Sir Arthur could concern himself with children uprooted by war, even when he was engaged in his biggest battle against arbitrary officialdom.

The Air Board had decided, without consulting the Trustees, to requisition the British Museum as headquarters. To this "breaking in of the jungles" Sir Arthur reacted like a man at the barricades, defending every principle and value by which he measured civilized society. He would not have those bureaucrats "prancing" through the halls of art, he fumed. His letters of protest to *The Times,* the *Morning Post,* and *The Manchester Guardian* were calls to action. The storm of indignation he raised, both in public meetings and private conversations, gave the generals and functionaries something more to think about than office space. It took them only nine days to decide that they did not need the museum after all. Unfortunately, the damage had been done. Overzealous underlings had already removed priceless objects of art to make room for clerks.

Evans, in a speech that reverberated in carpeted offices, spoke passionately about the "weeks of labour in the clearing out of three large galleries, to the final undoing of the work of a century and a half." He lashed out against this "treatment of the British Museum, the incalculable destruction there of the results of generations of learned labour and classification." He fulminated against panic action, which "threatens at every turn the very sanctuaries of learning." In a final outburst of fury he credited politicians with scorn for scholars as "a very inferior race," but he reminded them "that even the lowest tribes of savages have their reservation."

Though superior Allied military force would finally end World War I, the battle of Evans versus the Philistines was among the notable blows struck on behalf of civilization. His was not a single campaign but a continuing struggle, which reached a peak in September 1916. Sir Arthur, as president of the British Association for the Advancement of Science—an office he held until 1919—was due to deliver the presidential address at the forthcoming meeting at Newcastle. Almost simultaneously came the news that Lance Freeman lay gravely wounded in a field hospital in Abbeville, France—that same Abbeville where Sir John had had his historic meeting with Boucher de Perthes more than a half-century before. Lance's condition was so critical that Evans boarded the first train leaving for the English Channel.

The journey, strenuous even in peacetime, was nightmarish. More anxious with each lurch of the train, each rocking of the boat that brought him closer to Lance, Evans composed the speech he would deliver on his return to England to the elite of British intellectuals. Two years had gone by since the outbreak of war and there was no end in sight. A young life lay precariously in the balance in a crowded hospital ward. The world was somber and starless. Yet Evans focused his myopic eyes, more suited to bright study than to dark night, upon the future. First he arranged to have Lance transferred to Somerville College in Oxford, which had been converted into a hospital, so he could be closer to him. Then he returned home in time for the meeting, where he made one of his most eloquent speeches.

We, indeed, who are here today to promote in a special way the cause of truth and knowledge have never had a more austere duty set before us. I know that our ranks are thinned. How many of those who would otherwise be engaged in progressive research have been called away for their country's service? How many who could least be spared were called to return no more? Scientific intercourse is broken, and its cosmopolitan character is obscured by the death struggle in which whole continents are locked ... there seems to be a real danger that the recognition of truth as itself a source of power may suffer an eclipse. ... It is at such a time and under these adverse conditions that we, whose object it is to promote the advancement of science, are called upon to act. It is for us to see to it that the lighted torch handed down to us from the ages shall be passed on with still brighter flame.

During the war years Evans put his quill pen to powerful use. Sometimes he used it as a torch illuminating truth, sometimes as a sword in the fight for Slav liberation. As early as January 1916, with Europe still a raging battlefield, he had publicly advocated the establishment of a free and independent Yugoslav state. The occasion was a meeting of the Royal Geographical Society. To understand the reasons for creating "this new entity in political geography," he told his audience, one had to go back to Roman times.

He described the area's physical duality: the rugged mountains populated by a race of indomitable highlanders; the semitropical coastline with its roots in Latin culture. He traced its history from the days of Illyrian tribesmen through the Roman conquest in A.D. 9 to the successive waves of occupation by Slavs, Magyars, Tatars, Venetians, Turks, and Austrians. The most enduring result of foreign domination, he said, had been the forging of a South Slav nationalism. Now the time had come to grant autonomy to a people long oppressed.

Moreover, this new state must have easier access to its European neighbors. The ancient Roman road, Evans pointed out, that ran from east to west along the Save River valley was still the main avenue of communication. He proposed that it be reestablished as a railroad by joining Brood to Belgrade and Gradisca to Ljubljana to create a direct route from western Europe to Belgrade and the East. Five years later Evans' concept became reality when the Simplon Express was built. It provided a much shorter railway link between western and southeastern Europe as an alternative to the route followed by the Orient Express.

In that same year of 1916 Allied intelligence forces learned that the Germans were planning to conscript all Serbian youths from the ages of fifteen to eighteen into the kaiser's army. To save them from this enemy call-up the boys were secretly rounded up, marched over the Carpathian mountains to Fiume and Trieste, and then shipped to England. Evans brought scores of them to Youlbury, where he housed them in tents alongside the scouts until they could be dispersed to more permanent quarters throughout England. The boys swimming in the lake and speaking Serbian would never forget the man who fed and housed them, bought them indoor games, spoke their language, and bolstered their spirits. Nor would their elders overlook any opportunity to seek his advice and his help.

In July 1917 Slav leaders called upon Evans to meet with them on the Greek island of Corfu. He was the only outsider present. The subject of their deliberations was national unity. The men grouped around the table included hardy mountaineers, seasoned revolutionaries, suave statesmen from Ragusa—and the small, firm, aristocratic Englishman with his walking stick. Evans was accepted as an equal partner among Slav patriots. He helped to shape the meeting's final action, a formal resolution to establish a single united South Slav nation. It was one step forward, one positive act in a world that seemed bent on self-destruction.

Lance, still recovering from his wounds and with one arm in a sling, had been discharged from hospital and brought back to Youlbury. Because of the condition of his lungs, the doctors said, he needed to sleep in the open air. Evans converted the tree house on the grounds into semihospital quarters and looked after him tenderly. He continued to pore over Minoan pots and Linear B tablets and to set up new trestle tables in his library, seeking solace in *The Palace of Minos* from the daily casualty figures. But with Lance constantly as a reminder, he was never far from the battlefield.

Despite the fact that America had joined the Allied forces the previous year, the outcome of the war and the prospects for peace looked very dark in the spring of 1918. A German offensive, launched on March 21, succeeded in driving a wedge through British lines to a depth of sixty-four kilometers. A second and third offensive brought the kaiser's troops to the Marne River on May 30, only fifty-nine kilometers from Paris. The secret meetings Evans held at Youlbury in June with still another group of Slav leaders were both a preparation for the peace everyone prayed for and for the ongoing battles to achieve it. James Candy, many years later, recalled a particular June evening with a clarity so sharp as to relive the event.

There would be no billiards after dinner that night, Sir Arthur told him, nor was he to come into the library. But instead of going to bed, Jimmie, with a boy's natural curiosity, hid on the upstairs gallery to see what was going on. He heard the cars arriving at midnight. He saw six or seven men scuttle across the entrance hall and into the library, where a maid brought sandwiches and coffee before the door was firmly shut. The next morning, after his usual prebreakfast swim, Jimmie met one of the midnight visitors sitting on a bench facing the lake, his eyes fixed on the shimmering water, his thoughts far away. His name, he told the boy, was Tomáš Masaryk (he was the man destined to be the first president of the still-to-be-created Republic of Czechoslovakia).

Tomáš Masaryk had fled to Paris at the outbreak of the war. Together with Eduard Beneš, who would eventually succeed him as president, he had formed the Czech National Council, a government-in-exile, and had helped to create Czech legions in the heartland of the Austrian Empire to fight on the side of the Allies. Each morning for a week, shortly after sunrise, Masaryk chatted with Jimmie about the scout movement and promised to send him stamps for his collection. But only Sir Arthur was privy to what went on during the rest of the day and late into the evening at Youlbury, in Oxford, and farther afield. Evans' opportunity to honor and justify the trust placed in him by his Slav friends would come later, when hostilities finally ceased.

By the time the Great War ended, a generation of young men had been decimated and the Europe inherited by the survivors was a shambles. Fighting had gone on with unabated violence for four years. Peace negotiations, which began in Paris after the Armistice was signed on November 11, 1918, would drag on with no letup in rancor and bitterness. When Evans realized the low priority accorded to the Yugoslavs, whose right to an independent state he had publicly proclaimed three years earlier, he immediately left Youlbury to join the Slav leaders assembled in the French capital. They welcomed him as a valuable, if unofficial, member of their delegation. Sir Arthur could enter doors that were closed to obscure partisans with unpronounceable names. His confidential memoranda and letters helped to enlighten politicians whose ignorance of Balkan history, geography, and ethnic loyalties was abysmal. Even more important, Evans was instrumental in winning over the British foreign secretary Arthur Balfour to the South Slav cause.

It was a long struggle, by no means to his liking. One could picture him attending interminable meetings with repugnance, recoiling from political maneuvering, restraining tongue and temper. Youlbury must have loomed as a scholar's haven. Yet Evans interrupted his reconstruction of the Minoan past long enough to insure the Balkan future.

His first act on his return home was to erect a war memorial to the boys who had once played at Youlbury, the scouts who had roamed its woods and never returned. He chose a quiet and poetic spot. The ground on one side of his house, which stood high over the lake, fell steeply into a deep ravine planted with tall fir trees through which hardly any light penetrated: a place of gloom and darkness recalling the war years. Then the land slowly climbed up again to a sun-flooded and tranquil heath overlooking the bank, symbolizing a world once again at peace. On this memorial site he planted cypress trees and two scarlet oaks. He bordered it with a semicircular bench. In the grassy center he set a sundial, engraved with his own moving dedication to the fallen and surmounted by the motto: I count the sunny hours alone. Only five years later he added another name to the rolls of the fallen when Lance Freeman finally succumbed to his war wounds.

Evans went frequently to count the sunny hours alone, when not even the Minoans could distract him from the political proceedings taking place in a succession of venues: Paris, Versailles, Saint-Germain, Neuilly, Trianon, Sèvres, Constantinople. Not until November 1920 were the boundaries of a new Yugoslav state finally established and the world became accustomed to calling Ragusa by its Slavic name, Dubrovnik. For Evans this fulfillment of a people's dreams was a landmark, the culmination of one strand of his life. The following year marked important progress in the second strand, when Volume I of *The Palace of Minos* was published.

The scholarly community had waited long for this report— too long, its author ruefully admitted in his preface. But the reasons for the delay rested with the Minoans themselves. "In the case of the palace site of Knossos," Evans wrote, "not only the immense complication of the plan itself, with its upper as well as its lower stories, but the volume and variety of the relics brought to light—unrivalled perhaps in any equal area of the earth's surface ever excavated—have demanded for the working up of the material a longer time than was required for the actual excavations."

The publication of Volume I of *The Palace of Minos* aroused excitement among prehistorians and archaeologists of all nations, even those recently at war. While Europe still wore its peace uncomfortably, like an ill-fitting mantle, the cessation of hostilities brought quickly renewed fervor to the exploration of the Aegean past. Fortunately, Mackenzie reported to Evans, the war had inflicted little damage on the Palace of Knossos or the Villa Ariadne. He was already busy clearing the grounds, removing weeds, and checking inventories in preparation for another season. The Greek archaeologist Joseph Hazzidakis announced the discovery of a Minoan palace at Mallia, while his compatriot Stéphanos Xanthoudídes was exploring new tombs and caves elsewhere in Crete. The French had sent a team to follow up the work at Mallia. Alan Wace, an Englishman, was back at work in Mycenae, extending Schliemann's excavations. The American Carl Blegen was investigating other sites on the Greek mainland, discovering new treasures that betrayed unmistakable Minoan traits. Evans laid aside his notebooks, folded up the trestle tables, and prepared to return to Crete in the fastest possible way.

He had added a new mobility to his life: flying. Always a poor sailor, he was one of the earliest enthusiasts of air travel, at a time when people still craned their necks and shook their heads in wonderment at the sound of an airplane's roar. Evans had only one complaint after his first flight from London to Paris: "I should have liked a little more soaring and diving." The mere thrill of flying, apparently, wasn't enough for a man already turned seventy.

Chapter XVIII
A New Era in Reconstruction

In the spring of 1922 the Villa Ariadne was framed in color. The scarlet pomegranate blossoms were in full bloom, the rose bushes ablaze. April 20 began like any other working day, with Evans taking a quick stroll around the garden before going off to the excavations. As usual, there was more digging going on than he had planned for: walls suddenly emerging and requiring pursuit, evidence of a stepped portico, paving blocks calling for investigation. In the valley below the basement level of the Domestic Quarter some workmen were exploring the artisans' houses which had been crushed by huge blocks of masonry hurled from the palace during that fateful earthquake in approximately 1580 B.C. They had just cleared "The House of the Sacrificed Oxen." The four severed horns still lay in front of the terra-cotta altars where the Minoan priest had placed them, in poignant appeasement to the gods.

Suddenly, at exactly 12:15 p.m., "a short sharp shock, sufficient to throw one of my men backwards, accompanied by a deep rumbling sound, was experienced on the site and throughout the whole region." To the superstitious Cretans standing among the ruins of an earlier disaster this new tremor was like a wrathful outcry from the past. Did it come from that same Minoan priest who, after presiding over the sacrificial rites, had commanded that this house remain sealed?

197

Was he warning ordinary mortals not to tamper with his functions? At the very least, Evans noted wryly in *The Palace of Minos,* it was certain "that the task of clearance was not accomplished without a token of the Earth-Shaker's displeasure."

Yet even more than earthquakes, the biggest threat to fragile ruins was the Cretan climate itself. Its violent extremes ran from searing desert winds to torrential rains, from near tropical heat to sodden humidity. In the dry air of Egypt and Mesopotamia ancient walls, columns, and beams could retain their original state for thousands of years. In Crete the dampness eroded and destroyed whatever it penetrated. Furthermore, the mighty buildings of Egypt had been constructed of stone, the massive structures of Mesopotamia of brick. Far different was the Palace of Knossos. Much of its masonry walls had been cradled in a framework of wood, with wooden posts and columns supporting the beams overhead. But the forest timber available to King Minos was far more abundant than what the island now offered. The original woodwork throughout Knossos was of cypress, bearing out the Roman historian Pliny's description of Crete as "the very home of cypress." In reconstructing the Grand Staircase Evans had used pinewood—imported at great cost from the Tyrolean Alps, where it lasted for generations—only to see it disintegrate into rotten powder within a few years. To save the exposed past from exposure was a continuing battle.

The task of preserving the Grand Staircase had gone on season after season. Wooden beams were replaced by masonry. Columns were laboriously cut out of stone. Pavements were supported by brickwork arches resting on iron girders, brought from England at enormous expense and not always without mishap. (Two of the largest girders, having arrived in Candia during an exceptionally heavy storm, lay at the bottom of the harbor.) Evans' delight when technology came to the rescue in the 1920s was understandable. With the use of ferroconcrete, which was reinforced by an interlacing web of steel wires, a whole "new era in reconstruction" could begin.

The new material was durable and easy to handle. It could be quickly recognized, so that no visitor would fail to distinguish old beams or columns from new. And it was cheap.

With supplies and wages skyrocketing in the postwar inflation, cost was becoming important even to a man as rich as Evans. Already he had had to sell some of his father's collections— reluctantly, but knowing that Sir John would have approved.

Columns that used to be hewn and carved from stone, one by one, could now be "cast wholesale" by pouring concrete into wooden molds made on the spot by Evans' carpenters. Carbonized beams and posts were reproduced in the same way. Whole pavements could be quickly laid out, and roofs, too. The introduction of reinforced concrete brought some of Evans' more expensive dreams of a restored Knossos within reach. In the process of restoration, however, every effort was made to remain faithful to the Palace of King Minos himself.

Modern concrete was never substituted for ancient stone when it was possible to recover the original. The new resident architect Piet de Jong, a lean man from Yorkshire, saw to that. If there was a groove in a decayed wall, showing where a timbered beam had once fitted, his trained eye spotted it. The beam itself would be replaced in concrete, painted pale buff to indicate wood, but the wall was rebuilt insofar as possible from the original blocks. Every fragment of stucco and every piece of stone saved by the spade were reused by the restorers. Though much of the framework of Knossos had to be reconstructed, an impressive proportion of the masonry seen by today's tourists was what the Minoans saw thirty-five centuries ago.

Evans' recompacted Grand Staircase was a magnificent sight. His prose in *The Palace of Minos* took flight as he described it. "With its charred columns solidly restored in their pristine hues, surrounding in tiers its central well, its balustrades rising, practically intact, one above the other, with its imposing fresco of the great Minoan shields on the back walls of its middle gallery, now replaced in replica, and its still well-preserved gypsum steps ascending to four landings, it revives, as no other part of the building, the remote past."

So much so, that the Grand Staircase haunted and lured him. One night, unable to sleep "during an attack of fever," he wrote, "and tempted in the warm moonlight to look down on the staircase-well," he was suddenly transported in time.

"The whole place seemed to awake awhile [sic] to life and movement. Such was the force of the illusion that the Priest-King with his plumed lily crown, great ladies, tightly-girdled, flounced and corseted, long-stoled priests, and, after them, a retinue of elegant but sinewy youths—as if the Cup-Bearer and his fellows had stepped down from the walls—passed and repassed on the flights below." They were as real to him as himself. All that separated them were thirty-five hundred years.

Was he, then, as some archaeologists claim, carried away by his imagination? Did he go too far in his restorations? The architect Piet de Jong, for one, did not think so. Years later he told Leonard Cottrell, author of *The Bull of Minos*, that "one of Sir Arthur's greatest gifts was his capacity for *visualizing*. He could tell, just by looking at a few broken stones, a fallen column, and a few bits of fresco, exactly how the whole room or building originally looked. And he'd get *most* impatient if his architect couldn't see it just as quickly. Yet when the architect had surveyed and measured the site, and studied all the architectural evidence, the fact is that Sir Arthur was nearly always right."

Most of Evans' own contemporaries agreed with de Jong. Few of them questioned either the necessity to preserve Knossos or the methods used to do so. Evans admitted, at a lecture delivered on December 9, 1926, to the Society of Antiquaries, that "To the casual visitor who first approaches the site and sees before him an acre or so of upper stories the attempt may well at times seem overbold, and the lover of the picturesque ruins may receive a shock." But heads nodded when he went on to say that without restoration much of King Minos's domain would have returned to the earth from which he had rescued it.

Lively discussion followed the speech. Mr. Carr Bosanquet, then director of the British School of Archaeology at Athens, found the reconstruction "convincing and dignified," and felt that all those present at the meeting deeply appreciated Evans' "wise and self-sacrificing efforts." The architect Christian Doll had no professional doubts about the Grand Staircase. It could be reconstructed on exact mathematical lines, he told the audience, since the dimensions were multiples of one another and the tread three times the riser. Professor John L. Myres expressed the consensus of the meeting by affirming that the "methods employed give promise of permanent preservation of much of the old Palace, for which future generations should be thankful."

Nevertheless, only four years later the Austrian archaeologist Camillo Praschniker blasted Evans' reconstruction of Knossos. He had made it, he said, "a movie city," an acid description to which other excavators added epithets ranging from unnecessary to ugly, and even to downright wrong. On the other side of the archaeological trenches stood Professor Georg Karo, the distinguished German scholar who had contrived to send Evans the proofs of his monumental work on Mycenaean shaft graves during World War I. Karo wholeheartedly agreed with his English colleague that the site of Knossos would be a heap of ruins today but for the restorations. Not only were Evans' interventions essential and mandatory, he wrote, but any careful examination of the immense remains would reveal how surprisingly few were unnecessary. To this view the great Greek archaeologists Nikolas Platon and Spyridon Marinatos, and the Italian Doro Levi, also ascribed.

The controversy continues. There are the purists today who unfavorably compare Evans' vividly reconstructed Knossos with Halbherr's serenely unrestored Phaistos. More practical souls answer them by pointing out that Phaistos, unlike Knossos, was built on level ground, so that Halbherr was not faced, as Evans was, with the problem of preventing his palace from slipping down a hillside. Some archaeologists feel, moreover, that the mysterious and labyrinthine Knossos of today gives a truer impression of its Minoan original than does Phaistos, with its broad expanse open to the sky and its aura of spacious harmony.

None of these arguments would have swayed Evans. His choice lay, he never doubted, between reburying ruins or restoring them. He began his "new era in reconstruction" in the year 1922 in order to conserve Knossos and would be less surprised than his critics to learn that to this day the annual cost of defending the Minoans from the elements is considerable.

The Cretan climate seemed determined, during that season of 1922, to display all its extremes. In April the earth rumbled and shook. In June the sea, whipped by tempestuous winds, foamed over banks and turned quiet coves into whirlpools. Would Evans have postponed his expedition had he foreseen what was in store? Probably not. He never missed the opportunity, during a pause in the excavations, to explore Crete.

This time, accompanied by a retinue which was less elegant but more functional than the priest-king's, he set out to cross the wild and rocky mountains that ran east-west through the island's narrow girth like a spinal cord, and then to continue on to his destination—the place called Fair Havens at the southernmost tip, on the Libyan Sea. They made quite a party: Duncan Mackenzie and Piet de Jong, Manolaki the current foreman, blue-eyed Kosti the cook, and a boy as handyman.

Manolaki's full name was Emmanouel Akoumianakis. He had started to work for Evans as a young boy fresh from his village and had worked his way up to replace the aging Gregori as foreman of Knossos. By now his mustache, too, had a touch of gray in it and his wrinkled face was nut-brown from the sun. The "Old Wolf," everyone called him. He had an uncanny eye for a site, like the master, and was equally inexhaustible.

At seventy-one Evans was still capable of riding twelve hours at a stretch on muleback through rough, uninhabited countryside and in temperatures that reached 105 F. degrees in the shade. Nevertheless, he was glad to pitch his tent when they finally arrived at Fair Havens. Near the sea, he specified to Manolaki, indicating the exact place. The rest of the party chose spots farther inland.

During the night came the wind, a wind so angry and violent that it lashed the sea into frenzied waves which rose higher and higher before they crashed onto the shore. Had it not been for some sailors whose own boat was being swamped, the reconstruction of Knossos might have ended then and there. The sailors aroused the campers—not without difficulty over the roar of the sea—and together they succeeded in removing Evans and his tent just in time. But "not before a large wave broke into the middle of it," Evans wrote home with gusto. "Next morning breakers rolled where my tent had been pitched!" It was quite weird, he admitted; and very much to his taste, though he didn't say so. He thrived on adventure.

He was also insatiably interested in anything that could throw light on his own Minoan research. Proximity took him most frequently to Phaistos, where he and Halbherr compared notes, but he didn't neglect any of the other Cretan sites being excavated. One such site was at Mochlos, where the American archaeologist Richard Seager was at work. Seager had found lovely little stone vases dating from the Early Bronze Age. From tombs he had unearthed funerary furniture of fine gold and a cup identical in shape to the famous Vapheio cups. The two men became such good friends that when Seager died, in 1925, Evans paid him the highest compliment of which he was capable: "He was the most *English* American I have ever known."

For some of his French colleagues he had less admiration. In order to get to Mallia, where they were excavating, Evans had to spend two nights camping out on mountaintops. (The trip took comparatively less time than the dig would, Evans caustically observed, since the French had only two men and three boys at work.) Nor did he confine his investigations to Crete. A quest for a gold signet ring found in a Mycenaean tomb took him to the Greek mainland. He went to Egypt to track down a seal. And what he didn't go in search of himself, others, not necessarily scholars, brought to show him at the Villa Ariadne.

Even remote villagers were on the lookout for artifacts. Peasants working their fields turned up with broken potsherds. Little boys followed him across the road from the villa to the palace with dirty coins which Evans gravely examined, paid for, and then gave back to them. It reminded one of the days in Ragusa when antique dealers and even total strangers brought their treasures to the man they called Milord Inglese—with the difference that then, as a young journalist, all he had was the lordly manner. During the grand years at the Villa Ariadne, Sir Arthur did in fact live like a lord.

The fame of Knossos and its excavator brought tourists

to Crete by the boatload. For those lucky enough to be invited, a tea party in the garden of the Villa Ariadne capped their visit. During one month alone Evans entertained three separate groups of English tourists, each numbering 100 to 150 people. There were parties of Swedes and Danes, too, and of Germans and Americans, including the famous millionaire J. Pierpont Morgan, who arrived in his yacht. "Quite pleasant people" were the words Evans summoned up to describe them. In the same letter he added that "Mrs. Edith Wharton the novelist is due, so you see this is really the hub."

Over the bustle of the waiters hired from Candia—wearing their enormously baggy breeches, cummerbunds, fringed jackets, and high boots—over the tinkle of spoons on saucers, Evans' elegant soft voice, rather high pitched, was the sound people listened for. He was always impeccably turned out, and always wore a yellow rose in his lapel. His small compact figure dominated all gatherings, whether of tourists making mental notes for their diaries or of colleagues discussing ancient trade routes. As a host he was gracious and lordly. As a scholar he spoke with authority. But it was the man himself, with his overwhelming vigor of mind and body, that no one was likely to forget. Already well into his seventies, he seemed indestructible. Ageless.

The same was not true of "poor Mr. Mackenzie," as Evans primly referred to his assistant in a letter home. Although Mackenzie was eight years younger than his redoubtable employer, his health was beginning to falter. It was not surprising, after twenty-five years under the Cretan sun, supervising and recording the numberless minute details of a dig like Knossos. The Scotsman no longer appeared at native weddings. He walked like an old man, stooped over and stumbling. Things bothered him, little things. "He told me," Evans wrote incredulously, "that the nightingales (who now sing all night and most of the day) had given him a 'set-back!' " Nightingales! Worse, he "drinks *warmed* bottled beer and reposes most of the time." It was hard to tell which of these shortcomings Evans found most unsettling.

Nevertheless, "poor Mr. Mackenzie" still rode his donkey to the site every day. New digging was in progress on the southern slope below the palace, where Evans had found traces of a monumental portico. Now he was looking for the approach road which must surely have led up to it. A trial excavation at a likely spot had immediately exposed the large blocks of what seemed to be a Minoan paved way. Exceptionally heavy rains brought out "certain other features which suggested the advisability of further probing." It was the familiar story of the spade following the clues.

Twenty men worked in shifts for six weeks. What they eventually uncovered was not merely a road but a road built over a viaduct. It was proof once again of the enterprise and engineering skills of the Minoans. And of their remarkable ability to conserve and channel water, that precious commodity—so overabundant during Crete's rainy season and so sorely lacking the rest of the year.

No one except Evans, however, would have expected the Minoans to solve the chronic water shortage at the Villa Ariadne. Everyone agreed that an additional source was needed, but the question was where to sink a new well. The native workmen expressed preference for an obscure corner of the vineyard. Evans had other ideas. "Acting on some vague inference from the contour of the hillside above, I drew a cross in the earth surface beside a large block that happened to be standing at that spot and bade them dig there." Then he went off on one of his periodic explorations of Crete. When he returned a few days later, he "found all the world agog."

The men had removed no more than thirty centimeters of the topsoil before coming on the choked opening of a Minoan well, some ninety centimeters in diameter. At the bottom of the well, about twelve and a half meters down, "was an abundant spring of water which proved to be of better quality than any for miles around, and still supplies the house." Nor was that all. The Minoans had thoughtfully left behind a pair of two-handled pitchers, dating from approximately 2100 B.C., for the convenience of those drawing the water. "To the workmen," he gleefully recorded, "the + mark was a sign of supernatural guidance and I found myself suddenly hailed as a miracle-worker!"

It was a splendid story to take back to England. Evans liked to tell it at dinner parties at Youlbury, straight-faced but with unabashed enjoyment. The anecdote joined the epigrams he collected, the sly lampoons and puns with which he bridged a gap in conversation or changed the subject. He had the gift of hospitality. There were very few weekends when the guest rooms in the big house weren't occupied, sometimes by colleagues alone, sometimes by their wives and children as well. In the latter case the servants' quarters accommodated the chauffeurs and maids who accompanied their distinguished employers. No matter how distinguished, however—and the guest list included some of the most famous archaeologists, historians, and scholars of the day—a visitor at Youlbury was quickly inducted into the formal routines set by their genial but imperious host.

Everyone knew that dinner was served promptly at seven. Oysters, of which Evans was inordinately fond, were a frequent first course. In front of each guest was a little menu offering a choice for the main dish: pheasant, roast beef, duck, game, the best of whatever was in season. Only the finest Madeira and port wines graced a connoisseur's table; on special occasions, champagne. If there were to be ladies present, Sir Arthur usually asked his cousin Josephine Phelps to assist him as hostess. She was much taller than Evans, an angular and rather forbidding woman whose training as a registered nurse added crispness and certitude to her Victorian formality.

Ladies, unless they were house guests, wore their wide-brimmed, flower-bedecked hats at the table and were expected to withdraw, at a given signal from Miss Phelps, so that the men could pursue their own elevated conversation before coffee. This was served in beautiful Royal Derby cups—in the octagonal room in summer, when the twilight still offered a view over the gardens and lake; in the drawing room during the winter, where a parlormaid preceded the guests to throw rose petals into the roaring fire in the fireplace. Emma came in after the coffee was served with a silver ewer of liqueur and a silver bowl, carved in the shape of a horse and filled with biscuits.

Guests or no guests, Evans liked to go to bed early. He was far too courteous, however, to leave his company if it included ladies, and it fell to the evening's hostess to make the first move to retire. By nine-thirty or ten o'clock he was in bed, leaving the other men to continue their discussion of Early Minoan prisms or the Ubaid phase of occupation at Ur in about 4300 B.C.

Sir Leonard Woolley, the renowned excavator of the Royal Tombs at Ur, was a frequent weekend visitor at Youlbury. The historian H. R. Hall, author of the *Ancient History of the Near East*, was another; Gordon Childe, whose *Dawn of European Civilization* marked a starting point for prehistoric archaeology, still another. Among guests of such rarefied knowledge it was not surprising that some of the less erudite were happy to retire when Sir Arthur did.

Not all of the social life at Youlbury revolved around archaeology. Men of distinction in other fields had followed Evans to live on Boars Hill and there was much visiting back and forth among them. He went for long walks with the poet laureate Robert Bridges, who wore a hat like Rembrandt's and a coat like Sherlock Holmes's, and who often brought Evans home to have tea with him and Mrs. Bridges. The Classical scholar Gilbert Murray, professor of Greek at Oxford and translator of Greek drama, was a friend and a neighbor. John Masefield, a future poet laureate as well as a novelist and playwright, lived nearby and had built a small theater on his grounds in which to stage amateur plays. Evans firmly refused invitations to performances. He cared neither for theater nor for movies, perhaps because his eyes could make out so little of either. Nor did he ever permit social visits to interfere with his own schedule.

Promptly at six, in the middle of a conversation, he would make for the door of whichever house he might be in and return to his library to write letters before dinner. He enjoyed the intellectual companionship Boars Hill afforded, but his preferred place was his own home. The seat at the head of his table seemed a natural habitat for Sir Arthur. As comfortably as he wore his mud-splattered raincoat in Crete, he slipped into black tie and stiff collar at Youlbury.

Surprisingly, he could look equally at home in scout uniform. In February 1926, at a ground-breaking ceremony presided over by Sir Robert Baden-Powell himself, the chief scout of England, Evans was by far the oldest participant wearing khaki. He had presented the scout movement with a large plot of land on his estate for a training center, plus freedom of the Youlbury woods and lake, a house for the warden, a substantial headquarters building, a place for the boys' bicycles, and an area for putting up tents. To all that he added a handsome contribution toward a maintenance fund. It was a truly munificent gift.

The donor, his small figure still trim and wiry, his hair white now but still thick, left the platform when the speeches were over to mingle with the boys and their leaders. They were the ones who would carry on the work of a generation decimated by war. Lance Freeman, barely into his thirties, had died of his wounds the year before. Many others who should have been present at this ground-breaking ceremony had lost their lives on the battlefield. This training center for Boy Scouts was Evans' way of keeping their memories alive; this and the commemorative services he held every year on Armistice Day at his own memorial to the fallen.

One month after he had donned the scout uniform Evans returned to Crete. These days he always flew—first to Paris, where he changed planes for Athens. (It was "a record flight to Paris," he reported with delight; "245 miles in an hour and 29 minutes, which works out at over 150 miles an hour.") From Athens he got Imperial Airways to allow him to fly as far as their refueling stop on the Athens–Egypt route, which in those days of seaplanes was no farther than the Gulf of Mirabello in eastern Crete. It could be a bumpy ride in bad weather, but was preferable to a rough journey by sea. From Mirabello he hired a car to take him to the Villa Ariadne.

At Knossos he found Piet de Jong hard at work, continuing to replace rotted wood with reinforced concrete. The new era in reconstruction was producing daily results. Solid floors, walls, and ceilings made palace tours no longer hazardous. The downward-tapering columns, so distinctive a feature of Knossos, were as sturdy as the beams they supported. As the concrete-pourers grew more familiar with their material, they worked with increasing speed, a speed which turned out to be providential. And which proved, at least to Evans' awestruck workers, that their master was not only uncannily intuitive about past earthquakes but could foresee future ones as well.

Writing after the event in *The Palace of Minos,* Evans admitted to a certain premonition. "Occupied as I largely was in the spring of 1926 with tracing seismic action in the phenomena presented by the ancient remains at Knossos, the imminence of a fresh convulsion had become to me a kind of obsession, when on June 26 of that year, at 9:45 in the evening of a calm, warm day, the shocks began."

This time it was not merely a token of the Earth-Shaker's displeasure but the real thing.

Chapter XIX
Clash of Spades

Afterward, everyone who was in the Villa Ariadne on June 26, 1926, had his own story to tell about what happened. Piet de Jong had just taken some guests—the historian H. R. Hall and John Forsdyke, who was exploring a Minoan necropolis—up to the roof to see the night view. When the first shock came they rushed down to the lower terrace, where the round stone table on its thick Roman base was executing a crazy dance. The whole house creaked and groaned. An ominous rumbling came from its very depths. Out in the open the trees were swaying madly, threatening to fall at any moment. The roofs of two small houses located outside the garden gate caved in with a thundering crash. Women shrieked. Children screamed with terror. As shock followed shock with increasing intensity, the three men looked vainly for Evans.

Evans was inside the Villa Ariadne reacting to events— perhaps not quite with the scholarly detachment with which he later described them, but certainly with curiosity. He had just been studying medieval and modern records which showed that Crete suffered an average of two serious earthquakes every century. Since the "last really good specimen" had occurred in 1856, this present example was long overdue. He was instantly alert but not surprised when the first shocks came.

"They caught me reading on my bed in a basement room of the headquarters house—the Villa Ariadne—and trusting to the exceptional strength of the fabric, I decided to see the earthquake through from within. Perhaps I had hardly realized the full awesomeness of the experience, though my confidence in the strength of the building proved justified, since it did not suffer more than slight cracks. But it creaked and groaned, heaved, and rocked from side to side, as if the whole must collapse. Small objects were thrown about, and a pail, full of water, was nearly splashed empty."

This rocking movement, he later wrote to his half sister, Joan, probably lasted no more than a minute, but it gave him the same queasy feeling he got on board ship during a storm. "Earth sickness is a new complaint!" Still, it didn't occur to him to leave the house.

"A dull sound rose from the ground like the muffled roar of an angry bull; our single bell rang, while, through the open window, came the more distant jangling of the chimes of the Candia Cathedral. . . . Meanwhile, a dark mist of dust, lifted upwards by a sudden draught of air, rose sky-high, so as almost entirely to eclipse the full moon, house lights reflected on this cloud bank giving the appearance of a conflagration wrapped round with smoke."

Through his open window Evans could see the mist rising, like a preternatural shroud flung up from the depths. His basement room encased and magnified the sounds rumbling and reverberating through the house. Such must have been the experience of that Minoan priest who sealed up "The House of the Sacrificed Oxen." So must the priest-king himself have felt the anger of the Unseen. "It is something," Evans wrote, "to have heard with one's own ears the bellowing of the bull beneath the earth."

Almost the whole population of Candia poured out of the city gates and spent that fearful night, and many more, camping out in the open for fear the tremors would recur. Not until morning was it possible to assess the destruction. In the city itself some fifty houses were in ruins. The belfry and dome of the cathedral were badly damaged and the museum, housing the principal treasures of Knossos, suffered considerable harm. In the neighboring villages the havoc was

even greater. Whole streets were filled in, as those of the
Minoans had been, with the debris of fallen houses. A crazy
quilt of stones tossed like pebbles lay in haphazard jumble.
But the Villa Ariadne had withstood the angry bull.

At the first light Evans, Mackenzie, de Jong, and their
guests went over the house stone by stone. There were a
few cracks here and there, some damage to the furnishings:
nothing important. Its framework of steel and cement was
as solid as before. Had modern technology also safeguarded
the excavations? With trepidation they went across the road
to the palace.

"Thanks largely to the ferro-concrete of the floors," Evans
reported in *The Palace of Minos* with almost audible relief,
"very little damage was done to the works of reconstitution
in the upper stories of the Palace. The upper part of a masonry
pillar of recent construction"—obviously the concrete had not
yet solidified—"which was moved bodily several centimetres
due south supplied, indeed, a good index of the prevalent
direction from which the waves of disturbance came." But
the Grand Staircase was unharmed. The copies of the Cup-
Bearer and the other processional figures still appeared in
their proper places on the walls, and the priest-king looked
down triumphantly on the corridor approaching the Central
Court. This time, with Evans' help, Knossos had defied the
Earth-Shaker.

He continued to reconstruct the palace even when the site
was no longer "his" Knossos. Shortly after the earthquake
Evans presented the excavations and the Villa Ariadne, together with it olive groves and vineyards, to the British School
of Archaeology at Athens. It was a princely gift, which he
augmented with an endowment to pay the salary of a resident
director and for upkeep. Fittingly, his faithful assistant Duncan
Mackenzie, though failing in health, was appointed the first
curator of Knossos.

Neither looking nor feeling his age, Evans turned a spry
seventy-five on July 8, 1926. His friends and colleagues
marked the occasion by presenting him with a handsomely
bound volume entitled *Essays in Aegean Archaeology,* written
in his honor by leading historians and archaeologists from

many countries. In the preface Lewis R. Farnell expressed their collective admiration for the "gifts and qualities which have made you so illustrious a discoverer in the world of archaeology: your bold imagination guided by critical judgement and severe historical scholarship, your unflagging energy and hopeful enthusiasm, your singular FLAIR in the discovery of unexplored sites where the treasures of the past lay hidden."

All of the essays added carefully documented facts to the Cretan story. One in particular, however, joined past to present by describing a very human everyday link between the Minoans and the people still living on the island. The essay of the Cretan archaeologist Stéphanos Xanthoudídes was entitled "Some Minoan Potter's Wheel Discs." Xanthoudídes had long surmised that the clay discs found at Gournia were parts of a potter's wheel, the rest of which, being made of wood, had disintegrated. He found confirmation in the hamlet of Silamos, just beyond Knossos: the village craftsmen were still using identical clay discs to hold the fresh clay which they applied to the upper wooden discs of their potter's wheel. The Minoan artisans who had lived three thousand years before in Gournia, the "industrial town" excavated by the young American Harriet Boyd, would have found a common working language with the potters of Silamos.

Xanthoudídes' essay also drew upon the present for the answer to another puzzling question from the past: by what means were the ancients able to fashion their giant jars, some of them taller than a man? The village of Thrapsanos supplied the secret. Thrapsanos was known to every Cretan as the village of the *pithos* makers. Starting in the middle of May until about the tenth of August, its potters traveled all over the island in parties of five to twelve men, directed by a master potter whose technical skills and experience placed him at the apex of his craft. Xanthoudídes watched one of the parties dig ten deep holes in a row and line the insides with small walls like a hearth. In each hearth they placed a tournette, a small potter's wheel with a wooden disc set upon a wooden axle which ended in a metal point. A wooden bar, passing horizontally through the axle, afforded two handles by which the potter spun the wheel in the socket of a stone or metal base.

He made the circular base of the first *pithos* and then went on to the second and third. By the time he had finished the tenth jar the base of the first one was dry. He then added a cyclindrical section about one-sixth of the desired height to the first *pithos* and continued doing the same down the line. Each time he returned to the first jar he added another section, three in all, bound together by a belt of clay. When he had completed the last section—a procedure known as "fitting on the collar"—he then "eared the *pithos*" by equipping it with three large handles. By sunset the master potter and his helpers had produced ten enormous jars.

Like the potters of Silamos, those of Thrapsanos kept a stock of the same clay discs the Minoans had used. Their traditions of pottery-making, the villagers claimed with pride, went back hundreds of years. They would have been astonished to know *how* many; or that they owed the discovery of their artistic predecessors to a stubborn Englishman who had started digging on their island primarily in search of written records.

Evans at seventy-five had reached the pinnacle of fame. It was he who had added the Minoan chapter to the history of civilization. He had invented the very name by which every schoolchild now called a long-forgotten people. To illustrate and enliven the story he had reconstructed ruins and covered walls with frescoes. Where footnotes were needed for clarification, he had provided them: maps, references, interpretations, and intuitive deductions, sometimes from evidence so small that another explorer might have overlooked it. Both in the public press and in scholarly journals his name was indelibly linked with the Minoans, while he himself had become obsessed, almost proprietary, about those lively and endearing people. They were "his" Minoans and not many archaeologists dared to question either his theories or his conclusions. It took courage to argue with Evans, but there were a few intrepid souls who were beginning to.

Half a century had passed since Schliemann began searching for Troy; more than a quarter of a century since Evans opened excavations at Knossos. A whole new generation of archaeologists were now at work both in Crete and on the Greek mainland. None of them was rich. Supported by university grants or public subscription, they could not afford to explore like Schliemann for Homeric treasures, or to indulge like Evans in expensive restorations—even had they wanted to; and most of them did not. Both their aims and their methods were different. Field archaeology had ceased to be an adventure and was on the road to becoming a science.

Although Mackenzie especially, and Evans as well, had been pioneers in the study of Minoan pottery, this newer breed of archaeologist went far beyond either of them in elevating the ordinary potsherd to an indispensable tool in dating the past. Moreover, they were learning new ways to excavate a site so as to disturb its stratification as little as possible. They proceeded much more slowly than Evans; more slowly still as time went on.

It was becoming an accepted rule not to clear a whole area simultaneously. To record finds accurately, to analyze them scientifically, and to publish them promptly were as important as the finds themselves. Though there would always be something of the treasure hunter in every archaeologist, the excitement of pure treasure hunting was over. Archaeologists were no longer looking primarily for gold headbands like the one Sophia Schliemann posed in, or for sculptures of human-headed winged bulls like those Austen Henry Layard shipped from Nimrud to the British Museum. A simple clay pot, an inscribed tablet, bones, seeds of wheat or barley, a humble grave could tell them more about when and how an ancient people had lived.

Two of the most gifted men among the younger excavators were the Englishman Alan Wace and the American Carl Blegen. They were both working on the Greek mainland and systematically uncovering the remains of a vigorous, prehistoric Bronze Age civilization which Evans claimed was an offshoot, a transplant from Crete. And they were running headlong into conflict with the formidable Evans as they drew their own conclusions; Wace especially. He was more impetuous than his American colleague in questioning what he considered outworn viewpoints, less cautious, and without Blegen's ability to express controversial theories in words of quiet understatement.

Wace, director of the British School at Athens at the time,

worked in Mycenae from 1920 to 1923 with results almost
as fruitful as Schliemann's. The German's pioneering work,
and that of his assistant Wilhelm Dörpfeld, had been followed
up by the Greek archaeologist Chrestos Tsountas. Tsountas
published a brilliant book on *Mycenae and Mycenaean Civilization* in 1893—seven years before Evans laid spade to
Knossos. In the twenty years following his excavations, however, the Minoans had preempted the spotlight on the stage
of prehistory and the man in the prompter's box had been
Evans. The mystery of unraveling the past took a dramatic
turn when Wace dared to question some of Evans' most cherished theories.

Wace had already run into trouble with Evans when he
co-authored with his friend Blegen an article entitled "The
Pre-Mycenaean Pottery of the Mainland." The two younger
men had undertaken a study of hundreds of thousands of
potsherds extracted from ancient mounds which had lain outside the major sites of habitation and whose strata were therefore less disturbed. From their study they had reconstructed
a sequence of ceramic fabrics, shapes, and decorative motifs
that kept recurring in more or less the same order on the
different sites. They then published their findings.

Wace and Blegen began their article innocuously enough.
"The glory of Tiryns and Mycenae," they were careful to
point out, "was the climax of prehistoric art on the mainland
of Greece and, as shown conclusively by Sir Arthur Evans
. . . is derived from Crete." However, they continued, "though
Minoan in origin, the Mycenaean civilization is not merely
transplanted from Crete, but is the fruit of the cultivated
Cretan graft set on the wild stock of the mainland. . . . The
underlying mainland element influenced the dominant Minoan
art so as to make it Mycenaean as opposed to Cretan."

This was a direct challenge to one of Evans' most basic
assumptions: that from about 1600 B.C. onward the mainland
was completely dominated by Minoan culture and probably
also under political control. Only after 1400 B.C., Evans insisted, did the base of power in the Aegean shift from Knossos
to Mycenae.

Wace and Blegen went further. They proposed that Evans'
all-inclusive term "Minoan" be changed for their area to "Hel-

ladic"—from "Hellas," the name by which the Greeks both ancient and modern have always called their country. And they continued to pit their picks and shovels against the old master's reputation and prestige, not hesitating to publish conclusions which might arouse furious reaction. And did. Sir Arthur was as ready at seventy-five as he had been at twenty-five to defend his ideas and convictions with vigor, whether they concerned the Slavs' claim to independence or the Minoans' to preeminence. Nevertheless, to his credit, he proved himself a generous opponent by giving Wace financial assistance to continue his work.

Wace had undertaken the project of reexamining the nine *tholoi* at Mycenae, correlating his findings with the stratigraphical and structural evidence emanating from Tiryns, where Professor Georg Karo was excavating at the same time. The beehive tombs, both of them concluded, were constructed later than the shaft graves, which they dated between 1600 and 1500 B.C. The *tholoi* were, and still are, among the architectural wonders and mysteries of Mycenae. While Wace was not able (nor has anyone been to this day) to pinpoint their architectural origin, he was sure of one thing: the direct source was not Crete. Furthermore, while allowing for the pervasiveness of Minoan artistic influence on the mainland, Wace insisted on granting the Mycenaean culture its own creative individuality. He pointed out, for example, that the engraved daggers found by Schliemann in the earlier shaft graves were Minoan in style only. Their subject matter— scenes of hunting and battle—reflected the life-style of a warrior people exposed to enemies, not of islanders protected by the sea. The Mycenaeans had gradually blended their own ideas with those imported from Crete and had developed their own significantly different culture.

Wace published his findings and the battle was on. Evans fired the first shots in two issues of *The Journal of Hellenic Studies*—a vehicle used customarily to express views with more restraint than the tone reflected in his articles. First he disputed the date of the *tholos* tombs. They were earlier than the shaft graves, he insisted. Then he questioned both the classification and dating of "Late Helladic Pottery." Wace replied in a third issue.

The younger man began, wisely, by marshaling his forces. Professor Karo and the excavators of Tiryns, he wrote, had welcomed the report of his work at Mycenae and had expressed general agreement with the results. Wace then went on to deal separately with the two points raised by Evans. In doing so, he cautioned that "every care must be taken to prevent the danger of allowing theories or preconceived prejudices to outweigh the facts, that is to say, the archaeological evidence obtained by excavation." There followed a long technical discussion intended to remove "misunderstandings" about pottery styles and fabric and then came the conclusion, which did nothing to mollify Evans. After the fall of Knossos, Wace flatly stated, "Crete was decaying, while the Mainland, released from the cultural overlordship of Crete, was free to express itself."

Now Blegen, independently and perhaps unwittingly, entered the battle. He published a study on *Zygouries: A Prehistoric Settlement in the Valley of Cleonae.* In discussing the problem of establishing a chronology, he wrote: "The system is naturally modelled on Sir Arthur Evans' classification, which laid the foundations for all subsequent study in the field of Aegean chronology, but when applied to the mainland or to any other area outside of Crete, the subdivisions should and must correspond, not with a system worked out on the basis of internal evidence for Crete itself, nor with any fixed mathematical formula, but with the actual facts as revealed by excavations in the region in question. If they are to have any meaning in themselves they should and must correspond with the stratification."

The pages of *The Journal of Hellenic Studies* were no longer sufficient to contain Evans' reactions to such iconoclastic ideas. His reply came in 1929 in the form of a handsomely printed monograph called *The Shaft Graves and Beehive Tombs of Mycenae and Their Interrelation.* In it he paid tribute to Wace's careful work in a footnote—it was "a great advance on any preceding accounts"—and then proceeded summarily to dismiss his conclusions. "Parenthetically, it may be observed that to call this civilization 'Helladic' is both untrue to fact and misleading to students." So much for nomenclature. "The higher aspects of the culture revealed to us at Mycenae must in any case be recognized as belonging to the Minoan world. That world doubtless included provincial areas, of which, as in the case of the Western part of Crete itself, we as yet know nothing. It may already have absorbed colonial tracts on the East Aegean shores. There was room within it for many local variations and divergent customs. But Minoan Crete is still its centre, and—as will be fully demonstrated now—down at least to the close of the Palace Period—the influence of Knossos itself, the 'Great City,' was still predominant."

Two years later Evans made use of his introduction to Emil Ludwig's biography *Schliemann of Troy* to continue his polemic. He railed against "that School of Archaeology who still regard the question from its Mainland aspect," and once again asserted that the beehive tombs predated the shaft graves. To think otherwise was "preposterous and perverse."

Nevertheless, the fight was not over; had hardly begun, in fact. One of its first victims was Wace himself, whose reappointment as director of the British School of Archaeology at Athens, it was darkly hinted at the time, was refused because he had crossed swords with Evans. But Wace would eventually return for a second round of digging at Mycenae. Blegen, too, would still be heard from and others after him, when the great pioneer would no longer be present either to accept new theories or to demolish them in print. Back in the year 1927, however, Evans was still very much alive and had other things on his mind besides tirades against Wace or any future heretics.

The library at Youlbury again looked like an obstacle course, bristling with trestle tables. Volume II of *The Palace of Minos* was in the final stages of prepublication, which was to say that Evans and the printers were arguing over costly corrections to page proofs. And letting errors slip by no matter how minutely the typesetters pored over Sir Arthur's handwriting: "erotic" for "exotic," for example, and "sky-totes"—an inspired word—for "rhytons." The manuscript turned out to be so bulky that it had to be bound in two volumes. In the introduction Evans expressed his gratitude for the "Memorial Volume of Essays on Minoan subjects that has just reached me—the work itself of a select group of scholars and presented to me, in honour of my 75th birthday, under the auspices of the Oxford Philological Society, on behalf of a much larger number of well-wishers. . . . It is a touching tribute and a great encouragement."

An encouragement, presumably, to continue working. By the time Volume II appeared in the year 1928, its author was back in Crete.

True, the Villa Ariadne was no longer "his." It now belonged to the British School of Archaeology at Athens. But the uniformed chauffeur was on hand to meet Evans. Maria wore a starched white apron over her black dress. Kosti outdid himself in the kitchen, there was French wine on the table, and Manolaki came up from his house in Candia to supervise matters. When the master was in residence, life at the Villa Ariadne resumed its stately ways and everyone in it was aware of Sir Arthur's presence. These days, in addition to Mackenzie, de Jong, and the constant visitors, there were also students from the British School at Athens.

Earnest young heads were bent over potsherds, studying and classifying them. Willing young hands joined in the work at the site, learning the techniques of excavation. There was a hushed silence in the library, broken only by the sound of pages turning. It was the way Evans had planned it. His Cretan home had become a center for research into the Minoan past.

To its other facilities he now added an annex. At the bottom of the garden stood a small vine-covered house which everyone still called the Taverna. The neighboring villagers used to gather there to sing their "table songs" about love and freedom and to relax over a bottle of raki. Evans had it remodeled into a two-bedroom cottage with sitting room, workroom, and kitchen "for the use, at any time, of members of the School independently studying the antiquities on the spot." For the next two years the Cretan peasants who used to frequent the Taverna were replaced by transient archaeologists. Then the Taverna underwent another change, substituting for its monastic air of scholarship an unexpected bustle of domesticity. It became the home of the new curator of Knossos, John Pendlebury and his wife, Hilda.

"Poor Mr. Mackenzie" was no longer able to cope with growing responsibilities. Though no one had realized it at the time, his complaints that the nightingales kept him awake at night had been the first signs of deep psychological disturbance. Gradually he grew more and more silent, morose, fearful. He spent longer hours alone in his room. He also began drinking heavily, or so it appeared to Evans and others. The Scotsman's failing health and frayed nerves deteriorated eventually into a mental breakdown from which he never recovered.

Evans had shown admirable forbearance with his assistant's aberrations up to now. The day came, however, when he felt forced to retire the man who had worked with him for almost three decades. It was a tragic moment for both men. "I think it broke his heart," Evans said years later, still recalling that moment; but the Minoans took precedence over sentiment. With the departure of the ailing Mackenzie and the advent of the young Pendleburys, the work at Knossos passed, at least symbolically, from the hands of the pioneering discoverer and his able lieutenant into those of the new generation of trained excavators.

John and Hilda Pendlebury were both archaeologists. John was twenty-five when he became curator of Knossos in 1930. Sir Arthur was seventy-nine. Yet for all their difference in age and experience, the two were remarkably similar in character. The one was a superb athlete, despite the fact that he had lost an eye in infancy and wore a glass eye. The other, for all his night blindness and need for Prodger, could still climb mountains on muleback. The young man in his mid-twenties was as tenacious as the man nearing eighty. Both were quick-tempered and outspoken. Enormously active. Adventurous. In choosing a successor to Mackenzie, Evans had found in John Pendlebury the quality of mind and the energy he was looking for. He was very pleased with his new curator.

Pendlebury's feelings about Sir Arthur, on the other hand,

were more mixed. Though he liked and admired the old giant, he found him irksome to work with. Evans' autocratic assumption of authority often struck Pendlebury as interference. The old man's demands seemed unreasonable. His pertinacity translated itself into sheer stubbornness. Even when Evans was far away in Youlbury his personality seemed to dominate the Villa Ariadne. When Milord descended on Crete, one could imagine his presence stirring the Minoans themselves. There was excitement in the air, expectancy on the site. What would he be up to next?

Professionally, what troubled Pendlebury most about Evans was his reconstruction of Knossos. Like other archaeologists of his generation, Pendlebury took a severely purist approach to restoration. He felt that a site should be preserved against the inroads of weather and tourists but not tampered with. He himself wanted no part of Evans' reconstructions, though he did defend them—perhaps out of respect only, or to maintain the courtesies—in his *Handbook to the Palace of Minos*: "Without restoration, the Palace would be a meaningless heap of ruins, the more so because the gypsum stone," of which so much of Knossos was built, "melts like sugar under the action of the rain, and would eventually disappear completely."

Nonetheless, the young Pendleburys, like everybody else, found themselves fascinated by Sir Arthur. However warily they might tread during his peripatetic visits to the Villa Ariadne, they spent endless hours talking about him after he left, recalling his stories and the way he laughed at his own jokes. And remembering his generosity. A remark from Pendlebury that he would like to build a really fine archaeological library at the villa immediately produced a check. Evans also insisted on brightening the Taverna with the colorful Cretan embroideries he loved, and went on a buying spree for new curtains, furniture, and rugs.

Sir Arthur was in Youlbury when the Pendleburys' first child was born. His reaction to the event was one of delight: "A Knossos nursery will be a new feature!" Reading his letter of congratulations, the new parents could picture the old man running a hand through his hair to scratch the far side of his head, that puckish gesture of his when he had said something clever or was raising a scholarly eyebrow.

You could disagree with such a man, even resent him, but it was hard to resist him—and even harder to keep up with him.

Evans had flung himself into a new cause: the preservation of the English countryside.

Chapter XX
So the Legend Was True

Though ecology was not yet a familiar word, Evans' vocabulary was quite equal to his purposes: to protect the peak of Boars Hill from building speculators and to safeguard its broad view over Oxford and the tranquil countryside. The "truly spacious outlook," as he described it, rejoiced the eye and invited quiet contemplation. From this spot the poet Matthew Arnold, sitting in the shade of a cascading umbrella tree, had found the foreground for his poem "The Scholar Gypsy" and for "Thyrsis," one of the loveliest elegies in English literature. When speculative builders, more interested in profits than in poetry, began exploiting so incomparable a view in advertising brochures, Evans sprang into action. The Oxford Preservation Trust had been alerted to the threat, but it was moving much too ponderously for his taste. Sir Arthur took personal command of the summit of Boars Hill.

First he bought it. Then he constructed a mound 162 meters in circumference and rising 15 meters above the crest of the hill. He called it Jarn Mound, after the local name for the spot. The crown—and crowning jewel—was a "dial of indication" made of copper plate and protected by a thick disk of unbreakable glass. Engraved on the copper and inlaid with red, black, and blue enamel was a plan of the principal points of interest spreading out from Oxford over green valleys and winding rivers all the way to London. Though not all the sites indicated were visible from Boars Hill, the dial fixed their location in the topographical mosaic: St. Paul's Cathedral in London, more than eighty-six kilometers southeast; the river Thames intersecting the landscape in great loops; the important roads and courses of the ancient Roman way.

It took almost three years to construct Jarn Mound. The first attempt failed when the clay used for the structure suffered what Evans described as "a general slump." He tried again, using a different material. An average of twenty men worked daily for thirty-four months, with the aid of a motor hoist and trucks running up inclined rails, to complete the mound. "For the benefit of future archaeologists," Evans solemnly explained, he buried "freshly minted coins of the realm" at the base. The "dial of indication" drew visitors to the top. To ease their climb he made a hollow iron railing, but to discourage small children from sliding down and risking a fall, he saw to it that little spikes protruded from the railing at spaced intervals. Then, on the sloping sides, he planted dwarf Cornish gorse, the purple lizard heath and the rosy variety of Dorset. These would form "a fitting center for an experiment in wild gardening," he wrote in his booklet telling the story of Jarn Mound.

At Jarn Mound, Evans the botanist came into his own. He ringed the circumference with the flora of all Britain, taking care to set the plants in such order, "their prime shifting with the seasons," as to insure year-round color. He set snowdrops and grape hyacinths, foxgloves and cornflowers along the curving paths and formed thickets of all the principal varieties of British roses. He planted monkshood and elecampane, grass of Parnassus with its beguiling yellow-and-white flowers, and the guelder rose, also known as highbush cranberry. Special preference, he wrote, was given to wild cherry trees, "equally lovely in their Spring blossoms and Autumn foliage." He provided place for shelter in case of rain; designed a rockery; went himself with a trowel to find wild flowers.

A special section was set aside so that Evans the conservationist could provide "additional asylum for local species threatened with extermination." Here the purple orchises, the cowslips, the bluebells and primroses, the white-and-purple fritillaries would be shielded from "plough, urban growth, picking, and marauders who are professional hawkers and find ready sale for their spoils in Oxford." In this protected environment botanists would carry out scientific observation and further experiments relating to the local soil and climate.

And all the while, Evans the archaeologist had been toiling away on Volume III of *The Palace of Minos.* It was published in March 1930. Needing release from his library and with Jarn Mound midway to completion, Sir Arthur decided to set aside his quill pen and his gardener's trowel for the spade. On this next visit to Crete, however, he intended to devote all his time, "apart from some minor investigations," merely to completing the work of reconstruction, especially in the Throne Room and its antechamber. But it appeared, he cheerfully noted, that "the great Goddess of the spot" had other plans in mind.

It was early April. Sir Arthur had just arrived, the Villa Ariadne had barely had time to shift gears. Guided, perhaps, by the Great Goddess herself, Evans set some men to work making exploratory soundings beyond the western limits thus far excavated. Within a few days they turned up a startling new discovery. Before either Evans, Pendlebury, or de Jong knew quite what was happening, "it became necessary to embark once more on a campaign of excavation comparable to that of earlier years."

Fifty additional workmen were taken on. A "massed attack," as Evans called it, of some six weeks' duration exposed sixty meters of a wall running due west; then turning at right angles at its southern end, it continued east for another thirty-one and a half meters. Some of the mixed filling of the wall contained potsherds dating back to Neolithic and Early Minoan times. From these and the stratigraphic evidence there could be no doubt that it was the wall of the first Palace of Knossos, built somewhere around 2000 B.C. It went back, then, to the very beginning of the palace history, stretching the boundaries of Knossos both in time and in space. Volume III of *The Palace of Minos,* published only one month before, was already incomplete. This new addition to the Minoan story would have to await Volume IV.

Work on the site continued until August and ended with the traditional *glendi*. Old-timers at the party were reminded of those exhilarating early years when the "Saint" had emerged from the earth, the first inscribed tablets, the Cup Bearer, the bull. Would the Knossian surprises never end? The master himself had thought that "something like finality might seem to have been attained." But he was mistaken. The Great Goddess was holding still another revelation in reserve for the following year, when Evans would be eighty.

Like an omen of what was ahead, the 1931 season began with a series of uncommon occurrences. Just as Evans was preparing to leave Youlbury for Crete, there was an earthquake in Macedonia. All land communications with Greece were cut off. He flew to Paris, then had to travel by way of Italy and finally reached Piraeus, the port of Athens, just in time to board the Greek steamer anchored out in the harbor. The boat was due to leave for Crete within hours when a freak snowstorm—the worst anyone could remember—put departure out of the question.

Evans had been on board only long enough to create a scene. And to teach a lesson to the men he called the "Pirates of Piraeus," the boatmen who rowed passengers to and from the shore in those days before modern piers. One of them, he wrote home, "had tried to prevent my entering the saloon, demanding four times the fare, 100 instead of 25 drachmas—though, as the weather was bad, I had tendered him 50." Always prepared to be generous, Evans would not tolerate extortion.

"Next he pursued me into the small saloon, where among the passengers seated—all of whom knew me—was the Greek Minister of War and other officials, who all looked away terrorized by this representative of the Piraeus *Camorra*!" The Camorra Evans referred to was a secret criminal association, the Italian Mafia of its day.

What terrorized a minister of war, however, only enraged Sir Arthur. He decided to wait out the snowstorm in Athens and then take the seaplane to Crete. Meanwhile, he took the opportunity to write a blistering letter to the newspaper *Estía* about the Pirates of Piraeus. Whether thanks to his prose or his signature, he received an immediate reply. After offering fulsome apologies, the captain of the port assured Sir Arthur that the proper steps had been taken.

Evans' adventures were not over. The seaplane landed at Spinalonga, a small lagoon off the east coast of Crete. From there, his letter continued, "I had to cross about seven miles of open sea to reach St. Nicholas, the nearest port, in a motor-boat. This was too small for its job and, though the English captain was very plucky, a gale blowing from just the wrong quarter made the sea so rough that we were beaten back three times in trying to make the headland that we had to pass, and returned ignominiously to the little hamlet of Elunda whence we had started."

Most octogenarians who suffered from seasickness would have delayed their journey until the gale blew over. Not Evans. "I managed," he blandly went on, "to secure a larger motor-boat which took us through."

And now here he was at the Villa Ariadne, with the Pendleburys and the de Jongs, about to demonstrate once more his incomparable flair for ferreting out the past.

Something had been puzzling Evans since the early explorations. Knossos, he was convinced, had been as much a sanctuary as a palace, the home of a succession of priest-kings who were invested with both religious and temporal authority. The Knossian earth abounded with relics testifying to this dual function of the reigning sovereign. Yet in three decades of excavation no trace had been found of a truly royal burial place: a burial place at once tomb and shrine, a fitting monument to a ruler who combined earthly and divine powers.

Evans had all but forgotten his earlier hopes of finding a "temple-tomb." Still, the feeling persisted that somewhere underground lay the final resting place of a priest-king. Moreover, there was legend to go by—a legend that was old even when the Sicilian historian Diodorus wrote about it in the first century A.D., in one of his forty books of "Universal History."

The last King Minos, according to Diodorus, had been murdered in Sicily, where he had gone in pursuit of his runaway architect Daedalus. Minos's reverent subjects, told that their ruler had been the victim of an accident, had brought his body back to Crete and buried it with magnificence in a tomb hidden deep in the earth. Over the tomb, visible to all, they had erected a temple dedicated to the Goddess.

A haunting legend. A nagging intuition. Both might have remained just that, had it not been for a small boy bringing up his father's midday meal to a vineyard south of the palace. It was one of those bright clear days in April when pebbles gleamed like diamonds in the sun. A glittering object on the tilled earth beside the vine caught the child's eye. It turned out to be a massive signet ring of solid gold, weighing about twenty-seven grams, with a beaded hoop. On its bezel was a carved intaglio design showing the passage of the Goddess from one rock sanctuary to another across an intervening stretch of sea.

The ring had been fashioned by a master goldsmith around the middle of the sixteenth century B.C. So resplendent an ornament could have graced only the hand of a king. It was a princely relic. Was it part of the treasure buried with its exalted owner? A symbol of his priestly and royal office? Evans' "uncanny sense for antiquities, almost like a dog's smell," as J. N. L. Myres described it, vibrated like an antenna in the wind. His intuition was intensified a few days later by the owner of the vineyard. This worthy, in the course of cultivation, had struck some large blocks not far from where the boy had found the ring. Evans surveyed the area, organized another "massed attack," and found the temple-tomb of Minos the priest-king. "Where I looked for it," he wrote home.

Magnificent it was. A single-storied pavilion led into an open paved court guarded by a gateway at the far side. (The lintel of the gateway was found *in situ*.) This in turn led into a divided passage. One side opened out into a pillar-crypt freely incised with the sacred double axe sign. The other side ended in a flight of stairs rising upward—to what? Evans had a pretty good idea. But first came the clearing of the pillar-crypt and whatever lay beyond.

Patiently, carefully, the men cleared the debris. Along the south side of the pillar-crypt they found walled compartments containing the bones of some twenty individuals. Who were

they? Worshippers, Evans speculated, come to pay their respects at the royal shrine and trapped there by the Earth-
Shaker; then given a decent burial by the survivors of the
earthquake. His men continued working. Suddenly the wall
masonry of the pillar-crypt showed a break. There was a
short passageway. It led, as Evans knew it would, to an
interior chamber cut out of the original rock: the sepulcher-
chamber of one or more of the priest-kings of Knossos.

It was a square room, paved and lined with slabs of gypsum.
Its central pillar of gypsum was still standing, although the
cypress beam it had supported was gone. A little pit on
the floor contained the tomb's only remains—not, alas, those
of a priest-king but of an elderly man and a child, laid
to rest in the early fourteenth century B.C., a date fixed by
the clay pots found with them. Clearly a cult of the dead
had continued at this spot until the final destruction of Knossos
and even after. The roof of the burial chamber had been
painted a bright celestial blue, as could be seen from traces
of paint still visible on the chalky limestone surface. The
Minoans had chosen the color, Evans wrote in one of his
more poetic passages in *The Palace of Minos*, so that "Despite
the darkness of the vault—without artificial lighting, impen-
etrable by mortal eye—the dead might still be given the
illusion of the blue sky above."

And the flight of stairs? As though magnetized, the spade
was drawn upward to emerge on an open terrace above the
pillar-crypt. Here stood the upper shrine, a double-tiered col-
umnar temple to the Goddess approached by three steps.
Its walls had been coated with stucco of Venetian red and
it stood open to the air, accessible to all, just as Diodorus
had written. The subjects of King Minos could come to pay
homage both to their Goddess and their sovereign without
disturbing the royal remains laid to rest in the rock-cut chamber below.

So the legend was true. The temple-tomb had existed. At
eighty Evans had again shown his undiminished flair for discovery.

At eighty-one he demonstrated his unflagging zest for travel.
Accompanied by his sister-in-law Helen Freeman, he went
to Ragusa.

Half a century had passed since the day when his wife, Margaret, and his sister Alice had collected him from jail and the three of them had boarded a steamer headed for England. During the interval new houses had been built on the outlying slopes, but within its walls the old town was unchanged. It was still the Ragusa he loved, as beautiful as ever. Some of the flowering shrubs he and Margaret had planted in the garden of the Casa San Lazzaro still miraculously survived. The piazza was there, the café, the hidden courtyards, the antique shops—and the jail. He revisited the cell block marked *Condannati.* He remembered the bread with its baked-in secret messages. To the bewildered jailer who showed him around Evans remarked, "I come back here every fifty years." Was there a ghostly innuendo that he would continue the habit?

Only two things had changed in Ragusa. Were she living there now, Margaret would not order her beef from the butcher in Italian. Slav was the universal language. As for Sir Arthur himself, he would have no need to hide or burn papers, to skulk home after midnight or write messages in code. The new Ragusa, now known as Dubrovnik, welcomed him home as a hero.

Two years later he was again honored in England. The Society of Antiquaries had just instituted the Gold Medal, to be awarded for distinguished services to archaeology, and chose Evans to be its first recipient. Sir Arthur had delivered more learned addresses to this august body, but his speech of thanks was surely the most moving. He spoke of the Society's long history and his own memories of its activities, going back almost seventy years. And he paid tribute to its series of distinguished presidents during that period: "All of them my friends, and one of them my father."

Evans was rooted in the past and Victorian in his habits, but he also strode with the present. He had owned the first automobile on Boars Hill. He flew in an airplane before the days of built-in safety devices. He ardently fiddled with the knobs on his new "wireless set." He was also among the first archaeologists to publish an aerial photograph of his excavations, a *"desideratum,"* he wrote, that "had long remained unsatisfied." He was delighted when a pilot of Imperial Airways finally succeeded in taking a snapshot of Knossos from the air. The photo showed almost the whole range of the palace site. Blurred though it was, Evans' eyes could make out details as small as a mule path, hair-thin. His historical imagination, however, could see things no camera could record because they no longer existed.

The House of Minos had been larger than Buckingham Palace, containing perhaps fourteen hundred rooms. The main approach to it had been magnificent, across a bridge or viaduct spanning the valley and the Kairatos stream. Once arrived at the vast structure, the visitors separated according to their rank and business. Artisans or merchants, or peasants come to trade their wares, turned toward the West Court where they waited for the functionary who would weigh or measure their goods or to whom they paid their taxes. A stone seat along the shady side of the court helped to ease their waiting.

The high-ranking visitor—an ambassador, perhaps, or an important man of commerce—entered through the northern gate. Having satisfied the sentries of his purpose, he then ascended a narrow ramp to an antechamber where he came face to face with the fresco of a charging bull. Just as the replica made by Gilliéron reminds the tourist of today, so the original fresco must have impressed upon the traveler in antiquity that he had penetrated into the capital of the Minoans.

From this antechamber the visitor now proceeded to the Central Court around which the whole structure had been built. The façade of the west wing of the palace rose three stories high. Within its sumptuous walls were the Throne Room, the ceremonial halls, and the religious shrines. Across the Central Court on the eastern side lay the Domestic Quarter, built into the sloping hill, with broad descending flights of stairs. Here were the Queen's Megaron and other spacious rooms, and a maze of workshops, corridors, and chambers. Studying the aerial photograph of the palace, Evans was both pleased with what he had resurrected and saddened by that which was forever destroyed. He recorded his mixed reactions in *The Palace of Minos*.

"Had the Fates, indeed, allowed Daedalos, the legendary builder and adorner of the House of Minos, and Father of Aviation, to take part in this later flight, there are many features that he would have sought in vain." The terraces and roof gardens, the arena of the bull-sports, the dancing ground—all had disappeared with the centuries. "But the old ground plan of the palace," Evans continued with satisfaction, "still stands four square, partially roofed over in places, as first conceived by its great architect, with its Central Court clearly defined and the main entrances to it from N and S easily discernible." Daedalus, a man of no mean imagination himself, would have recognized what remained of his blueprints.

The aerial photograph of Knossos received special mention in the preface to Volume IV of *The Palace of Minos*, published in two parts in 1935. In that same preface Evans summarized his final stubborn conclusions about the downfall and disappearance of Knossos, withholding full credit for Mycenaean power and originality to the bitter end.

> The end was sudden, and the evidence once more points to an earthquake as the cause, followed by a widespread conflagration and, doubtless, ensuing pillage of the ruins left. But on this occasion the catastrophe was final. Squatters, indeed, after a short interval of years, occupied the probably considerable shelter still offered by the remains of the fabric. But the Minoan augurs may have satisfied themselves that the Powers of the Underworld were not to be exorcized. The long experiment was given up, and there are reasons for supposing that the residence of the Priest-Kings of Knossos was, perhaps not for the first time, transferred to a Mainland site, quite probably, indeed, to Mycenae, at this time redecorated according to the latest Knossian fashion.

Volume IV of *The Palace of Minos* was Evans' literary farewell to the Minoans and, alas, to many of his own colleagues. At eighty-four he had outlived most of his own generation. He dedicated the book to Federico Halbherr, the great Italian excavator of Phaistos. But he reserved his most touching tribute for Duncan Mackenzie, who died in Italy while Evans was still going over the proofs of his manuscript. His "vexed Spirit had found release at last," Evans wrote of his assistant, friend, and colleague with a tenderness that few people, including Mackenzie himself, knew he possessed.

> His Highland loyalty never failed, and the simple surroundings of his earlier years gave him an inner understanding of the native workmen and a fellow-feeling with them that was a real asset in the course of our spade-work. To them, though a master, he was ever a true comrade. The lively Cretan dances revived the "reels" of his youth. No wedding ceremony, no baptism, no wake was complete among the villagers without the sanction of his presence, and as sponsor, godfather, or "best man," his services were in continual request. There yet fall on my inner ear the tones of that "still small voice" as he proposed the toast of a happy pair—with sly jocose allusions, fluently spoken in the Cretan dialect of modern Greek—but not without a trace of the soft Gaelic accent.

Pendlebury, who was on hand to greet Sir Arthur when he arrived at the Villa Ariadne in 1935, had hardly known Mackenzie. The young curator of Knossos was much closer in age to the students swarming over the villa than to the patriarch of Cretan archaeology or his former assistant. By confiding the Minoans to younger hands, Evans had signaled, consciously or unconsciously, the end of one era and the beginning of another.

This was to be the grandest of Sir Arthur's visits to Crete. He intended to investigate a stone passage that had come to light near the Temple Tomb, though he would not attempt, he said in all seriousness, "any considerable dig at present" (he was eighty-four!). The islanders used this occasion to honor the man who had been their single most outstanding benefactor. Evans had stood by the Cretans in their fight for liberation from the Turks. He had provided a livelihood to countless families during decades of economic stress. But beyond anything else, Sir Arthur had uncovered for them an illustrious ancestry which brought pride to the humblest of peasants. This ceremony was the collective cry of gratitude to Evans from the citizens of Candia, the city now known by its Greek name Herakleion.

Ten thousand visitors packed the palace court where foreign emissaries had come millennia ago to pay homage to the priest-king. So immense was the gathering that people crowded the upper floor of the palace, spilled over onto trees and thronged outside the gates. There were scores of dignitaries among them: Professor Spyridon Marinatos, then director of the Herakleion Museum; the British consul, the bishop of Crete, the Metropolitan himself from Athens; representatives of all the learned societies on the island and mainland. But mostly they were the simple inhabitants of Herakleion and the neighboring villages. All eyes were focused on the slight figure with the thatch of white hair, still radiating energy and accompanied, as always, by Prodger.

Evans was made an honorary citizen with all kinds of privileges, exemption from dues, and even the right of asylum! The climax of the occasion came with the unveiling of a bronze bust of the discoverer and restorer of Knossos. It was inscribed with his name—Sir Arthur Evans—and underneath were written six simple words: "The people of Herakleion in gratitude." His "brazen image," Evans wrote home, set "on a—happily—high pillar," was placed at the entrance to the palace where it greets all visitors to this day. There were seven speeches, all of them in Greek. Then came Evans' reply, which he had carefully composed "in the proper mixture of old and new Greek" for the benefit of both scholars and laymen.

"We know now that the old traditions were true," he told his reverent listeners. "We have before our eyes a wondrous spectacle—the resurgence, namely, of a civilization twice as old as that of Hellas. It is true that on the old Palace site what we see are only the ruins of ruins, but the whole is still inspired with Minos' spirit of order and organization, and the free and natural art of the great architect Daedalos. The spectacle, indeed, that we have before us is assuredly of world-wide significance. Compared with it how small is any individual contribution! So far indeed, as the explorer may have attained success, it has been as the humble instrument, inspired and guided by a greater Power."

The applause was thunderous. No curtain ever rang down more triumphantly on a stirring drama. The next day at another ceremony in Herakleion Sir Arthur received a laurel crown, after which he gave a splendid reception for hundreds of guests in the garden of the Villa Ariadne. But it was, indeed, the last act. When Evans left Crete shortly after the festivities, it was for the last time.

Not that he knew it, or would have brooded over the fact had he known. There was work waiting for him at Youlbury. England was preparing to celebrate the silver jubilee of King George V. The Boy Scouts were to be responsible for a nationwide chain of beacons, one of which would be lit at Youlbury. As one might have expected, Evans began studying old records to determine the classic English form of the beacon. Then he reproduced it at Youlbury and wrote a long article entitled "News by Fire" for *The Times*.

He recounted the history of beacons in England and described the model he had built. Only the straight trunk of an oak tree, cut expressly for the purpose, would do. It had to rise six meters aboveground. At its top a "fire cage," with a fire of tow steeped in pitch and helped out by wood and coke, would burn for over two hours. He knew it would because he had tried it.

Of the many honors conferred on him by every learned society in England, none pleased Evans more than the Silver Wolf, the highest award of the scouts, which he received in the spring of 1936. In gratitude he undertook to write a Boys' Guide to Holland, where they were to hold a jamboree in the fall. That meant, of course, flying to Holland for material. And why not, once in the air, continue on to Göttingen, where he had attended the university some sixty-five years before?

Was it, like the return visit to Ragusa, the nostalgic looking back of an old man? Far from it. After noting that Göttingen had changed surprisingly little—a few new lecture halls, a building here or there—Evans hurried home to Youlbury to prepare his next undertaking.

Chapter XXI
Bombshells
and Bombs

In 1936 the British School of Archaeology at Athens, which counted Evans among its founders, attained its fiftieth anniversary. To celebrate the event the school organized an exhibition at Burlington House in London with the active participation of the excavator of Knossos. Sir Arthur had agreed to arrange the whole Minoan gallery at his own expense; to deliver a lecture during the exhibition; and to write for the printed catalogue the section on Cretan archaeology, which turned out to be thirty-nine pages long. It was no small undertaking for a man approaching his eighty-fifth birthday. He would need help, but there were few budding young archaeologists, especially males, who were willing to test Evans' reputation for being difficult and irascible. The most suitable candidate turned out to be Mercy Money-Coutts, mainly because she was a young woman. No matter how rude or ruthless Sir Arthur could be with a man, he was still far too Victorian to lose his temper with a member of the opposite sex.

Mercy Money-Coutts, as a student at the British School of Archaeology at Athens, had lived at the Villa Ariadne. She had helped John Pendlebury in the monumental job of cataloguing the two thousand boxes crammed with Minoan potsherds which had been stored at Knossos. In Crete, she had amply demonstrated her patience and diligence. In London, she would have to summon all her tact and forbearance.

237

But the obstinate Evans proved to be congenial and easy to work with, though no less opinionated than expected, and Money-Coutts ended up like so many before her by both liking and respecting the formidable but benevolent little tyrant.

Her biggest argument with him was over labels. She wanted the objects displayed in the showcases to be set off to their best advantage. He wanted them to be accompanied by an explanatory label so large, since he conceived the whole exhibition as a résumé of Minoan history, that sometimes the label obscured the object. Many years later, recalling those days and those arguments, Money-Coutts wondered whether Sir Arthur's insistence on large labels was due to his own peculiar eyesight. Perhaps even with glasses he could only see one object at a time and was not disturbed by the feeling of clutter in the showcases, as other viewers might be. It was even possible, judging from the sometimes overvivid restorations of the Knossos frescoes, to suspect him of not seeing colors quite like other people. Still, she thought that the restorations were justified and based on valid evidence, though the two of them did have one notable argument over the famous fresco called the "Saffron Gatherer." The young woman insisted that the Blue Boy was really a Blue Monkey. The old man finally admitted that she might be right. "But of course by the next morning it was a Blue Boy again!" Admitting error was not easy for Evans.

Obstinate he indeed was, and maybe it was a good thing. A less determined man of his age might have failed to be on hand for the opening of the exhibition. Only a day or two before the appointed date Evans was seized by a violent chill. However, he "took a desperate remedy, and had his breakfast in bed," and was on hand for the inaugural evening, feeling strong enough to give vent to a burst of anger. Sir Arthur was irate about the Duke of Kent's opening speech. The man clearly knew nothing about archaeology and didn't pretend to.

Now Evans was standing before the lectern about to begin his lecture on the work at Knossos. The hall was packed. Arriving at the last moment, the students from the sixth form at Harrow, who had come en masse to honor their most famoùs graduate, had to sit on the floor. Sprawled among the gangling seventeen- and eighteen-year-olds was a boy of fourteen who had managed to tag along with his seniors.

The audience sat spellbound as Sir Arthur told the Minoan story, thirty-five hundred years old and yet still so new. Some of his older listeners could remember the day when they had opened *The Times* and first learned about a people nobody knew had existed. A marvelously gifted people. The tables and glass cases around the lecture hall held pottery of a fineness rarely seen in Europe from the decline of the Roman Empire until the seventeenth century A.D. The gold jewelry was the work of unsurpassed craftsmen. Exquisitely carved sealstones and signet rings filled case after case. Many of the treasures were from Evans' own collections and would end up in the Ashmolean Museum for all the world to admire. For those fortunate enough to be present that night it was a superb presentation of the extraordinary art of the Minoans.

When his lecture was over, Sir Arthur joined the crowd eagerly examining the objects on display. Stopping to chat with friends, to answer questions or point out some significant detail, he moved from showcase to showcase more like an urbane host than an eminent scholar. When an eccentric woman buttonholed him to discuss some wild theory she had about the Minoan scripts, he found the tact to tell her he was busy at the moment, and signaled Mercy Money-Coutts to come rescue him. At last he came to the table on which lay a number of Linear A and Linear B tablets. Riveted to the spot was the fourteen-year-old boy who had temporarily insinuated himself into the sixth form at Harrow. His name was Michael Ventris.

Shy in the presence of the great archaeologist yet persistent, the boy asked Evans why the tablets had never been deciphered. What were the difficulties, the problems? Sir Arthur explained that the scripts were very old. They seemed to be related to no known tongue. Most important, however, was the fact that no bilingual clue had yet been discovered.

Michael nodded his head. He had learned about the Rosetta Stone and the Behistun Rock when he was eleven, but had been fascinated by hieroglyphics and cuneiform writing even before. Indeed, when he was only seven he had bought and

studied a German book on hieroglyphs. Languages, all languages, interested him, but especially ancient ones. This new
script, he wondered, would anyone ever decipher it? How
would one go about it? Thanking Sir Arthur for his explanations, Michael Ventris returned home determined one
day to try his hand at deciphering the Minoan script. Sixteen
years later he succeeded. By then, however, it was too late
for Sir Arthur—too late to remember a boy's questions in
a crowded lecture hall or be astonished at the answers he
proposed.

Long before Michael Ventris was old enough to begin his
life's work, Evans was putting the finishing touches to his
own. *The Palace of Minos,* that flowing saga of the Minoans,
was perhaps the most comprehensive and masterful record
of an archaeological discovery ever written. Yet there was
one more task to be completed. Without an index the four
volumes—really six—were like a detailed road map from
which all place names had been omitted. Even the most seasoned traveler into the past, trying to locate a specific landmark, would be lost in the three thousand pages of text
without an alphabetical guide. Evans' half sister, Joan, had
undertaken to prepare one.

With both training in archaeology and experience as a
librarian, Joan Evans was admirably suited to the job. She
had what her brother called "a slavish respect for the alphabet"—indispensable for someone preparing an index—
plus inexhaustible patience. It was the latter quality, it soon
turned out, that would be taxed more than the former. The
kind of index Evans had in mind was not merely something
one ran one's finger down, looking for the right letter of
the alphabet, but a summary of all the knowledge contained
in the whole monumental work.

Argue with Evans? Hardly. But Joan did arrive at a *modus
operandi.* She saw to it that the bulk of the index followed
the normal course of the alphabet. Those sections dealing
with subjects which Evans considered indivisible into mere
abc's—like religion, pottery, frescoes—he handled himself.
It took him twenty-eight pages, for example, to deal only
with "Seal-stones," and with good reason. There were almost
six hundred entries, all of them, as he explained in italics,

Chronologically arranged and specimens approximately placed.
It was what Evans called an "orderly presentment" of the
subject.

Gradually, after the publication of the index, the library
at Youlbury also took on a more orderly presentment. With
The Palace of Minos finally completed, there was no longer
any need for the trestle tables. One by one they were folded
away. Though Evans still descended on the Ashmolean Museum to offer advice or to sneak a new artifact into an already
overcrowded showcase, the intervals between visits grew longer. His eyesight was failing. Often he was alone, except for
his sister Harriet, a close friend, or James Candy. The Jimmie
who had been almost a son to Evans was now a married
man with sons of his own, kept busy by a growing family
and the dairy business he was trying to establish. However,
he still spent one evening a week with Sir Arthur and contrived
to look in on him whenever he could.

The walks they occasionally took together were no longer
as strenuous as they had once been. Evans' step was less
springy. He leaned more heavily on Prodger, using it not
only as an antenna but for support when he took his daily
strolls around the gardens or up to Jarn Mound. One of
his favorite walks, especially on a cold but sunny day, brought
him to the little revolving summerhouse he had had built
close to the lake. It was just big enough to hold comfortable
chairs for two people, and light enough so that he could
easily turn it on its axle. When the sun moved, so did he.
The spot he had chosen for his revolving retreat was close
to where Youlbury's natural stream flowed into the lake. He
built waterfalls for the stream: he loved the sound of running
water falling from a great height. Listening to the melodious
splash, sitting with the sun shining on him, he would take
his time with *The Manchester Guardian.* Or read the latest
issue of one of the many scholarly journals he kept up with.

There was little going on in the archaeological world that
escaped Evans' notice. Mortimer Wheeler, the young man
whose career he had helped launch twenty years earlier by
doubling his annual income, was now a full-fledged archaeologist in his own right. Wheeler was engaged at the time
in excavating the vast prehistoric fortification at Maiden Castle,

near Dorchester in Dorset. Looking up from his work in the fall of 1937, Wheeler hastened to greet an unexpected and distinguished visitor. "Sir Arthur Evans, small and frail, was blown across our skyline like an autumn leaf before the south-wester which was our normal accompaniment."

In 1938 Evans was told that he had to undergo an operation. His sister Harriet came to Youlbury to be with him. Since the death of their brother Lewis eight years before, the two of them—the last surviving siblings of their generation—had become increasingly attached. Shortly after she arrived she was taken ill and died within a few days—and though Evans pulled through the operation, the loss of Harriet was a blow from which he never really recovered. Until now he had been merely growing older imperceptibly. Suddenly he became an old man. He began to have great difficulty in swallowing and James Candy, alerted by Mrs. Judd, the faithful housekeeper, sent thick cream to Youlbury every day so that she could make ice cream for Sir Arthur. And yet, such was his resilience and intellectual vigor, he continued to work.

In the following year he turned over his collections to the Ashmolean Museum and personally supervised the arrangement of the Minoan Room, with the help of Mercy Money-Coutts. A few months later, accompanied by a nurse, he flew to Switzerland to see an exhibition of paintings on loan from Madrid's Prado Museum, and stopped over for a last look at Strasbourg before returning home. He even undertook some more digging. Almost half a century before, when he bought Youlbury, he had made note of Roman remains on Boars Hill and filed it away in his mind for future investigation. Now the mental note surfaced with the discovery of a Roman road traversing his property from Oxford to the south coast.

Evans' delight was matched only by his chauffeur's despair. No longer able to tramp over fields and through underbrush or climb hills, Evans used his car instead of his legs. Where he thought the Roman road led he bade the chauffeur to follow, at the risk of ruining tires, axle, and chassis. Sir Arthur was determined to map out the ancient thoroughfare, which he identified with the "Swan-Way" (*Swan-rade*) mentioned in *Beowulf*. He also exposed it at several points, with the help of some undergraduate students at Oxford. But though his mind still vibrated to every stimulus, his physical stamina was gone. There could have been no greater proof of his waning strength than when he failed to respond publicly to an archaeological bombshell.

Carl Blegen had continued to explore for remains of the great Mycenaean civilization that Evans considered an offshoot of the Minoan. Moreover, the American archaeologist, like his English colleague Alan Wace, had continued to build up evidence against Evans' Knosso-centric theory of Cretan colonization of the mainland. Wace and Blegen published a joint article in 1939 entitled "Pottery as Evidence for Trade and Colonization in the Aegean Bronze Age." They had painstakingly counted the foreign pottery found at various Egyptian sites dating from the middle of the second millennium B.C. The pots of mainland Greek origin, they discovered, outnumbered those from Crete by five to one. Clearly Egypt, if not Evans, had considered Mycenae a more important trading power than Knossos. "The theory of a Cretan conquest or colonization of the Mainland has been taken too much for granted," Wace and Blegen wrote. ". . .This theory should therefore no longer be allowed to cloud the historical implications of the archaeological evidence of the Late Bronze Age in the Aegean."

In that same year, coincidentally timed to return the fire, John Pendlebury published his admirable book *The Archaeology of Crete* in which he upheld the great Evans' most cherished theory. "So Minoanized does the rest of the Aegean become that it is impossible for the present writer at least to avoid the conclusion that it was dominated politically by Crete." It also seemed absurd to Pendlebury to alter Evans' chronological framework in "the present state of our knowledge. . . . Until we have got something better to put in its place, the terminology which has acted so well for so long must be kept." Pendlebury did, however, "unrepentantly" adopt the term Late Helladic I, II, and III to mark important dates on the Mycenaean calendar. The term Helladic, he wrote, "does not attempt to ram the name of a city down the throat of a country, and, as we shall see, we must have some dis-

tinction between Crete and the Mainland." He also dared
to question Evans' earthquake theory as the cause of the
final destruction of Knossos. "Everything, indeed, points to
a deliberate sacking on the part of enemies. . . ."

Such were the arguments Evans followed from afar as he
revolved with the sun in his summerhouse by the lake, or
sat in his library with a rug over his knees, sometimes talking
to Jimmie, more often alone; playing a solitary game of patience, watching the squirrels come to gather nuts; listening
to music on his wireless; wishing, perhaps, that he were
younger so that he could join in the debate. It was he who
had written the Cretan chapter, but there were appendices
in the making.

On April 4, 1939, Blegen was digging at a site overlooking
Navarino Bay on the west coast of the Peloponnese in Greece.
Within a few hours of laying out his first trench he knew
that a very large building—perhaps a complex of buildings—
had stood on this spot and been destroyed by fire toward
the end of the Bronze Age, around 1200 B.C. Location, legend,
and subsequent excavation would eventually identify it as
the Palace of Nestor, a legendary hero of Homer's *Iliad* and
King of Pylos in ancient Greece. But the archaeological bombshell—which by then Sir Arthur was too old to react to—
fell on the very first day of digging.

With an incredible luck equal only to that of Evans, Blegen's
workmen exposed the ruins of a little room in which lay
hundreds of broken clay tablets inscribed in Linear B writing.
The find in itself, though remarkable, might yield to reasonable
explanation—in fact, it might reinforce Evans' theory of Minoan domination—but the dating of the palace raised troublesome questions indeed. If the palace at Pylos had been
burned to the ground in 1200 B.C., what were Linear B
tablets like those from Knossos—destroyed two centuries earlier—doing in its ruins? Did this mean that mainlanders had
overrun Knossos and adopted its writing system? If so, when?
Was it possible that Evans' chronology was wrong? That
Knossos was destroyed later than 1400 B.C.?

Evans, at eighty-eight, kept to himself whatever theory
he may have formulated (although he would have been pleased
to know that archaeologists are still debating among them-

selves what they refer to as "the problem"). Nor was Blegen able, during that fateful year of 1939, to do much more than laboriously remove small groups of the tablets, leave them to dry in the sun, photograph, sketch, and number them. Adolf Hitler, the madman of Germany, was threatening to engorge all of Europe. War was in the air. Blegen had deposited his precious Linear B tablets from Pylos in the vaults of the Bank of Greece for safekeeping and then left for America, taking the photographs of the tablets with him. A few months later the first shells exploded.

For the second time in his life, Evans would see the countries he most loved overrun by tanks and bombarded from the air.

Only twenty-one years, a tiny tick of the second hand on nature's clock, separated the end of the First World War from the beginning of the Second. In one year and two decades a defeated Germany had become a military colossus astride Europe. A nation of inflamed "supermen," led by a demented rabble-rouser, was bent on world domination; on rule by terror wherever Nazi boots trod. In March 1935 Hitler had invaded Austria and annexed it to Germany. One year later saw the annihilation of Czechoslovakia, in whose founding Evans had played a role. The Republic's first president Tomáš Masaryk had been a guest at Youlbury. Now his son Jan Masaryk was a refugee in Paris, helping as his father had to set up a government-in-exile. On September 1, 1939, Germany invaded Poland. Two days later England and France declared war on Germany. The most lethal conflict in human history had begun.

Within eight months German troops occupied Denmark and Norway. German tanks overran the Netherlands and Luxembourg. In Belgium the priceless library at Louvain, destroyed in 1914 and rebuilt in 1928 as a gift of the American people, again lay in ruins. It was a symbolic reminder of what had been, a mere token of what was to come. This time around, it would have done Evans little good to rage at the Philistines. There were few civilized values left to defend when sheer survival was at stake. Rockets, missiles, and bombs had replaced trench warfare. In this new kind of war women and children were as vulnerable as uniformed soldiers. They would constitute one-third of the casualties. The front line was everywhere.

In June 1940 the French Army was forced to surrender to Germany and the enemy occupied three-fifths of France. Great Britain evacuated most of its expeditionary force from the beaches of Dunkirk barely in time to prepare to defend its own isles. Hitler sent one thousand German bombers in wave after wave to blast British skies as far north as Scotland. The roar of planes overhead drowned out the soprano voices of Boy Scouts playing in the Youlbury woods, while an increasingly lonely old man sat in his library following the progress—bitter, paradoxical word—of German troops over "the civilized marches of Europe." For the second time in his life Evans was cut off from Crete.

There was a new curator at Knossos, Robert W. Hutchinson, a Cambridge archaeologist and prehistorian past military age, who was known to his friends as the "Squire." Hutchinson did his best to maintain standards on the site and at the Villa Ariadne with a calm that was remarkable under the circumstances. A sense of impending crisis pervaded the island. The tension of a people awaiting their turn to be invaded was alleviated only by a grim determination to resist. If the Germans came to Crete, they would find the Cretans ready to fight.

Mustachioed herdsmen and peasants gathered in mountain caves to plan guerrilla warfare when the time came. Villagers met secretly. In Herakleion men tapped one another on the shoulder and went silently to hidden outposts. Cooperating with them was the former curator of Knossos, John Pendlebury—now Captain Pendlebury on special service with the British forces stationed on Crete. "Blebbery," the Cretans called him, unable to master his language as he had theirs. Fluent in the native dialect, familiar with every cove and peak on the island, Captain Pendlebury together with his Cretan friends—including the foreman of Knossos, the faithful Manolaki—organized the underground resistance movement. The Cretans would fight Nazi terror with guns, with knives and, if necessary, with sticks.

On April 6, 1941, German troops poured into Yugoslavia and Greece. Two weeks later the Greek Army surrendered and King George II fled with his family to Crete. The Villa Ariadne, which Evans had planned as a center of study, became a haven for royalty. The crowned heads of Greece slept in the bedrooms built in the basement for coolness. The new curator of Knossos tried to make his guests comfortable. But it was a temporary haven indeed. There was scarcely time for the Squire to take His Majesty on a tour of the Knossos excavations. As the roar of Nazi cannons and the rumble of German tanks drew ever closer, the Greek royal family fled into exile.

During the night of May twentieth came the German airborne invasion of Crete. Parachutists fell from the sky, like gigantic flakes in a snowstorm, swarming by the thousands over the island. Superior enemy air power blazed away at the British cruisers and destroyers anchored in Cretan waters. Within forty-eight hours the German swastika flew over the power station in Herakleion and Captain Pendlebury—wounded on the day of the attack, ruthlessly executed by the Germans the day after—was buried in an unmarked grave on the outskirts of the city.

By the end of May the fighting on the island was over. In a Cretan replay of Dunkirk, the British evacuated as many of their troops as were left and the Germans occupied Crete. The Villa Ariadne became the military headquarters of the enemy.

Yugoslavia, Greece, Crete—countries Evans knew and loved, the names of whose tiniest hamlets were familiar to him—all had fallen to the Germans. For the last time in his life the old man was stirred to anger. The barbarity of the present seemed to him a betrayal of man's long and productive past. "Civilization," he had written in 1919, "might perhaps be defined as a social condition inherited from long experience of life in an ordered State." By that definition mankind had reverted to savagery. Were the simplest Minoan potter to be awakened from his grave, he would look with horror upon a world from which all orderly coexistence had vanished.

Weak, frail, almost blind, Evans went to London at the end of May to inquire at the Hellenic Society about friends and colleagues left behind in Greece and Crete. The death of John Pendlebury, only thirty-six years old and so full of promise, was a heartrending shock. Manolaki Akoumianakis, fifty-eight, had also fallen: both of them heroes of the Cretan resistance. Both of them gifted explorers of the past, felled by the inhuman present.

Feeling his way with Prodger, Sir Arthur went from the Hellenic Society to the British Museum. He found it burned and blasted by enemy bombs. The Numismatic Room, to which both he and his father had contributed so many coins, was a smoking ruin. Irreplaceable books were a heap of ashes in the library. How passionately he had fought against the requisitioning of the museum in that other war as a threat to "the very sanctuaries of learning." How futile such defense of knowledge in this war. London was a city of gaping holes. Historic landmarks were forever obliterated. London was a city without children. They had been evacuated in order to preserve them. These were bitter, agonizing sights for a man nearing the end of his life.

On July 8, 1941, after recovering from a second operation, Arthur Evans celebrated his ninetieth birthday. His cherished friend John Myres was among the group of colleagues who came to Youlbury to present him with a scroll commemorating his extraordinary contributions, in so many areas, to the common human heritage. But above all, the scroll concluded, his friends "delight in commemorating his never-failing inspiration and encouragement to all workers in these wide fields, his initiative and wise counsel in the advancement of learning and research on many occasions, his lifelong and strenuous devotion to the cause of freedom in thought and in action."

Evans received his friends in his library, where he had been busily mapping out the remains of the Roman road which crossed his property. They found him sitting at his desk, Myres reported. "On his knees was a well-used ordnance map, showing his Roman road, and in reply to a question he showed the fair-copy of his account of it, and said brightly,

'It is finished, it will go to *Oxoniensia.*'* It was his last contribution to learning."

Three days later, scholar-explorer to the end, Evans died, leaving behind a legacy so personal and provocative that even today his ghost hovers over the dais at conferences on Cretan archaeology. Many decades have passed since Sir Arthur Evans staged his last "massed attack" on Knossos. Many teams of younger field archaeologists, armed with the latest scientific tools, have excavated new sites all over the island. They have contributed new evidence to the still incomplete picture of the Aegean Bronze Age, but they have only added fuel to some of the fires kindled by Evans, one of the greatest and most controversial of their predecessors.

Evans towered over his contemporaries during his lifetime. His stamp of authority on a Minoan potsherd seemed as indestructible as the potsherd itself. So powerful was his impact that archaeologists are still arguing about his theories and his reconstructions, his dating and his methods. The discussions often become heated, but seldom so acrimonious as at the First Cretological Congress held in 1961. It was a pity that Sir Arthur, who so much enjoyed a fight, wasn't there to participate in the proceedings.

*The annals of Oxford.

Chapter XXII
Following Evans Street to Knossos

The Cretological Congress held in 1961 in Herakleion was an event without precedent but with far-reaching repercussions. As the first international gathering of its kind it brought together Aegean archaeologists, as well as experts from other disciplines, from over a dozen countries. The delegates were housed in the Villa Ariadne, now the property of the Greek government. The British School of Archaeology at Athens had handed over the keys nine years earlier, severing the last link between the sturdy stone house and the man who had built it a half-century before. Yet to the distinguished gathering Sir Arthur still seemed to preside as the regal if invisible host. Few of the guests were unaware that the Villa Ariadne was a resounding platform from which to subject the awesome, the unassailable Evans to criticism; quite violent criticism, in fact. When Leonard Palmer, professor of comparative philology at Oxford University, finished his lecture, the audience was too shocked to applaud.

Palmer vigorously disputed the master's dating of Linear B script, whose invention Evans placed at about 1450 B.C. That was the year, Evans claimed, when catastrophe overtook all of the Cretan palaces except Knossos, where "a change of dynasty" took place. The tablets owed their very survival to the final conflagration that felled Knossos in 1400 B.C.

Palmer disagreed. Drawing philological conclusions from the
tablets Blegen had found at Pylos, and Wace at Mycenae
some years later, he propounded a much later date for the
Knossian archives and suggested that the final destruction
of the Palace of Minos took place at the very end of the
Bronze Age, around 1150 B.C. As though that weren't sac-
rilegious enough, Palmer implied—more than implied—that
Evans' methods of excavation and of recording were an in-
evitable invitation to error.

The Cretan scholars in the audience were horrified. The
archaeologists present—including Sinclair Hood, then director
of the British School at Athens, and John Boardman, reader
in classical archaeology at Oxford—were profoundly disturbed.
After the initial stunned silence came a barrage of reactions
and the war of words was on. Charges and countercharges
were hurled. The language so often strayed from scholarly
understatement that Palmer warned: "These are not admissible
modes of scientific discourse."

The two men who would have played leading roles on
this verbal battlefield were both dead: the formidable Evans
himself and Michael Ventris, who had begun puzzling over
Linear B script as a fourteen-year-old schoolboy listening to
a lecture in London. Ventris's tragic death in an automobile
accident only five years before, at the age of thirty-four, still
haunted the delegates as his name came up again and again.
It was his astonishing feat of scholarship that had precipitated
the present debate.

Although trained as an architect, Ventris had managed in
his short lifetime to decipher Linear B writing. His study
of the script, begun so long before, was intensified in 1951
when the Pylos tablets were published. It so happened that
one year later the BBC asked him to give a talk on the
Third Programme in connection with the publication of *Scripta
Minoa* II, edited by Sir John Myres. Myres's efforts on behalf
of his life-long friend Evans had finally made the Knossian
tablets available to the scholarly community and gave Ventris
the additional evidence he needed to make his startling announcement: "During the last few weeks, I have come to
the conclusion that the Knossos and Pylos tablets must, after

all, be written in Greek—a difficult and archaic Greek, seeing that it is 500 years older than Homer and written in a rather abbreviated form, but Greek nevertheless."

Among Ventris's listeners there was one who reacted immediately. John Chadwick, a young Cambridge philologist specializing in ancient Greek dialects, got in touch with Ventris and the two men began a fruitful collaboration destined to affect all future research into the Aegean past. Their volume of over five hundred pages, entitled *Documents in Mycenaean Greek*, appeared in 1956, the very year of Ventris's fatal automobile accident. The brilliant young scholar had lived only long enough to establish the fact that the language inscribed on the tablets was not Minoan, as Evans had thought; not Etruscan or Indo-European or Hittite or Basque, as other scholars had suggested; but ancient, archaic Greek.

What a new set of questions *that* raised! If the scribes at Knossos had written in Greek, then obviously that was the language of the educated and ruling class at the time. But what Greek-speakers, other than conquerors from the mainland, could they have been? Did this mean that Knossos was toppled not by an earthquake, as Evans had believed, but by foreign invaders? And what about dates? How could Knossos have been destroyed in 1400 B.C. if the palace at Pylos, where the same language and writing was in use, was still intact in 1200 B.C.? What *happened* during those puzzling two hundred years?

Even before the First Cretological Congress Palmer had kicked up an archaeological dust storm by raising such questions and giving his own answers. In order to prove that Evans' dating was wrong, Palmer had gone back to Mackenzie's original Day Books, now part of the Ashmolean archives. Between them and Evans' final summation of the evidence, he charged, there were serious discrepancies and inaccuracies. He hinted at a suppression, perhaps even a misrepresentation of certain facts. His own study of the tablets and of the archaeological context in which they were found, Palmer asserted, indicated that Knossos had been destroyed after 1200 B.C. There would have to be some serious rethinking of Evans' theories.

Thus the philologist Palmer. Now the archaeologists had

their say. With Sinclair Hood as field director, the British School at Athens had just completed some new excavations that cleared up at least one point about dating raised by some of Evans' critics. Evans insisted that the other great sites in Crete were destroyed in 1450 B.C. Knossos, on the other hand, still had another fifty flourishing years in store under a powerful new (Minoan) dynasty. Those fifty years were marked not only by the invention of Linear B writing but by the splendid, even grandiose "Palace Style" of the pottery produced uniquely in the Knossian workshops. Not so, said the critics, and they, too, brandished the enduring clay pot to prove their theory that all the Cretan palaces were destroyed at the same time. Evans, they pointed out, had classified a particular style of vase decoration as Late Minoan Ib and assigned it to the years 1500–1450 B.C. This kind of pottery had turned up in abundance almost everywhere but at Knossos. Why, the critics wanted to know, had it never been found in the House of Minos? Did this not indicate that Evans' famed "Palace Style" was merely contemporary with the less imperial Late Minoan Ib vases? Did it not follow, then, that all of the palaces had been destroyed by the same conquering invaders in 1400 B.C.?

But now Sinclair Hood had found the missing vases at Knossos. Whether or not his report in *The London Illustrated News* in 1962 convinced Evans' doubters, its very title reflected the prevailing embattled mood: "Sir Arthur Vindicated." The British dig just completed, Hood wrote, had made new stratigraphical tests at Knossos and turned up "a remarkable discovery"—a hoard of the troublesome vases in question in exactly the stratum where they should have been to confirm Evans' dating. "At one blow, over 60 years since he began his great excavations at Knossos, the views of Evans have been confirmed in a most unexpected and dramatic manner." Hood went on to say that "This LM Ib deposit is probably the most important of its kind that has been found in Crete. When the material from it is fully digested it may cause a minor revolution in Minoan studies. It would be more true to speak of a counter-revolution, since the evidence from it essentially confirms the correctness of the views held by Sir Arthur Evans."

But the dust clouds raised by Palmer only thickened. At the beginning of the controversy he and John Boardman—the one a philologist, the other a classical archaeologist—had planned to collaborate on a book presenting the evidence on the Linear B tablets. However, when Boardman came to studying the material, he found that he disagreed with Palmer not only on the evidence but the conclusions. The way out of *this* dilemma resulted in two glaringly opposed books printed in 1963 under one cover by the Clarendon Press at Oxford. The Publisher's Note explained why: "... Prof. Palmer and Mr. Boardman found that they differed not only on the conclusions to be drawn from the evidence but also on how to utilize it. Since, however, they were agreed in thinking that it should be made available to scholars as soon as possible, the Delegates have agreed to publish two independent studies of the material, neither of which has been seen by the author of the other before it was in print."

Duncan Mackenzie would have taken comfort in Boardman's defense of his Day Books. "Mackenzie wrote clearly and legibly." His notebooks were "a mine of interesting information about the excavations and a revelation of the care and observation of detail exercised by Mackenzie, itself a reflection on the judgment of Evans, who chose him as his Field Director for so many years." Boardman pointed out that the notes kept day by day on a site were necessarily only fresh impressions. More considered deductions might change as the work progressed. After two seminars on the subject, press and radio reports, and exchanges in the periodical *Antiquity*, it seemed to Boardman that "the correctness of Evans' dating has been generally accepted by scholars."

Meanwhile, more tablets turned up. In the very year that Palmer and Boardman published their two-in-one book, the Greek archaeologist Nikolas Platon discovered fragments of Linear B tablets at Thebes among the ruins of a Mycenaean palace. In the same deposit with the tablets was a Babylonian cylinder seal which could be ascribed to approximately 1350 B.C. Did this anchor Linear B to still another date? The evidence, it seemed, compounded the confusion more by being unearthed than by remaining buried. The debate went stubbornly on. The only voice missing was that of Sir Arthur, which however soft would assuredly have made itself audible above the din.

More than the polemics, Evans would have enjoyed following the Minoan story as it continued to unfold. In 1962 Platon discovered a fourth palace at Zakro on the eastern coast of Crete. Though not as splendid as Knossos or Phaistos and somewhat smaller than Mallia, it was just as elaborately planned. There were the ceremonial apartments, the Domestic Quarter, the Central Court, the storerooms, workshops, and shrines. Moreover, because the palace had been destroyed by fire around 1450 B.C., its buried treasures had escaped plunderers. The earth yielded extraordinary finds, from a bowl filled with olives still preserved by water to an exquisite rhyton made of rock crystal with a jewel-like handle of rock-crystal beads.

From Zakro on the east to Kastelli on the west, archaeologists were at work. On site after site they excavated Minoan cave sanctuaries and mountain shrines, Minoan homes and villages, as well as the layers of habitation that overlay them. A team from the British School of Archaeology at Athens even went back to Knossos to investigate Evans' "Unexplored Mansion" and found that it was exactly what he had said it was, so many decades before: a Greco-Roman house. By 1977 the Unexplored Mansion had been fully uncovered and the marbled wall paintings Evans had described still survived where he had failed to dig.

And still the search continues, sometimes producing facts about Evans' Minoans that their great discoverer might find unnerving. In 1979 the Greek husband and wife team of archaeologists, Ioannis and Effie Sakellarakis, completed their fifteenth year of digging near the village of Arkhanes on the slopes of Mount Juktas. In unearthing a Bronze Age cemetery they came upon what seemed to be a scene of human sacrifice interrupted by an earthquake around the seventeenth century B.C. The shrine contained the skeletons of two men and a woman. Two, perhaps a priest and a priestess, had been killed when the ceiling collapsed. The third had died from a knife blow which pierced the artery in his neck; the heavy bronze dagger still lay across his ribs.

One year later, in 1980, Professor P. M. Warren of Bristol

University, excavating just west of Knossos near Sir Arthur's "Little Palace," disclosed an even more disturbing cache of human bones. The knife marks on them led him to the "disagreeable" conclusion that they gave evidence of cannibalism. Scholars continue to study this grisly possibility, but there is yet so much more to know. Fortunately, the Cretan earth seems inexhaustible. The body of knowledge grows. Facts denied to Evans, Hogarth, Halbherr, even to Wace and Blegen, emerge both to clarify and to cloud the historical record.

Answers to one problem raised questions about another. One of the most puzzling—the question of when and how so brilliant a civilization had disappeared—was given a dramatic new dimension by the Greek archaeologist Spyridon Marinatos when he began his excavations in 1967 on the volcanic island of Thera, known today as Santorini. And considered by increasing numbers of scholars as the fabled Lost Atlantis, buried in legend, literature, and folk memory for more than thirty centuries.

Thera is the most southerly of the thirty-nine islands called the Cyclades which form part of the Aegean archipelago. Only a hundred and twelve kilometers of open sea separate it from the northern coast of Crete. Small but lovely, Thera was once about sixteen kilometers in diameter and covered by steep cone-shaped peaks, topped at the summit by a soaring volcano. Its deep valleys were verdant with vines and its volcanic soil was fertile. Its people and its culture thrived until, somewhere around 1500 B.C., one of the most stupendous events in all history took place.

Triggered by a fearful earthquake, the volcano exploded in a series of eruptions so violent that the center of the island literally collapsed, plunging downward to form a vast sea-filled *caldera*, or crater, where once had been dry land. The inrush of water into this *caldera* raised tidal waves, *tsunamis*, of almost unimaginable size which spread in ever-widening circles to crash down upon the neighboring coasts. One's mind could scarcely encompass such a paroxysm of nature were it not for the single parallel event in modern history: the eruption of Krakatoa in A.D. 1883.

In that year two-thirds of the volcanic island of Krakatoa—

lying between Java and Sumatra and, like Thera, situated on one of the earth's great faults—plunged from sight into the sea. Its boiling peak began erupting in May. The volcanic activity kept increasing in intensity until it reached its cataclysmic climax on the twenty-sixth and twenty-eighth of August 1883. The island was blown into almost total extinction with a roar which could be heard in Australia, some thirty-five hundred kilometers distant.

A billowing black cloud rose an estimated twenty-five kilometers into the sky. Seacoast towns on neighboring islands were completely washed away by tidal waves that reached thirty meters high. Of such incredible force were the *tsunamis* that they raised up the Dutch ship *Berouw* from its mooring at Sumatra, carried it nearly three kilometers inland, and left it in the middle of a forest nine meters above sea level. For months after the eruption the atmosphere was filled with particles of volcanic ash. The noise of the explosion was so frightful that the sound waves of the air went three times around the earth before calming down.

Evans, of course, was alive at the time of the Krakatoa eruption, which occurred only yesterday in geological time. He would have been fascinated by what Marinatos found on Thera, destroyed thirty-five hundred years earlier. Still buried under a thick layer of volcanic ash were the remains of houses two and three stories high; of rooms covered with frescoes unmistakably Minoan in their lively naturalness, yet infused with a genius all their own. Marinatos found magnificent vessels of pottery, stone, and bronze—some made by local artisans, others imported from Crete and the mainland, testifying to the active trading carried on by a prosperous seagoing people.

Dominated by their powerful neighbors in Knossos, the people of Thera had nevertheless added a scintillating footnote to the Minoan chapter. And then, through an almost supernatural phenomenon—Marinatos estimated that the force of the eruption could have been four times as great as that of Krakatoa—this highly advanced society disappeared from sight in approximately 1500 B.C. It is impossible to fix exact dates. Though volcanologists agree that some time elapsed between the beginning of the eruption on Thera and the final, culminating paroxysm which produced the *caldera,* they cannot say for certain how long the gap was.

Marinatos believed that it was the fearsome eruption of Thera, followed by gigantic tidal waves, which brought the brilliant Minoan civilization to an end. The great palaces of Crete were leveled by the earthquake which triggered Thera's volcano. Engulfed by the surging sea as well, they could no longer be rebuilt. Knossos alone, because it stood on higher ground, survived; but so weakened, now, that it was easy prey to Mycenaean conquerors from the mainland.

The final destruction of Knossos, then, came through invasion and not earthquake, as Evans thought. Not all archaeologists today accept Marinatos's reconstruction of events, but most of them agree that the throne of Minos was captured by the Mycenaeans, or Greeks from one of the other mainland centers, sometime during the fifteenth century B.C. The "change of dynasty" which Evans said took place in 1450 B.C., and which introduced the glittering "Palace Style" of pottery, did indeed occur; but the new rulers who occupied the throne of Minos were not Minoans but Greeks. Other archaeologists, Wace among them, advance still another theory. Knossos was destroyed in approximately 1400 B.C., they say, not by the invaders but by the subject Minoans themselves, who set fire to the palace in revolt against their conquerors. So there is still no single, unanimous answer to the question of how and when the Palace of Knossos, and with it one of the most extraordinary civilizations in antiquity, ceased to be.

Indeed, one voice has dared to suggest that the civilization evoked by Evans never existed at all. A German professor of geology named Hans Wunderlich wrote a book called *The Secret of Crete* in which he set out to prove that the Minoans built their great palaces not for the living but as sumptuous mortuaries for the dead. One of his main arguments—he was, after all, a geologist—revolved around the fact that the principal building material used at Knossos was gypsum, a stone so soft and porous that it seemed particularly unsuitable for a vast building inhabited by many hundreds of people. This alone led him to believe that the palace could never have been lived in at all. He cited other reasons, too—for instance, the fact that most of the rooms were windowless, lighted only by the indirect light of an air shaft: more suited for the cult of the dead than the comfort of the living. So plausible did some of his arguments seem that the book aroused considerable furor, particularly among laymen. Archaeologist Jacquetta Hawkes, however, in reviewing his book, could only conclude that "Professor Wunderlich is aptly named." To dismiss the findings, she wrote, "to which hundreds of able archaeologists, historians and epigraphists have devoted their learned lives" was a fantastic absurdity. But the book showed what problems besides dating an archaeologist can come up against.

The arguments continue. There are scholars today who even question Ventris's decipherment of Linear B script. Is the language *really* Greek? New disputes arise over the Thera catastrophe: some Aegean archaeologists widely separate the eruption from the Minoan collapse. Political scientists and economists add their theories to explain the erosion of Aegean hegemony in the ancient world. The swirling controversies make Evans' contribution to human knowledge all the more remarkable. He may have been obsessed with his Minoans and their role in antiquity, but the great bulk of his findings have firmly stood the tests of time and technology.

The spade can only uncover, not interpret facts. To help him in the reading of the evidence, the modern excavator calls in scientists from a score of other disciplines, some of which didn't exist in Evans' day. Atomic physics has provided radiocarbon dating. Spectroscopy can specify the origin of the clay used in ancient pottery. Thermoluminescence can determine when the pots were fired. Restorations are carried out in laboratories, stones can be "injected" with preservatives. Aerial photography, underwater archaeology, computer-processed data—all are tools in the explorer's kit. New hyphenated specialists answer new questions: palaeo-ethnobotanists, palaeo-pathologists. Long words are coined: archaeoastronomy, archaeomagnetism, dendrochronology. From atomic physicists to zoologists, the scientists who work today with what were once called "antiquarians" run the gamut of the alphabet.

Not all archaeologists are pleased with these new developments. Jacquetta Hawkes warns that though a technological approach to the buried past may produce much scientific knowledge, there "will be no one great humanist who could weld it all together and make it into history." Professor R. J. C. Atkinson, the expert on Stonehenge, worries that these many new tools "can lead to what I would call gadgeteering, which is only in a sense another name for mistaking the means for the end."

One thing is certain: there are no substitutes in archaeology for flair and intuition, for scholarship and an instinctive feeling for typology. With these qualities Arthur Evans was abundantly endowed. Were he alive today, his thirsting mind would surely welcome any scientific collaborators who could help to interpret or verify a find. However, he would add to their technical data that extra ingredient of divination which would illuminate the object under scrutiny and bring it and the people who fashioned it back to life.

Evans was not the only pioneer who foreshadowed the day when archaeology would marry into the exact sciences. Other names besides his are forever linked with the place of their discoveries: Heinrich Schliemann with Troy and Mycenae, for example; Flinders Petrie with Egypt; Austen Henry Layard with Nineveh; Leonard Woolley with Ur. But Evans is the only one of the early great archaeologists who so suffused his work with his vision that the two became almost inseparable. His intuition and imagination added visual dimension to what his spade found, until ruin and reconstruction together produced a latter-day awakening of life in the court of King Minos. Knossos is as much the crowning jewel of Crete today as it was thirty-five hundred years ago.

Evans' Candia is now Herakleion, the metropolis of the island. Hotels encroach upon its beaches. Merchants display bright native hangings and embroidered dresses outside their shops, making the streets colorful. Strangers bargain and buy, and ask directions in a multitude of tongues. Yet like Crete itself, Herakleion too—despite its modern tangle of television antennas, its jumbo jets and car rentals, its highways of newly gleaming concrete—has a long memory. The music blaring from café radios may be the latest out of Athens, but the songs still piped by shepherds recall more distant times. The souvenirs in tourist shops reproduce ancestral gods and goods. And somewhere, deep in every Cretan's subconscious, there are traces of the sea people.

To a sightseer strolling among the avenues and alleys of Herakleion, bearing polysyllabic street signs—Paraskevopoulou, Themistokleous, Zanthoudhidhi, Konstantinou—the name Evans Street falls like a gavel in a noisy hall, calling the meeting to order. It makes a statement. And indeed, on the city bus following its route down Evans Street to Knossos, any local passenger—from the plump housewife struggling to contain a live chicken in a straw basket to the elderly hatted gentleman eating grapes—could tell you who Evans was. They might have more trouble guiding you through Knossos, but that, as everyone knows, is a labyrinth.

Evans himself might be put off course (and out of kilter) were he to approach the vast excavations today via cafés and kiosks, rest rooms and souvenir shops, and the huge turn-around where tour buses disgorge tourists and guides herd them into groups. Once inside the palace grounds, however, the old master would be content. The legendary home of King Minos is still all there and all his. The busloads of tourists following polyglot guides are marveling at his restored frescoes. The magnificent staircase they climb up and down, pausing for explanations, is the one he labored to preserve. The sacral horns, the double axes—all are his. The visitor fancies a look of proprietary pleasure on the face of his bronze bust and has an eerie feeling that from his pedestal Sir Arthur still keeps an eye on Knossos.

One feels his presence on Boars Hill, too, even though Youlbury no longer exists. Evans' home was requisitioned after his death during World War II by the Royal Air Force, a bit of historical irony he would have appreciated: his Villa Ariadne in Crete a headquarters for enemy dictators, his Oxford labyrinth sheltering the defenders of freedom. Valiant efforts were made when the war ended to preserve Youlbury. There were thoughts of converting it into a recreation center, perhaps, or a youth hostel. A syndicate was formed with the idea of turning it into a convalescent home. But the immense sprawling mansion with its magnificent trappings belonged to another era. Too expensive to maintain, Youlbury, the house over which Sir Arthur presided with such urbane elegance, disappeared from Boars Hill. Only two legacies remain of the mound's most famous resident. One is Youlbury Camp, the large area he gave to the Boy Scouts for use as a training site, and which has by now developed into an international camping center with every kind of facility. The other is Jarn Mound, a living reminder of the man whose whole life reflected the "truly spacious outlook" he sought to preserve.

Arthur Evans' buoyant step still seems to accompany the visitor idling his way along the sinuous paths, stopping to admire the red cherry trees, the wild oak, the mountain ash; the boggy places and the rockery; the tender patches of wild flowers, some of them planted by Sir Arthur himself. On June 17, 1978, the grateful members of the Boars Hill Association, joined by scores of dignitaries and scholars, gathered to honor the man who had created Jarn Mound. Some of those taking part in the ceremony could recall when the spreading trees were mere saplings. They could remember the "dial of indication" which had once crowned the summit. Chatting among themselves as they waited for the ceremony to begin, they reminisced about the Christmas parties at Youlbury, the cricket matches, the flower shows. No one present, however, treasured more personal memories than James Candy.

Candy had been asked by the Oxford Preservation Trust to suggest an appropriate monument. From a local quarry a "menhir" of unblemished beauty was selected, a single vertical standing stone about 2.5 meters in height and weighing over ten tons: a monolith as enduring as the stone burial markers still surviving in Ireland and southwest England from the days of the Bronze Age. In its simplicity, dignity, and timelessness, no memorial could have been more fitting. James Candy on behalf of the boy Jimmie had found a noble way of paying tribute to Sir Arthur.

The Greek ambassador, the honored guest of the occasion, brought the gratitude of a people to whose present freedom

and ancient past Evans had contributed so much. It had
been everyone's hope that Joan Evans would be present to
unveil the plaque inscribed to the memory of her brother.
Alas, the event came too late. Shortly before her death the
year before, knowing that her health was failing, she had
expressed the wish that someone acquainted with Evans' great
work in Crete should replace her; and thus the honor fell
to Sinclair Hood.

Hood had never known Evans personally. Nevertheless,
he said, "for those of us who have worked, as I have been
doing for over thirty years now, at the site of Knossos in
Crete, Sir Arthur is still very much alive." To those who
continued to explore the inexhaustible riches of the Knossian
earth, he was an ever-present guide and inspiration; just as
to those who lived in the region of Oxford, the very ground
on which the ceremony was taking place proclaimed their
enduring debt to Evans. Hood also spoke of the man who
had worked so tirelessly to help create modern Yugoslavia;
who had achieved distinction for his basic studies of the
Roman antiquities of Dalmatia; who had done so much for
the Scout Movement, for the British School of Archaeology
at Athens, for the Ashmolean Museum. It was reserved for
Joan Evans, however, to sum up the multiple achievements
of her brother's fruitful lifetime in a few simple words. Already
ill when she wrote it, she had composed the inscription engraved on the plaque:

TO
ARTHUR JOHN EVANS
1851–1941

WHO LOVED ANTIQUITY, NATURE, FREEDOM
AND YOUTH, AND MADE THIS VIEWPOINT
AND WILD GARDEN FOR ALL TO ENJOY

A few steps lead down to the spot where the "menhir"
stands. Wild heather covers the ground. There is a place
to sit, where the contemplative visitor can enjoy the viewpoint
and the wild garden, and reread the eloquent inscription.
Antiquity, nature, freedom and youth: the words draw one's

thoughts beyond the quiet beauty of the spot to Evans' more spacious outlook. Shortsighted though his eyes were, his inner vision had embraced the whole human adventure—from be-beginnings of the Minoan landmark on the long journey through time to the continuing road to the future.

Minoan Chronology

Date	Crete	Egypt
To about . . . 3500 B.C.	Neolithic Age	Predynastic Period
3500–2600	Transitional and Early Minoan I	Protodynastic Period
2600–2400	Early Minoan II	Dynasties V and VI
2400–2200	Early Minoan III	Dynasties VII–X (First Intermediate Period)
2200–2100	Middle Minoan Ia	Dynasty XI in Egypt
2100–2000	Middle Minoan Ib	and Hammurabi in Babylonia
2000–1900	Middle Minoan IIa	Dynasty XII
1900–1800	Middle Minoan IIb	
1800–1700	Middle Minoan IIIa	Dynasties XIII–XVII
1700–1550	Middle Minoan IIIb	and Hyksos (Second Intermediate Period); earliest Dynasty XVIII
1550–1500	Late Minoan Ia	Dynasty XVIII early
1500–1450	Late Minoan Ib	Dynasty XVIII Hatshepsut and Thotmes III

Date	Crete	Egypt
1450–1400	Late Minoan II	Dynasty XVIII Amenhotep II–III
1400–1250	Late Minoan IIIa	Dynasty XVIII late; sea
1250–1100	Late Minoan IIIb	raid in XIX (Merenptah) Dynasties XX–XXII; relations interrupted between Egypt and Aegean

Note: There is a tendency among archaeologists today, who consider Evans' chronological system overschematic and partly incorrect, to adopt the following dating and nomenclature:

Neolithic Period	?–2600 B.C.
Pre-palatial Period	2600–2000
Proto-palatial Period	2000–1700
Neo-palatial Period	1700–1400
Post-palatial Period	1400–1100

Bibliography

Alexiou, Stylianos. *Minoan Civilization.* Herakleion: Spyros Alexiou Sons, 1973.

Alsop, Joseph. *From the Silent Earth.* New York: Harper & Row, 1964; London: Secker & Warburg, Ltd., 1965.

Annual of the British School at Athens, The. Nos. VI through XII and No. XXXI. London: Macmillan & Co., 1900–1931.

Boardman, John. *On the Knossos Tablets: The Date of the Knossos Tablets.* Oxford: Clarendon Press, 1963.

Bosanquet, R. C. "The Realm of Minos." *Edinburgh Review,* July 1922.

Burrows, Ronald W. *The Discoveries in Crete.* London: John Murray, 1907.

Casson, S., ed. *Essays in Aegean Archaeology.* Oxford: Clarendon Press, 1927; Darby, Pa.: Arden Library, 1978.

Cottrell, Leonard. *The Bull of Minos.* London: Evans Brothers Ltd., 1953.

————. *Realms of Gold.* Greenwich, Conn.: New York Graphic Society Publishers, Ltd., 1963.

————. *Reading the Past.* New York: Macmillan, 1971; London: J. M. Dent & Sons, Ltd., 1972.

Daniel, Glyn. *The Idea of Prehistory.* London: C. A. Watts, 1962; Baltimore: Penguin, 1964.

Deuel, Leo. *The Treasures of Time.* London: Pan Books, Ltd., 1964.

Evans, Arthur. *Through Bosnia and Herzegovina on foot.* London: Longmans, Green & Co., 1877.

————. *The Slavs and European Civilization.* Lecture delivered at

Sion College, February 23, 1878. Longmans, Green & Co., 1878.

————. *Illyrian Letters.* London: Longmans, Green & Co., 1878.

————. *The Ashmolean Museum as a Home of Archaeology in Oxford.* An Inaugural Lecture. London: Parker & Co., 1884.

————. *Letters from Crete.* Oxford: Printed for Private Circulation by Horace Hart, Printer of the University, 1898.

————. *Scripta Minoa.* Oxford: Clarendon Press, 1909.

————. *The Adriatic Slavs and the Overland Route to Constantinople.* London: The Geographical Journal, April 1916.

————. *The Palace of Minos.* London: Macmillan & Co., Ltd. 1921–1936.

————. *Work of Reconstruction in the Palace of Knossos.* London: Journal of the Society of Antiquaries, Vol. VII, No. 3, July 1927.

————. *The Shaft Graves and Beehive Tombs of Mycenae and Their Interrelation.* London: Macmillan & Co., Ltd., 1929.

————. *Jarn Mound.* Oxford: Joseph Vincent, 1933.

Evans, Joan. *Time and Chance.* London and Toronto: Longmans, Green & Co., 1943.

————. *Prelude and Fugue.* London and Toronto: Longmans, Green & Co., 1943.

Faure, Paul. *La Vie Quotidienne en Crete au temps de Minos.* Paris: Librairie Hachette, 1973.

Graham, James Walter. *The Palaces of Crete.* Princeton: Princeton University Press, 1962.

Hall, H. R. *Aegean Archaeology.* London: Philip Lee Warner, 1915.

Harden, D. B. *Sir Arthur Evans Centenary Exhibition.* Oxford: Ashmolean Museum, 1951.

Hawes, Charles Henry and Harriet Boyd. *Crete, the Forerunner of Greece.* New York: Harper & Brothers, 1922.

Hawes, Harriet Boyd. "Memoirs of a Pioneer Excavator in Crete," *Archaeology,* Vol. 18, Number 2, June 1965.

Hawkes, Jacquetta. *The World of the Past.* New York: Alfred A. Knopf, 1963.

————. *Dawn of the Gods.* New York: Random House, 1968.

————. *The Atlas of Early Man.* New York: St. Martin's Press, 1976.

Higgins, Reynold. *Minoan and Mycenaean Art.* New York: Oxford University Press, 1967; London: Thames & Hudson, 1967.

Hogarth, D. G. *Accidents of an Antiquary's Life.* London: Macmillan & Co., Ltd., 1910.

Hood, Sinclair. "Sir Arthur Evans Vindicated." *The Illustrated London News,* archaeological section no. 2080, February 17, 1962.
———. *The Minoans.* New York: Praeger, 1971; London: Thames & Hudson, 1971.
Luce, J. V. *The End of Atlantis.* New York: McGraw-Hill, 1969; London: Thames & Hudson, 1969.
Ludwig, Emil. *Schliemann of Troy.* New York and London: G. P. Putnam, 1931.
Marinatos, Spyridon. *Crete and Mycenae.* London: Thames & Hudson, 1960.
———. *Some Words about the Legend of Atlantis.* Athens, 1972.
———. *Excavations at Thera VI (1972 Season).* Athens, 1974.
McDonald, William A. *Progress into the Past.* New York: Macmillan, 1967.
Mellersh, H. E. L. *Minoan Crete.* New York: G. P. Putnam, 1968; London: Evans Brothers Limited, 1967.
Myres, John Linton. "The Cretan Labyrinth: A Retrospect of Aegean Research." London: *Journal of the Royal Anthropological Institute,* Vol. LVII, July–December, 1933.
———. *Sir Arthur Evans.* From the proceedings of the British Academy, Vol. XXVII. London: Humphrey Milford Amen House, 1942.
Palmer, Leonard R. *On the Knossos Tablets: The Find-Places of the Knossos Tablets.* Oxford: Clarendon Press, 1963.
Pendlebury, J. D. S. *The Archaeology of Crete.* London: Methuen & Co., 1939; New York: Norton, 1965.
———. *A Handbook to the Palace of Minos.* Toronto: Clarke, Irwin, 1954; London: Max Parrish and Co., Ltd., 1954.
Platon, Nicolas. *Crète.* New York: Hippocrene Books, 1968; Geneva: Les Editions Nagel, 1968.
Powell, Dilys. *The Villa Ariadne.* London: Hodder & Stoughton, 1973.
Renault, Mary. *The King Must Die.* New York: Pantheon Books, 1958.
———. *The Bull from the Sea.* New York: Pantheon Books, 1962.
Sandars, N. K. *The Sea Peoples.* London: Thames & Hudson, 1978.
Wace, A. J. B. "The Date of the Treasury of Atreus." London: *The Journal of Hellenic Studies,* Vol. XLVI, 1926.
Wheeler, Mortimer. *Still Digging.* London: Michael Joseph, Ltd., 1955.
Willetts, R. F. *Cretan Cults and Festivals.* New York: Barnes & Noble, 1962; London: Routledge & Kegan Paul, Ltd., 1962.

Wilson, David. *The New Archaeology.* New York: Alfred A. Knopf, Inc., 1974.

Woolley, Leonard. *A Survey of Eighteen Archaeological Sites.* London: Ernest Benn Ltd., 1958.

———. *History Unearthed.* New York: Praeger, 1962; London: Ernest Benn Ltd., 1958.

———. *As I Seem to Remember.* London: George Allen & Unwin, Ltd., 1962.

Wunderlich, Hans Georg. *The Secret of Crete.* New York: Macmillan, 1975.

Index